HIGH PLAINS

The Joy of Alberta Cuisine

CINDA CHAVICH

photographs MIKE STURK

FIFTH
HOUSE

Design by Rachel Hershfield

The publisher gratefully acknowledges the support of The Canada Council for
the Arts and the Department of Canadian Heritage. We acknowledge the
financial support of the Government of Canada through the Book Publishing
Industry Development Program for our publishing activities.

First Published in the United States in 2008.

National Library of Canada Cataloguing in Publication Data

Chavich, Cinda.
    High plains: the joy of Alberta cuisine/Cinda Chavich.—Rev. ed.

Includes index.
ISBN 978-1-897252-38-3

    I. Cookery, Canadian—Alberta style. I. Title.
TX715.6.C535 2008   641.597123   C2008-900397-7

Printed in Hong Kong.

01/2008

Fifth House Ltd.
A Fitzhenry & Whiteside Company
1511-1800 4 St. SW
Calgary, Alberta, Canada
T2S 2S5

1-800-387-9776
www.fitzhenry.ca

Contents

TUESDAY
MALPEQUE OYSTERS
ROASTED & TOPPED # FRESH HORSERADISH
& AN APPLE CIDER VINAIGRETTE
2²⁰/ea

AHI TUNA CARPACCIO
WITH WARM HORSERADISH OIL, COLD
DRESSED CANOLA AIOLI & A
CAPER BERRY VINAIGRETTE
#12⁵⁰

LOCALLY RAISED FREE RANGE
PHEASANT
SEARED BREAST & FOIS GRAS
STUFFED ROULADE SERVED ON
MANITOBA WILD RICE WITH A HALF
BOSC PEAR POACHED IN
DANDELION HONEY, CREAMED FRESH
WALNUTS & A FOIS GRAS VEAL
REDUCTION
$29⁹⁵

PINTO

POPLAR BLUFF FARM

Introduction

I have been a food writer and journalist in Calgary for a very long time. And for a very long time I have wanted to collect the stories of Alberta's food producers and purveyors in a cookbook about this part of the world. This is that book.

After years of telling the stories of Alberta's best farmers and food producers, chefs and creative cooks, in newspaper and magazine articles, I have become an advocate of Alberta cuisine. By writing and collecting recipes for the four seasons in this most western extreme of the Canadian prairies, I have discovered our unspoken reliance on the foods produced in this very particular place.

Alberta is like any other region of the world. We gravitate to our own—the freshest corn in August, the best beef, the incomparable wild fish and game—for a modern style of eating that is both traditional and influenced by changing trends. You may still wonder what we mean by the term "regional Alberta cuisine." The concept of regional cuisine is evolving as we learn to meld the concepts of local and global to our best advantage. But it's safe to define it as a style of cooking that is connected to the land.

Here in Alberta the landscape sweeps from brilliantly stark wheat fields and big skies to steep foothills carpeted in hardy wild grasses that can feed free-ranging livestock and survive years of drought, prairie fire, and long stretches of sub-zero temperatures. Wide rivers wend their way across the prairies like satiny blue ribbons, rivers born in snowy mountain peaks and collected from tiny streams that sparkle and crash through rocky canyons. Made for the word majestic, the mountains thrust their rocky peaks above their heavily forested shoulders, where coniferous trees create the environment that supports wild mushrooms and a variety of small animals, birds, and big game like elk, moose, and deer. Game also abounds in the mixed forests of larch, pine, spruce, aspen, and poplar throughout the northern and central parts of the province. Above all, the sun almost always shines in this fertile province.

In today's world, professional chefs and savvy diners look in their own back yards for the tastiest, healthiest, and best-quality food they can find. Everyone knows that food coming directly from the land to the kitchen is superior to food that has travelled halfway around the globe. While we still must import many items, from coffee to citrus fruit to seafood, we can also make a commitment to cooking with foods grown close to home. We return to our roots: grains that form the backbone of our diet, animals that we have long raised or hunted, and fruits and vegetables grown and gathered during our short summers and stored through long winters. We celebrate the farmers who challenge the harsh prairie environment and use hands-on production methods, based on environmental and ethical principles, to produce the best and the healthiest food possible.

There are many success stories. Alberta-produced milk is now the basis for wonderful cheeses that rival any in the world, from aged Gouda and Parmesan-like Grana to creamy chèvre and sheep feta. We are raising tender bison and wild boar, growing flavourful heirloom tomatoes and gourmet greens, and our top restaurants are offering their own versions of cutting-edge prairie food for the first time.

This book celebrates Alberta with a contemporary collection of recipes inspired by local history and landscape and current trends in dining. Many people helped to make this book happen, from the producers, farmers, and chefs who graciously shared their time and expertise with me, to the publisher who believed that this project was worth pursuing. I want to thank all of those supportive and inspirational people, especially Fifth House publisher Fraser Seely, managing editor Charlene Dobmeier, and Mike Sturk, the fine photographer who travelled with me to tell the story of Alberta's food business with his artistic, evocative images.

I feel very lucky to have the chance to share these stories, insights, and recipes with Albertans and others who are devoted to showing the world what the best regional Canadian cuisine is all about. We have some fine examples of it here on the high plains. Join us and share in the joy of it.

Cinda Chavich

Appetizers: The Cheese Board

ANYTHING BUT ORANGE

When Canadians think of cheese, they usually think of basic orange Cheddar or processed cheese for macaroni and hamburgers. Until recently, the most exotic Canadian cheese produced in Alberta was a factory-made mozzarella or Monterey Jack. But something exciting has been happening in the cheese business in recent years. Today you can offer your guests an appetizer cheese tray that includes French-style, surface-ripened goat cheeses from Ponoka, real sheep feta from Innisfail, award-winning Gouda from Sylvan Lake, and even a dry grating cheese created exactly like the finest Italian Parmesan on a farm outside of Edmonton.

At the dawn of the new millennium, our appreciation for cheese is increasing. Nothing is simpler or more satisfying than a loaf of good bread, a glass of good wine, and a chunk of good cheese. It may be no coincidence that all of these ancient food products are created through the fermentation process caused by yeasts and other micro-organisms. Nor is it surprising that cheese, a concentrated and portable food, has long been eaten as a snack or simple starter everywhere in the world.

But it's taken us a while to realize that good cheese is a gourmet product worth producing and paying for. Better Alberta restaurants are adopting the European tradition of serving a variety of fine cheeses after dinner, and we are gladly relying less and less on imports and more and more on our own superb products.

Two of the earliest pioneers in the handmade Alberta cheese business were Peter and Christianne Welkerling. On their little farm near Innisfail, the young immigrants from Germany discovered a way to turn unwanted, excess milk from a neighbour's herd of meat sheep into a product that you'll now find on the best menus in the province.

On this summer afternoon, Christianne is beginning another batch of her creamy sheep's milk feta. In her tiny dairy, a small stainless steel tank is filled with fresh milk from their herd of fluffy East Friesen dairy sheep. The milk is pasteurized, cooled, and cultured in the morning, and by afternoon she is cutting the curd and pouring the soft, jiggly mass into square moulds to drain. Tomorrow the 8-kilogram blocks of fresh sheep feta will go into pails of salt brine, where they will age for only two weeks before being packaged and sent to supermarkets and restaurants.

When Peter calls his herd in for milking twice a day, a woolly mass of bleating ewes arrives at the barn, their swollen udders jiggling behind them like eraser-pink beach balls. They line up on the milking platform and dig into their dinners while waiting their turn to be hooked to the milking machine.

Last year the Welkerlings turned 24,000 litres of sheep milk into feta and Asiago cheese and thick, creamy live yogurt. Like their tender milk-fed lamb, it finds its way into Alberta gourmet grocery stores and the kitchens of the best chefs. The yogurt is a fresh, seasonal product only available between May and November, while the feta keeps well in brine throughout the year.

As their Shepherd Gourmet Dairy label says, theirs is "Alberta's first licensed sheep dairy and processing operation." The Welkerlings not only made the first sheep cheeses here, they raised the first dairy sheep.

While sheep milk is popular in Europe for making classic cheeses such as Greek feta, blue-veined French Roquefort, and Italian Asiago, it was impossible to find milking sheep in North America when the young couple first arrived in Canada a decade ago. The Welkerlings noticed that their neighbour's Rideau Arcott ewes (a meat-producing breed) were producing too much milk for their lambs, and realized it would be possible to breed them with East Friesen milking sheep. They began a breeding program, importing semen from European dairy sheep and finally, several generations of sheep later, imported the frozen East Friesen embryos that saw the first North American dairy sheep born on their family farm in 1996.

Christianne Welkerling

Today, breeding stock has become the biggest part of their business as the pioneering Alberta shepherds are helping to educate an entire continent in the joy of sheep-milk cheeses. The offspring of the Welkerlings' milking sheep can be found on farms in Canada, the United States, and even Mexico and Chile.

Like the Welkerlings' feta, the beautiful surfaced-ripened and ash-covered goat cheeses made at Natricia Dairy near Ponoka are sometimes hard to find. The production at this new $3-million, state-of-the-art plant is huge compared with the Welkerlings' operation, but still tiny compared with the large volumes of commercial cheeses produced by the big players in the cheese business. Many of these fine, handmade cheeses go directly to chefs and gourmet grocers, but you will be rewarded greatly if you seek them out.

Natricia Dairy was created a few short years ago by Virginia Saputo, daughter of mozzarella magnate Francesco Saputo, and her partner Mark D'Amato. The Montreal pair came to Alberta because it was here that they found the country's largest herds of milking goats. Today the milk from most of those goats, and many others, is being shipped directly to Natricia Dairy to be made into cheeses modelled after the best in the world. In addition, Natricia also markets fluid Alberta goat milk for those who are lactose intolerant.

To make sure that the cheeses she creates here in Alberta rival any in the world, Virginia not only travelled the backroads of France and Italy to learn her trade, she also imported moulds, cultures, and equipment. When her first Alberta goat cheeses were ready to sample, Virginia invited a government official from France to inspect her plant. His conclusion: she would easily achieve *appellation contrôlée* status (A.O.C.) if her dairy were located on French soil, indicating her full compliance with their strict cheesemaking standards.

Retailing at about $20 per pound, Natricia cheeses are not inexpensive, but they are the perfect addition to your cheese board, no matter which of the twenty distinctive varieties you choose. There are delicate, fresh cheeses to serve with fruit, runny wheels of Brie, salty goat feta, tiny, aged Crottin, no bigger than a stack of poker chips, and strong, assertive dry cheeses like Tome Chèvrine. Logs of surface-ripened St. Maure rolled in smoky ash are a favourite for slicing atop baguette rounds for grilled croutons to perch on the side of a salad or float in a bowl of onion soup. Snow-white Pannier crumbles easily over greens and melts perfectly inside an omelette. All have the complex flavour, white colour, and sharp acidity characteristic of goat-milk cheeses.

Central Alberta seems to be the place to make cheese. Most of the new cheese artisans are found on farms in the Red Deer region, where beef cattle ranches give way to dairy farms, berry farms, and vegetable growers. Until these players entered the scene, most Alberta cheeses (a lot of Cheddar, Havarti, and Monterey Jack) were created from pasteurized cow's milk. Small producers like Neapolis Dairy in

Didsbury, Alberta Cheese Company in Calgary, and Sunny Rose Cheese in Lethbridge were the earliest to break that mould, producing some of the first Camembert, Brie, Ricotta, and Gouda cheese in Alberta.

Today, Gouda has become a bit of an art form. Dairies like Sylvan Star and Eyot Creek produce award-winning aged and flavoured Goudas that are delicious eaten on their own or melted into sandwiches and other dishes. The mild Gouda from John Schalkwyk at Sylvan Star Cheese, a small family operation near Sylvan Lake in central Alberta, took top honours in the firm cheese category at the Canadian Cheese Grand Prix awards. Schalkwyk produces all of his plain and flavoured Gouda cheeses from milk from his own herd of dairy cows. The milk produced on Eyot Creek Farm near Leduc goes into their own unpasteurized mild, medium, and aged Gouda-style cheeses with flavours ranging from dill and black mustard to habanero pepper and stinging nettle.

The latest player in this cheesemaking tableau is Emanuela Leoni, who recently opened a facility in Camrose to make her Parmesan-style Leoni-Grana cheese. The first wheels of this aged cheese are still young, not yet as complex in flavour as top Italian Parmesan cheeses like Parmigiano Reggiano, but typically grainy in structure and nutty in flavour.

Leoni makes her big 15–22-kilogram wheels of Grana just like they do in Italy. The skill in making hard cheeses like this is in the cutting of the curd. A large rake-like cutter is drawn repeatedly by hand through the curd until it is broken into tiny pieces, each no bigger than a lentil. Because Grana is aged between six and twenty-four months, the law allows the makers to use unpasteurized milk, giving the cheese extra flavour and complexity. Like the makers of Parmigiano Reggiano, Leoni stamps her company name, the date of the cheese making, and the batch number in the rind, which becomes a golden buff colour as the cheese ages on wooden shelves in their climate-controlled warehouse.

Made from local partly skimmed cow's milk, Leoni-Grana is a strong cheese that goes a long way when grated into pastas and other dishes. As a first course or appetizer, it marries well with fresh figs, melon, pears, or prosciutto ham, and can be pared into large curling shards to top a peppery arugula salad.

After you have sampled some of the fine handmade cheeses being created at Alberta dairies, you are certain to expand your cheese repertoire to include these homegrown products. Sure, there are good Cheddars being made in Canada, too, but usually they're anything but orange.

COWBOY QUESADILLAS WITH AVOCADO CREAM DIPPING SAUCE

Quesadillas make an easy, impromptu appetizer, as long as you have fresh tortillas on hand. I like to cook quesadillas on the barbecue.

1 package flour tortillas (plain, tomato, spinach, or other)
1 cup (250 mL) spicy salsa
1/4 cup (50 mL) canola oil
1 avocado, peeled and thinly slivered
**1/2 cup (125 mL) cooked black beans
   (rinsed and drained well if canned)**
6 thin slices smoked chicken or turkey, slivered
2 cups (500 mL) shredded Monterey Jack cheese
1/4 cup (50 mL) chopped fresh cilantro

CHEESE TIPS

Cheese is an excellent source of calcium because it is a concentrated form of milk. In the cheesemaking process, milk proteins are broken down and digested by enzymes, creating a product that can be easier for adults to digest than milk.

• Sheep- and goat-milk cheeses are easier to digest than those made from cow's milk and are recommended for individuals who are lactose intolerant.

• Strong cheeses offer the most flavour for the least amount of calories and fat. Dry cheeses like Parmesan are particularly concentrated sources of protein and calcium—and calories. It takes more than sixteen litres of milk to make one kilogram of Grana cheese.

• Serve all cheeses at room temperature—never straight out of the fridge—to enhance their flavours and textures.

• Good cheese requires expert care and handling. Try to buy cheese from a cheese counter where it is stored at the proper temperature and cut to order. Better yet, go directly to the farm or rural market and buy from the cheesemaker, who can give you the best advice for handling and serving it.

• Cheese is killed when it is cut up and sealed in plastic. Wrap cheeses loosely in waxed paper rather than plastic. Large wheels of cheese should be allowed to breathe through their rinds. Natricia Dairy uses special perforated wrappers that allow cheeses to breathe and mature as they age.

• Use a short-bladed knife (similar to an oyster-shucking knife) to pry Parmesan or Grana-style cheeses into chunks for serving as a table cheese. This highlights its distinctive granular texture.

Avocado Cream Dipping Sauce
1 ripe avocado, mashed
1/4 cup (50 mL) mayonnaise
1/4 cup (50 mL) sour cream
2 teaspoons (10 mL) fresh lime juice
1/8 teaspoon (0.5 mL) salt
2 tablespoons (25 mL) chopped fresh cilantro
1 green onion, chopped
dash of garlic powder
dash of ground white pepper

1. For sauce, combine all ingredients in blender or food processor and whirl until smooth. Chill.
2. For quesadillas, brush one side of a tortilla lightly with oil and lay on a large plate, oiled side down.
3. Spread tortilla with a thin layer of salsa, right to edges. Top with a few slivers of avocado, a sprinkling of beans, some turkey or chicken slivers, and a smattering of cilantro. The trick here is to make the filling light (the quesadillas will fall apart if too much filling is used). Sprinkle evenly with shredded cheese.
4. Set another tortilla on top of filling, press down firmly and brush outside lightly with oil. Repeat, stacking tortillas on the plate until tortillas and filling are used up.
5. Heat a gas grill to high heat. Carefully slip quesadillas onto the grill, one at a time, using a large spatula. After a couple of minutes, check to see if tortillas are beginning to brown. Press to seal with melting cheese, then carefully flip each quesadilla over to cook the second side.
6. Repeat until all quesadillas are crispy and cooked through. Watch carefully so they do not burn. When cooked, set aside for a few minutes to allow cheese to cool slightly and set up, then cut each quesadilla into eight wedges. Serve with avocado sauce for dipping. Serves 6.

WHITE BEAN SLATHER WITH ROASTED ONIONS AND GOAT CHEESE

Spread this simple, savoury warm bean and onion purée on toasts or slices of dense ciabatta bread. It's also delicious served alongside roasted or braised lamb.

1 19-oz (540 mL) can white beans, drained and rinsed
3 tablespoons (45 mL) extra-virgin olive oil
1/2 cup (125 mL) roughly chopped fresh herbs (rosemary, sage, thyme)
2 cloves garlic, minced
1 teaspoon (5 mL) balsamic vinegar
dash of hot pepper sauce
salt and freshly ground black pepper

Roasted Onions
1/4 cup (50 mL) olive oil
2 cups (500 mL) chopped or slivered red or white onions
4 ounces (125 g) goat cheese, crumbled

1. Combine herbs, garlic, balsamic vinegar, and hot sauce in food processor and pulse to chop. Add half of the beans and half of the olive oil, and process until smooth.
2. Add remaining beans and olive oil and process in bursts until combined but still chunky.
3. Meanwhile, heat 1/4 cup (50 mL) olive oil and cook onions slowly until soft and caramelized. This should take at least 40 minutes.
4. Add bean purée to onions in the pan and stir to heat through. Sprinkle in the goat cheese, stir well, and remove from heat. Cheese should be melting but still visible in pieces. Serve warm or at room temperature. Makes 3 cups (750 mL).

CHILI PITA CHIPS

Here's a wonderful way to use up pita bread that has lost its freshness. Spice up these flavourful, low-fat chips with any of your favourite herbs and spices. Calgary's Byblos Pita Bakery supplies Middle Eastern bread and pastry to western Canada.

1 package (8) whole-wheat pita breads
1/2 cup (125 mL) olive oil
2 cloves garlic, crushed
chili powder, oregano, ground cumin, and garlic powder (or other dried herbs and spices like basil, thyme, rosemary, seasoned pepper, cayenne pepper, or Cajun spice)
sesame seeds (optional)
finely grated Parmesan cheese (optional)

1. Split each pita into two circles by cutting around the edge with kitchen shears, then cut each half into eight triangles.
2. Combine olive oil and garlic and set aside for 10 minutes to allow flavours to infuse. Combine herbs and spices.
3. Using a pastry brush, brush the rough side of each triangle very lightly with garlic-infused oil, then sprinkle with mixture of chili powder, oregano, cumin, and garlic powder (or your choice of herbs and spices). Top lightly with a mixture of sesame seeds and Parmesan, if desired.
4. Place chips, rough side up, on a baking sheet and bake in preheated 400°F (200°C) oven for 4–5 minutes. Watch carefully as chips burn easily.
5. Remove from pan, cool to room temperature, and store in a plastic bag or other container. These chips have a long shelf life and are delicious alone or with many different dips, from lentil hummus to White Bean Slather with Roasted Onions and Goat Cheese (page 4).

AIR-DRIED BUFFALO CARPACCIO STICKS

This is a great appetizer to serve with olives and antipasto from your local Italian deli when you're too busy to cook. Try the air-dried buffalo carpaccio made at Valbella Meats in Canmore, or use regular prosciutto ham.

grainy mustard (try a garlic or raspberry champagne mustard)
very thin slices of lean, air-dried buffalo carpaccio or prosciutto
thin Italian breadsticks

1. Trim any excess fat from buffalo or prosciutto and spread each slice with a little mustard.
2. Wrap the meat slices around one end of each breadstick. The mustard will help the thinly sliced meat adhere to the breadsticks.
3. To serve, set the breadsticks, wrapped ends up, in a jar or other tall container lined with a napkin.

> **TIP**
> To make your own rustic breadsticks, try this easy method. Partially thaw a loaf of frozen bread dough and cut it lengthwise into about twenty to twenty-five pieces. Roll and stretch each piece until it is about 15 inches (38 cm) long. Lay the breadsticks side by side on a large baking sheet brushed with olive oil. Brush tops of breadsticks with olive oil and sprinkle with coarse salt or other toppings (sesame seeds, poppy seeds, Parmesan cheese, or granulated garlic). Bake in a preheated 400°F (200°C) oven for 12–15 minutes, or until golden brown and crisp.

RED LENTIL HUMMUS

*At the River Café in Calgary, this creamy lentil spread is served
with flatbread and roasted garlic from the wood-fired oven.
You can also try it with pappadams or homemade pita chips.*

2 cups (500 mL) dried red lentils
2 whole garlic cloves
1/2 cup (125 mL) dried yellow tomatoes (or other dried tomatoes), chopped
3 tablespoons (45 mL) cumin seeds
1/2 cup (125 mL) flavourful extra-virgin olive oil
salt and freshly ground black pepper

1. Rinse lentils in two changes of cold water (or more) until water is clear. Cover with cold water and soak overnight. Drain.
2. Cover lentils with clean water and bring to a boil. Add garlic and yellow tomatoes. Reduce heat to simmer and cook for 15 minutes or until lentils are beginning to break up, skimming any foam that rises to the top. Drain any excess liquid. Using an immersible blender, blend lentils until smooth in pot (alternatively, purée lentil mixture in a food processor).
3. Place cumin seeds in a dry sauté pan and toast for a few minutes over medium-high heat, until fragrant. Remove, cool, and grind in an electric spice grinder or blender.
4. Stir cumin into lentil mixture and blend in enough olive oil to make a smooth dip. Season with salt and pepper to taste. Serve hummus with roasted garlic and flatbread or Chili Pita Chips (page 5). Serves 4 to 6.

Roasted Garlic
4 whole heads garlic, unpeeled
2 tablespoons (25 mL) olive oil
salt and freshly ground black pepper

1. Cut 1/4 inch (5 mm) off the top of each garlic head to expose the cloves. Toss garlic, salt, and pepper together with olive oil. Wrap heads loosely in foil and bake in preheated 350°F (120°C) oven for 45 minutes or until soft.
2. Serve whole heads alongside lentil hummus. Press roasted garlic from papery skin and spread on bread with hummus.

> **TIP**
> Soak all legumes in cold water for several hours to remove grit and sediment, and to help release some of the gaseous starches that give beans and lentils a bad name.

CORN AND CHILE PEPPER PANCAKES WITH SMOKED TROUT AND HORSERADISH CREAM

This is a simple, elegant way to present cold-smoked fish like the trout and salmon from Cunningham's in Pincher Creek. You can also serve these savoury corn and chile pepper pancakes as a light meal, topped with sour cream and fresh salsa, or as a side dish for grilled chicken or fish.

6 ounces (180 g) cold-smoked trout or salmon, sliced paper thin

Pancakes
3 ears fresh corn
2 fresh jalapeño chiles, seeded and minced
1 chipotle chile in adobo, chopped
2 cloves garlic, minced
1 red bell pepper, finely chopped
6 green onions, chopped
2 eggs
1 cup (250 mL) all-purpose flour
1/2 cup (125 mL) cornmeal
1 teaspoon (5 mL) baking powder
1 teaspoon (5 mL) salt
1 cup (250 mL) milk
1/4 cup (50 mL) plain low-fat yogurt
3 tablespoons (45 mL) minced fresh cilantro
freshly ground black pepper
2 tablespoons (25 mL) canola oil

Horseradish Cream
1/3 cup (75 mL) spreadable cream cheese
1 tablespoon (15 mL) prepared horseradish, drained
1 teaspoon (5 mL) wasabi powder
freshly ground black pepper
1 green onion, minced

1. Bring a pot of water to a boil and add corn. Cover and remove from heat. Let stand 5 minutes. Cool corn and cut kernels from cobs. You should have about 2 cups (500 mL). Set aside.

2. Place corn kernels in a bowl with jalapeño, chipotle, red pepper, garlic, and green onions.
3. In food processor, combine eggs, flour, cornmeal, baking powder, salt, milk, and yogurt and whirl until smooth. Add vegetables and pulse just to mix. Stir in cilantro and black pepper. Let stand at room temperature for 30 minutes.
4. To make horseradish cream, whisk together cream cheese and horseradish until smooth. Add wasabi and mix to combine well. Season with a little black pepper and refrigerate.
5. Meanwhile, heat 2 tablespoons (25 mL) of oil in a nonstick frying pan over medium heat. Pour in batter to make pancakes 1–2 inches (2.5–5 cm) in diameter for cocktails (or larger if serving as a side dish). Cook, turning once, until golden on both sides. Drain on paper towels and keep warm. Repeat with remaining batter.
6. To serve, place a dollop of horseradish cream on each pancake. Separate the thin slices of smoked fish and cut each in half. Roll each piece of smoked fish into a trumpet-shaped coronet and set one on each hors d'oeuvre. Sprinkle with a few pieces of minced green onion or cilantro and serve. Serves 6.

NOT FOIE GRAS PATÉ

A top chef recently commented to me that a recipe he'd read for a foie gras terrine in a food magazine "would cost $150 for the ingredients alone!" This creamy, old-fashioned paté from my student days certainly won't.

4 large shallots, minced
2 cloves garlic, minced
1 pound (500 g) chicken livers, trimmed and halved
2 tablespoons (25 mL) butter
2 tablespoons (25 mL) olive oil
1/2 cup (125 mL) white wine or sherry
1 bay leaf
1/2 teaspoon (2 mL) freshly ground black pepper
1/2 teaspoon (2 mL) dried thyme
1/2 teaspoon (2 mL) dried sage
1 teaspoon (5 mL) minced fresh rosemary
1/2 teaspoon (2 mL) salt
1/2 cup (125 mL) soft cream cheese or whipping cream
2 tablespoons (25 mL) brandy
3 tablespoons (45 mL) butter, melted
bay leaves to garnish

1. Sauté shallots, garlic, and chicken livers in butter and oil for 4 minutes at medium-high heat, until livers are firm but still pink inside. Remove livers and set aside.
2. Add wine or sherry, bay leaf, pepper, thyme, and sage to the pan. Simmer together for 10 minutes, until liquid has cooked down to about 1/4 cup (50 mL).
3. Transfer mixture to a food processor, discarding bay leaf. Add reserved livers, rosemary, salt, cream cheese or whipping cream, and brandy and process until smooth. Add melted butter and pulse to combine.
4. Fill small bowls or crocks with the paté and decorate the tops of each bowl with bay leaves. Cover and refrigerate overnight or freeze for storage. Serve paté with sliced French bread and tiny cornichon pickles. Serves 8.

APPLE, WALNUT, AND CHEESE STRUDEL

Make this savoury strudel with the award-winning Gouda from Sylvan Star Dairy, or opt for chunks of goat-milk Camembert or creamy blue goat cheese. For an elegant first course, artfully arrange two strudels atop an apple, walnut, and celery root salad.

1/2 pound (250 g) Gouda cheese, shredded, or surface-ripened goat cheese, chopped
1 Granny Smith apple, cored and cut into 1/4-inch (5 mm) cubes
1 tablespoon (15 mL) mustard
1/3 cup (75 mL) chopped walnuts
1 green onion, minced
freshly ground black pepper
1 package phyllo pastry, thawed
1/4 cup (50 mL) melted butter

1. Combine cheese, apple, mustard, walnuts, and green onion in a bowl. Season with black pepper. Set filling aside.
2. Lay a piece of phyllo on your work surface and brush lightly with butter. Top with a second sheet. Brush with butter.
3. Cut the phyllo into 3-inch (8 cm) strips. Place a heaped tablespoon of filling at the bottom of a strip, fold corner over so that it forms a triangle, and continue folding like a flag until the filling is completely enclosed and the pastry is used up. Brush the top with butter and set on a parchment-lined baking sheet. Repeat with remaining pastry and filling.
4. Bake strudels in a preheated 400°F (200°C) oven for 12–15 minutes, or until puffed and golden. Makes about 16 strudels.

WILD MUSHROOM TOASTS

Search for a supply of wild mushrooms at your favourite gourmet or ethnic grocery. Mo-Na Mushrooms in Edmonton supplies wild mushrooms collected in the mountains, and most supermarkets now sell dried morels, chanterelles, and other wild varieties in the produce section. For information on wild Alberta mushrooms, see page 100.

1 small onion, minced
3 cloves garlic, minced
3 tablespoons (45 mL) butter
4 cups (1 L) assorted fresh mushrooms (white, oyster, shiitake, chanterelle, or morel), sliced, or dried mushrooms
1/4 cup (50 mL) white wine
1/4 cup (50 mL) whipping cream
1 teaspoon (5 mL) fresh thyme leaves, chopped, or 1/2 teaspoon (2 mL) dried thyme leaves
salt and freshly ground black pepper
1 baguette, sliced thickly
extra-virgin olive oil or cold-pressed canola oil

1. If you are using dried mushrooms, reconstitute by boiling in a bit of water or wine for 3 minutes. Drain and measure 4 cups (1 L).
2. Sauté onion and garlic in butter until tender, about 5–10 minutes.
3. Add mushrooms to pan with white wine. Cook until mushrooms are tender and most of the liquid has evaporated.
4. Stir in cream and bring to a boil. Reduce heat and simmer until sauce is reduced and thickened. Season with salt and pepper to taste. Stir in thyme and set aside to cool slightly.
5. To make toasts, place baguette slices on a baking sheet and brown quickly under a hot broiler. Brush toasts lightly with olive or canola oil. To serve, pile a little warmed mushroom mixture on each piece of toast, and pass them with drinks, or use them to garnish a salad of mixed greens. Serves 4 to 6.

DEVILLED EGGS

There's nothing new-fangled about devilled eggs, but this retro dish is still popular at big country buffet dinners, like the ones that were served up by Rudy (Bernard) Vallee when he ran Memories Inn in Longview, once a popular hangout for local ranchers and rodeo cowboys.

6 hard-boiled eggs (see tip, below)
3 tablespoons (45 mL) low-fat mayonnaise
1 tablespoon (15 mL) fat-free sour cream
1/2 teaspoon (2 mL) salt
1/4 teaspoon (1 mL) pepper
1/2 teaspoon (2 mL) dry mustard
1 tablespoon (15 mL) minced fresh parsley
1 tablespoon (15 mL) minced chives
fresh dill leaves, baby shrimp, smoked trout, or capers (optional)

1. Peel hard-boiled eggs and slice in half lengthwise.
2. Remove yolks carefully and mash with remaining ingredients.
3. Heap or pipe back into egg white halves. Serve plain or garnish with optional toppings. Makes 12.

TIP

If you want to take devilled eggs on a picnic, transport whites and filling separately. Put halved eggs in flat container and fill a zippered plastic bag with yolk mixture. When you're ready to fill them, cut a corner off the plastic bag and pipe the filling back into the hard-cooked egg whites.

For a classic ranch country salad, drizzle fresh garden greens with homemade mayonnaise (or commercial mayonnaise thinned slightly with cream or buttermilk), and set some of these old-fashioned eggs alongside.

Marinated Feta and Dried Tomato Skewers with Cilantro Sauce

Use cubes of sheep feta or fresh, firm goat-milk cheese,
or substitute your own favourite fresh cheese.

1 pound (500 g) fresh feta cheese, preferably sheep or
   goat cheese, cubed
1/2 cup (125 mL) sundried tomatoes in olive oil,
   drained and slivered
1/4 cup (50 mL) roasted red pepper, cut into 1/2-inch (1 cm)
   cubes (see tip, below)
1/4 cup (50 mL) fresh cilantro leaves

Marinade
3 cloves garlic, minced
1/4 cup (50 mL) roasted red pepper
1/2 cup (125 mL) chopped fresh cilantro
1/4 cup (50 mL) good-quality extra-virgin olive oil
1 tablespoon (15 mL) balsamic vinegar
1/4 teaspoon (1 mL) freshly ground black pepper
1/4 teaspoon (1 mL) salt

1. Combine marinade ingredients in a mini-chop or blender and purée until smooth.
2. Cut cheese into 3/4-inch (2 cm) cubes and gently combine with marinade. Refrigerate several hours or overnight. Bring to room temperature.
3. To assemble appetizers, skewer a piece of cheese, a piece of sundried tomato or roasted pepper, and a piece of cilantro on a toothpick. Arrange picks, standing upright with cheese cubes at the base and cilantro on top, on a serving tray. Serves 6 to 8.

TIP
To roast peppers, place them under the broiler or on the barbecue and cook until charred and blackened on all sides. Place charred peppers in a paper bag to steam until they are cool enough to handle, then use a paring knife to scrape away the blackened skin. Don't worry if a little of the skin stays behind. Remove cores and seeds and cut peppers into strips. You can make all of your roasted peppers in the fall when big bags of peppers are sold at local farmer's markets. Freeze roasted peppers to use all winter for salads, pizzas, and stews, or simply tossed with garlic, olive oil, and basil pesto, and served as an appetizer on French bread.

Prairie Pickerel Ceviche

In Mexican coastal towns, you can have ceviche (marinated raw fish "cooked" in lime juice) in little thatch-roofed palapas restaurants along the beach. Use only the freshest firm fish or shrimp and scallops for this chilled summer entrée or appetizer. Canadian freshwater pickerel, or walleye, is perfect for this dish, but should be frozen for seventy-two hours and thawed before using.

**2 pounds (1 kg) fresh pickerel, sea bass, or red snapper fillets,
  cut into 1/2-inch (1.5 cm) cubes
1 cup (250 mL) fresh lime juice
3 tablespoons (45 mL) olive oil
3 cloves garlic, sliced
2 pounds (1 kg) ripe tomatoes, seeded and chopped
1 cup (250 mL) chopped onion
1/2 cup (125 mL) chopped fresh cilantro
1/2 cup (125 mL) ketchup
1 teaspoon (5 mL) hot sauce
1 tablespoon (15 mL) dried oregano
1/2 teaspoon (2 mL) salt
1/4 teaspoon (1 mL) freshly ground pepper
2 tablespoons (25 mL) finely chopped pickled hot peppers
2/3 cup (150 mL) chopped green olives
whole green olives and lime wedges to garnish**

1. Combine cubed fish and lime juice in a bowl and marinate for 2–3 hours at room temperature. The fish should be "cooked" by the acids in the juice. Don't overmarinate or the fish will become mushy.
2. Combine olive oil and garlic and heat for 3 minutes, just until garlic starts to sizzle. Discard garlic and set oil aside to cool.
3. Combine tomatoes, onion, cilantro, ketchup, hot sauce, oregano, salt, pepper, hot peppers, and chopped olives. Add garlic-infused oil and mix well.
4. Rinse fish well under cold running water. Place in a bowl, cover with cold water, and let stand 5 minutes. Drain well.
5. Combine fish with vegetable mixture. Pile into a straight-sided glass bowl or layer in individual champagne glasses. Cover and chill. Serve cold, garnished with whole olives and lime wedges. Serves 6 to 8.

Classic Swiss Fondue

Around the turn of the twentieth century, the Canadian Pacific Railway brought Swiss guides to the West to take would-be adventurers safely up Rocky Mountain trails and mountain peaks. Their Swiss/German food traditions continue to be important in the cuisine of the mountain parks.

1 clove garlic, halved
1 cup (250 mL) white wine
1 teaspoon (5 mL) fresh lemon juice
2 cups (500 mL) grated Gruyere cheese
2 cups (500 mL) grated Emmenthal cheese
2–3 teaspoons (10–15 mL) cornstarch
1 tablespoon (15 mL) kirsch or brandy
freshly grated nutmeg
1 loaf crusty French or Italian bread, cubed

1. Rub inside of a fondue pot with cut clove of garlic, then discard garlic.
2. Pour in wine and lemon juice and heat to boiling over medium-high heat. Reduce heat to low and stir in grated cheeses gradually, a handful at a time, stirring until melted.
3. In a small bowl, combine cornstarch and kirsch and stir into cheese mixture. Continue to cook for 2–3 minutes until mixture is thick and smooth, but do not allow it to boil. Season with freshly grated nutmeg.
4. Place fondue pot on its stand over a low flame to keep cheese mixture hot. Serve with bread cubes for dipping. Serves 4.

Potato Skins with Double-Smoked Bacon and Sheep Feta

You can use any kind of feta cheese or fresh goat or sheep cheese for this special treat.

6 large white potatoes (Burbank or Idaho)
8 ounces (250 g) plain or herbed sheep feta
2 tablespoons (25 mL) butter
2 green onions, chopped
3 slices double-smoked bacon, chopped
freshly ground black pepper

1. Bake potatoes in a preheated 400ºF (200ºC) oven until they are cooked through and skin is crisp, about 45–55 minutes. Cool and cut lengthwise into quarters. Remove most of the flesh, reserving it for mashed potatoes, and set skins on a baking sheet.
2. In a small sauté pan, cook bacon until crisp. Drain and discard fat. Set aside.
3. Mash feta with butter and onions. Divide cheese among potato skins. Season with pepper and sprinkle with reserved bacon.
4. Bake in a preheated 400ºF (200ºC) oven for 5–10 minutes, until cheese is melted and beginning to brown. Serves 4 to 6.

Salads, Dressed Prairie Style

COLD-PRESSED CANOLA OIL AND ITS KISSIN' COUSIN, GOOD, GRAINY MUSTARD

The deep golden oil dripping slowly through a plastic tube on Tony Marshall's farm near Aldersyde, Alberta, is a product like no other. It's a rare, gourmet version of basic canola oil, the vegetable oil that's become commonplace in every Canadian cupboard. But unlike that product, produced in huge quantities by larger manufacturers, the canola oil that Marshall makes at Highwood Crossing Farm is organic, non-genetically modified, and cold-pressed. Free of the usual oil-processing chemicals and bleaches, it retains all of the vitamins and essential fatty acids that make canola oil one of the healthiest dietary fats around. It's coming through this small press at a rate of only about three to six litres an hour, a far cry from the tonnes of canola seed pressed every hour in a huge oilseed processing plant.

The cold-pressed oil produced at Highwood Crossing is a rich, amber oil, with a unique, nutty flavour. Marshall calls it Canada's answer to extra-virgin olive oil. Creative Alberta chefs love the colour and intensity, using it as a final, flavourful drizzle over composed salads and grilled fish. Like great extra-virgin olive oil, it is a product to use sparingly, when you can enjoy its unique, robust flavour.

The canola and flaxseed oils pressed at Highwood Crossing are simply pressed in a small German-made oil press, then bottled. It's all done weekly on the family farm south of Calgary. What you buy in the store on Friday was likely pressed on Tuesday and bottled on Wednesday. Held in a pair of large, steel bins, the seeds are fed through the tabletop green machine by a basic auger. Like a big kitchen sausage maker, it presses the tiny buff-coloured seeds until they release their oily juices. A cake of dry husk is extruded, to become organic chicken feed, and a small amount of golden oil drips through a tube to a collecting barrel below. It's not as romantic as the big horse-powered grinding stones that are museum pieces in the olive-oil producing countries of the world, but Marshall says this kind of small press is used in European countries where fresh, unrefined oils are as common as other fresh foods.

The simple expeller press never heats the oil above 40°C (104°C), or exposes it to light or oxygen, preserving the oil's most valuable assets, the antioxidant Vitamin E and essential fatty acids like Omega 3 and Omega 6. Marshall says that's what makes his cold-pressed canola and flax oils special; both are low in saturated fats. The flax especially includes far more Omega-3 fatty acids than other fats and oils.

While both Omega-3 and Omega-6 fatty acids must be obtained from foods, current research suggests that the balance of these fatty acids is unhealthy in the modern Western diet, with Omega-6 fats over-consumed and Omega 3s, highest in flax and canola oils, and fatty fish like tuna and salmon, especially deficient. Increasing the intake of Omega 3s can lower blood cholesterol and triglyceride levels, reduce the risk of heart disease and stroke, protect against some cancers, boost the immune system, and reduce inflammation to improve conditions like arthritis.

The Highwood Crossing oil is perishable, needs refrigeration, and has a maximum one-year shelf life. Marshall uses freshly squeezed orange juice and powdered drink crystals as a

comparison. "We don't refine our oil at all," he says. "With the flax oil, we sell the residue that settles as nut butter. It's super high in lignans."

It's best to consume the oil while fresh and not to use it for frying because excessive heating can create free radicals in oils like this. Regular canola oil is a better choice for frying and everyday cooking, when the unique properties and flavours of the expensive cold-pressed oils would be lost. The Marshalls use their canola oil in baking, though, as the internal temperatures reached do not destroy the oil's beneficial properties. Their oil's nutty character adds a unique flavour to breads, muffins, and even cookies. If a recipe calls for a cup of butter or margarine, they recommend using ¾ cup (175 mL) of cold-pressed canola oil.

Marshall's farm has been in his family for five generations and he is the first to move to a fully organic operation. His product is unique and difficult to make, especially with nearly all of the cur-

rent canola crop in Canada grown from genetically modified (GMO) seed. Almost every week, Marshall gets calls from big food companies looking for non-GMO oil. With public pressure rising, manufacturers of chips, crackers,

Tony Marshall

cookies, and other processed foods are searching for sources of vegetable oil that is not genetically modified. That's a tall order, says Marshall. "Eighty percent of canola oil is GMO." Marshall uses a DNA test to ensure that the canola he presses does not include genetically modified seeds. "It's a real struggle, trying to find the organic, non-GMO canola for our products."

You can find Highwood Crossing cold-pressed canola oil in gourmet groceries, along with Chef Desmond Johnston's handmade Brassica mustards, flavoured with roasted garlic, cranberry, and dill. Whisked together they perfectly dress a salad, prairie style.

Mr. Stripey Beet and Chevre Salad

Beets are a classic prairie crop and now there are colourful gourmet versions, such as yellow beets and bi-coloured 'Mr. Stripey' or Chioggia beets, with concentric pink and white circles inside. They are wonderful steamed and dressed with a light vinaigrette and eaten with rounds of sharp goat cheese.

5 to 6 small to medium striped beets, with leaves
2 tablespoons (25 mL) olive oil
1 tablespoon (15 mL) honey
1 teaspoon (5 mL) balsamic vinegar
1 teaspoon (5 mL) chopped fresh thyme
1/8 teaspoon (0.5 mL) white pepper
2 small rounds of aged goat cheese
1 green onion, minced
1 teaspoon (5 mL) chopped fresh parsley

1. Cut off beet greens, leaving about 1 inch (2.5 cm) of stem intact. Reserve youngest and smallest greens for serving with beets.
2. Boil or steam beets for 15 minutes, or until tender when pierced with a sharp knife. Run beets under cold water to cool. Slip off skins and remove tops and roots. Slice beets across the grain to reveal the concentric white and pink circles inside.
3. Heat olive oil with honey, balsamic vinegar, thyme, and white pepper just until honey is melted. Pour over warm, sliced beets and allow them to cool to room temperature.
4. Slice cheese into thin rounds. Arrange reserved beet greens on four individual salad plates. Arrange sliced beets and cheese on top and sprinkle with green onions and parsley. Serves 4.

Pork Tenderloin Salad with Spicy Ranch Dressing

This is the perfect combination for a hot summer night on the back deck—cool greens topped with slices of grilled lean Alberta pork tenderloin and a creamy, kicky sauce.

1 tablespoon (15 mL) chopped garlic
1/2 teaspoon (2 mL) Asian chili sauce
1/2 cup (125 mL) soy sauce
2 tablespoons (25 mL) brown sugar
1/4 cup (50 mL) fresh lime juice
1 10-ounce (300 g) pork tenderloin
1/2 cup (125 mL) mayonnaise
salt and freshly ground black pepper
6 cups (1.5 L) romaine, chopped, or mixed greens
1/4 cup (50 mL) chopped fresh cilantro
1 avocado, peeled and diced
1 orange, peel and pith removed, then sliced

1. Combine garlic, chili sauce, soy sauce, brown sugar, and lime juice in blender or food processor and whirl until smooth.
2. Place tenderloin in a zippered plastic bag with 1/2 cup (125 mL) of the above mixture and marinate in the refrigerator for 2 hours.
3. Whisk remaining marinade with mayonnaise and salt and pepper to taste, or shake together in a jar to make dressing. Chill.
4. Grill pork on medium heat, turning frequently, until just cooked through and still pink, about 20 minutes in total. Set on cutting board and tent with foil to rest for 5–10 minutes, then slice thinly on the diagonal.
5. Toss salad greens with cilantro and enough of the dressing to coat lightly. Arrange on four individual plates. Top each salad with some diced avocado and pork, and arrange orange slices around the edges of the plates. Pass the rest of the dressing separately. Serves 4 as a main dish.

Bulgar and Pinto Bean Salad

Bulgar is a whole grain version of instant rice—pre-steamed and dried cracked whole-wheat that rehydrates quickly in boiling water. Cracked wheat is raw cracked grain that requires substantially more cooking. Bulgar, a traditional Middle Eastern ingredient used in tabouli salads, is now being produced from Canadian wheat on the prairies. Make this healthy, portable salad for a picnic or to take to your next potluck barbecue.

1 cup (250 mL) dried coarse bulgar
2 cups (500 mL) boiling water
1 cup (250 mL) corn kernels
1 large carrot, grated
1 red bell pepper, roasted and chopped (see tip, page 10)
1/2 cup (125 mL) pinto beans, cooked and drained
1/2 cup (125 mL) chopped red onion
1 jalapeño pepper, chopped
1 teaspoon (5 mL) each: ground cumin, chili powder, and oregano
1/4 cup (50 mL) fresh lemon juice
3 tablespoons (45 mL) extra-virgin olive oil
1/4 cup (125 mL) minced fresh cilantro
salt, freshly ground black pepper, and hot sauce

1. Place bulgar in pot. Pour boiling water over bulgar, cover, and set aside for 30 minutes to soften. Set aside in strainer to drain well and cool.
2. Place rehydrated bulgar in a salad bowl. Stir in corn, grated carrot, roasted red pepper, beans, and red onion. Combine jalapeño, cumin, chili powder, oregano, lemon juice, olive oil, and cilantro in a food processor and whirl until smooth. Pour over salad and toss well.
3. Cover salad and refrigerate for 2 hours. Season with salt, pepper, and hot sauce to taste. Serves 6.

Baby Greens with Blue Potato and Goat Cheese Croutons

I use small, local blue-fleshed potatoes topped with bubbly goat cheese atop this salad of mixed greens to start a dinner party. The sweet fruit vinaigrette makes the perfect counterpoint to the cheese's acidic tang, and the blue potatoes are always a conversation starter!

8 small blue-fleshed potatoes, about 2 inches (5 cm) in diameter
8 ounces (250 g) creamy goat cheese
8 to 10 cups (2–2.5 L) mixed baby salad greens

Dressing
1/4 cup (50 mL) raspberry vinegar
1/2 cup (125 mL) fresh or frozen raspberries, puréed and
  pressed through a sieve to remove seeds
2 tablespoons (25 mL) honey
1 tablespoon (15 mL) Dijon mustard
1 shallot, minced
salt and freshly ground black pepper
1/2 cup (125 mL) olive oil or cold-pressed canola oil

1. Steam potatoes for 10 minutes, until barely cooked. Cool and chill potatoes for several hours or overnight.
2. Cut potatoes into thick 3/4-inch (1.25 cm) slices, removing rounded ends so that slices will stand evenly. Place potatoes on a nonstick baking sheet. Slice cheese and place one slice over each piece of blue potato (if cheese crumbles and refuses to slice, pile it evenly over potato pieces and pat in place).
3. To make dressing, combine vinegar, raspberry purée, honey, mustard, shallot, salt, and pepper in a food processor or blender and purée. Add oil slowly, with the machine running, to emulsify. Add a tablespoon or two of water if vinaigrette is too thick. Set vinaigrette aside.
4. Just before serving, place potato and goat cheese croutons under a hot broiler and cook for 2–3 minutes, until bubbling and beginning to brown. Watch closely to prevent burning.
5. Toss salad greens with enough dressing to lightly coat, and divide among eight individual salad plates. Place a few warm potato and goat cheese croutons atop each salad, drizzle with a little more dressing, and serve immediately. Serves 8.

Warm Red Cabbage and Pecan Salad

Here's a warm salad reminiscent of old-fashioned sautéed red cabbage, but with the upscale addition of sharp cheese. Serve it in the fall or winter as a first course or side salad with roast pork, duck, grilled sausages, or meat pies.

1/2 cup (125 mL) pecans, whole or coarsely broken
1 teaspoon (5 mL), plus 1 tablespoon (15 mL) walnut oil,
  sesame oil, or other nut oil
salt and freshly ground black pepper
1 Macintosh apple
1 tablespoon (15 mL) fresh lemon juice
1 clove garlic, minced
2 tablespoons (25 mL) red wine vinegar or balsamic vinegar
1 tablespoon (15 mL) olive oil
1 small red onion, thinly sliced
1 small red cabbage (about 1 lb/500 mL) quartered,
  cored, and thinly sliced
salt and freshly ground black pepper
4 ounces (125 g) aged goat cheese, dry ricotta or feta, crumbled
1 tablespoon (15 mL) chopped fresh parsley

1. In a small bowl, toss pecans with 1 teaspoon (5 mL) walnut or sesame oil, and a little salt and pepper. Spread nuts on a baking sheet and roast in a preheated 350°F (180°C) oven for 5–10 minutes, or until just fragrant, watching that they don't burn. Set aside.
2. Core apple, cut into six wedges and slice thinly. Toss with lemon juice.
3. Combine garlic, vinegar, 1 tablespoon (15 mL) nut oil, and olive oil in a large sauté pan over medium-high heat. As soon as it begins to sizzle, add red onion and sauté 30 seconds. Next add the cabbage and continue to cook, stirring constantly, until it just starts to wilt, about 3 minutes. Season with salt and plenty of pepper. Add apple slices and toss to heat through.
4. Remove from heat and place in a shallow serving bowl. Sprinkle warm cabbage salad with crumbled goat cheese (or ricotta or feta), and mix lightly so that cheese stays intact but begins to soften and melt. Add toasted pecans and toss. Serve immediately, sprinkled with parsley. Serves 4 to 6.

ALBERTA MUSTARD

Alberta farmers produce nearly 45,000 metric tonnes of mustard seed every year. Much of it is exported to places that produce mustard (the condiment), notably the United States and Europe, while some is ground into powders for hot Asian mustards and Japanese wasabi, and even fillers for processed meats and sausages. There are many varieties of mustard—black, brown, and yellow seeds—harvested from plants that turn the prairies into patchworks of colour in mid-summer.

The sharp heat and peppery flavour of mustard has been enlivening food for centuries. From ancient Rome to France, Britain, Germany, India, and China, mustard has been used as a flavouring and medicinal ingredient. North American Natives dried the seeds and used them in their cooking. Mustard has an affinity for certain foods like grilled ham and cheese sandwiches, the zippy, tart mustard flavour cutting the richness to aid digestion. Use it straight as a condiment, on sandwiches or smoked salmon, as a rub before roasting and grilling meat or fish, in a cream sauce for chicken or roast pork, in Indian cuisine, and, of course, as a flavouring and emulsifier in your salad dressings, dips, and vinaigrettes, where it makes every vegetable shine.

Alberta now has its own excellent local gourmet mustard maker—Brassica Mustard.

MAKING MUSTARD

While Dijon in France is known as the mustard capital of the world (because it still makes half of the mustard condiment), much of the mustard powder or crushed mustard seed that finds its way into those French jars doubtless was grown on the Canadian prairies.

Making mustard is so simple, yet few people still actually mix up their own recipes. Just add cold water to ground mustard seeds and stir. Don't use hot liquid—an adverse chemical reaction occurs when the ground mustard is heated, leaving the final condiment bitter. After you add the water to make a paste, let the mustard stand for 10 minutes to allow the flavour to develop. The longer it

HEIRLOOM TOMATO SALAD WITH SHEEP FETA FRITTERS

Chef Dany Lamote developed the creative Alberta cuisine at the Ranche Restaurant in the restored historic Bow Valley Ranche house in Calgary. These fritters, encrusted with prairie oilseeds, are made with local sheep feta and garnish a salad of heirloom tomatoes provided by local grower Paul Hotchkiss. Dany suggests using a feta that is not too dry and crumbly for easier slicing.

3/4 cup (175 mL) all-purpose flour
1/2 bottle (3/4 cup/170 mL) beer
1/4 teaspoon (1 mL) freshly ground black pepper
1/2 pound (250 g) sheep feta cheese
1 cup (250 mL) mixed seeds (canola, mustard, flax, poppy seed, etc.)
1/4 cup (50 mL) regular canola oil
3 cups (750 mL) mesclun mix or mixed baby greens
6 to 8 vine-ripened, heirloom tomatoes
   (as many different varieties and colours as possible)
1 tablespoon (15 mL) cold-pressed canola oil
juice of 1 lemon

1. Whisk flour with beer and pepper to make a smooth batter. Set batter aside for 30 minutes. Thin with more beer if necessary.
2. Cut feta into 1/2-inch (1.5 cm) slabs and dip first in batter, then roll in seed mixture to coat on all sides. Shallow fry fritters in hot regular canola oil until golden brown on both sides, about 2 minutes per side. You must fry them quickly so that the outsides are browned before they melt and disintegrate. Set aside to cool slightly, but keep warm.
3. Arrange greens on four salad plates. Slice tomatoes and overlap to make a colourful display on each plate. Top each salad with two or three warm fritters and drizzle with cold-pressed canola oil. Squeeze a little lemon juice over salads and serve. Serves 4.

stands, the less potent it will be.

You can also flavour your mustard with wine, fruit juice, cider, vinegar, oil, herbs, and sweeteners like honey.

You can make your mustard to complement your recipe—basil mustard for tomato quiche, ginger mustard for Asian dishes, honey mustard for sweet cured ham, herbes de provence mustard for lamb, lemon mustard for fish sauces, etc. A jar of homemade or commercial mustard keeps indefinitely. Although its flavour will fade over time, homemade mustard should be cured in the refrigerator for at least two days before serving to allow the flavours to meld, and to cool some of the intense heat you get in homemade mustard mixtures. Don't panic if your mustard seems thin—the mustard will thicken as it sits.

BASIC MUSTARD

1/4 cup (50 mL) mustard powder
1/4 cup (50 mL) mustard seeds, brown or
    yellow, ground
1/3 cup (75 mL) cold water (or fruit juice, cider,
    beer, wine, etc.)
3 tablespoons (45 mL) vinegar (white, wine,
    malt, balsamic, etc.)
1–2 tablespoons (15–25 mL) brown sugar,
    honey, maple syrup, liqueur, preserves, etc.
1–3 tablespoons (15–45 mL) olive oil (optional)
salt and pepper, and your choice of other
    flavourings such as ground spices, minced
    garlic, fresh herbs, dried herbs, crushed red
    chilies, etc.

Use a spice grinder or mortar and pestle to grind mustard seeds. Combine all ingredients in a blender or food processor and blend until smooth, stopping frequently to scrape the container. Put mustard in a clean jar, cover tightly, and refrigerate at least two days before using. Makes about 1 cup (250 mL).

WATERCRESS SALAD WITH POACHED PEARS AND THYME-SCENTED WALNUTS

Serve this salad as a special starter at a dinner party or for a fall luncheon. Pomegranate seeds add a colourful festive touch if you serve the salad for Christmas events.

3 to 4 pears, peeled (choose a sturdy, underripe pear like
    Bosc or Bartlett)
1 bottle (750 mL) red Zinfandel wine
2 bunches watercress, thick stems removed
2 cups (500 mL) mixed baby greens
1 cup (250 mL) red seedless grapes, halved, or
    pomegranate seeds
Alberta Parmesan (shaved) or crumbled goat cheese

Thyme-Scented Walnuts
2/3 cup (150 mL) walnut or pecan halves
1 tablespoon (15 mL) brown sugar
1 tablespoon (15 mL) walnut or olive oil
1/4 teaspoon (1 mL) salt
2 teaspoons (10 mL) fresh thyme, chopped
pinch of cayenne pepper

Dressing
1/4 cup (50 mL) olive oil
2 tablespoons (25 mL) walnut or sesame oil
2 tablespoons (25 mL) raspberry or balsamic vinegar
2 tablespoons (25 mL) of the poaching Zinfandel
2 teaspoons (10 mL) Dijon mustard
1/2 teaspoon (2 mL) each: salt and freshly ground black pepper

1. Peel pears, leaving stem intact. Cut in half lengthwise and neatly remove cores using a melon baller.
2. Bring Zinfandel to a simmer in a deep sauté pan. Add pears and poach for 15 minutes, until cooked but still very firm. Poke pears with a skewer to check occasionally. Do not overcook or pears will be mushy. Let pears cool in the wine, then cover and refrigerate.
3. To make thyme-scented walnuts, spread walnuts on a baking sheet and toast in a preheated 350°F (180°C) oven for 10 minutes. While the nuts are toasting, combine brown sugar, oil, salt, thyme, and cayenne pepper in a large bowl. Add hot toasted nuts and mix well until coated with the flavourings. Cool or serve warm.
4. Trim coarse stems from the watercress. Wash watercress leaves and baby greens, and spin dry in a salad spinner. Arrange greens on six individual salad plates. Sprinkle each salad with some of the grapes or pomegranate seeds and thyme-scented nuts.
5. Slice pear halves lengthwise into 1/4-inch (5 mm) slices, leaving the tops intact. Fan one or two pear halves on each plate. Whisk or shake dressing ingredients together and drizzle over salads. Top each with some shaved or crumbled cheese and serve. Serves 6 to 8.

> **TIP**
> Poached pears take on a lovely red colour and distinctive flavour when poached in wine. But to simplify this salad, you can omit the poaching. Start with very ripe, flavourful pears and peel, core, and slice or chop them, then toss with some of the vinaigrette before using to top these composed salads. The thyme-scented walnuts also make great cocktail snacks.

SUMMER GRAIN SALAD WITH ITALIAN PARSLEY

Make this salad when the garden is offering up its fresh produce, and try it wrap style, rolled up in a warm pita bread with grilled flank steak and a garlicky yogurt sauce.

2 1/2 cups (625 mL) water
1 1/2 cups (375 mL) bulgar wheat
1/4 cup (50 mL) extra-virgin olive oil or cold-pressed canola oil
1 tablespoon (15 mL) water
3 tablespoons (45 mL) fresh lemon or lime juice
1 teaspoon (5 mL) salt
1/4 teaspoon (1 mL) freshly ground black pepper
1/4 teaspoon (1 mL) hot sauce like Tabasco or Durkee's
1/2 cup (125 mL) minced Italian parsley
6 large radishes, chopped
2 small tomatoes, seeded and chopped
1/2 cup (125 mL) freshly shelled peas
2 green onions, chopped

1. Heat water to boiling and stir in bulgar. Remove pan from heat, cover, and let stand 30 minutes to rehydrate. Drain if necessary and fluff bulgar with a fork.
2. Whisk together oil, water, lemon juice, salt, pepper, and hot sauce. Pour over warm bulgar and toss to coat. Chill.
3. Stir parsley into bulgar. Add radishes, tomatoes, peas, and green onions and toss to combine. Serve immediately or refrigerate and return to room temperature before serving. Makes 6 servings.

WARM LEMON LENTIL SALAD WITH GOAT CHEESE

Use greenish brown Laird or Eston lentils in this dish, or try yellow CDC Gold lentils. Lentil salad is a traditional French first course, but it also makes a tasty base for grilled fish or lamb chops.

1 cup (250 mL) green lentils
3 cups (750 mL) water
bouquet garni of 1 branch thyme, 1 branch rosemary, and 1 bay
    leaf tied together, or use 1 teaspoon (5 mL) each: dried thyme,
    dried rosemary, and a bay leaf in a tea ball
1 carrot, peeled and quartered
2 cloves garlic, peeled but left whole
1/4 cup (50 mL) roasted red pepper, chopped (see tip, page 10)
3 green onions, chopped
3 ounces (90 g) goat cheese or sheep feta, crumbled
mixed greens

Dressing
zest and juice of 1 lemon (about 3 tablespoons/45 mL juice)
1 tablespoon (15 mL) grainy Brassica mustard or Dijon mustard
1 teaspoon (5 mL) salt
2 teaspoons (10 mL) fresh thyme, chopped, or 1 teaspoon (5 mL)
    dried thyme leaves
1/4 cup (50 mL) extra-virgin olive oil
freshly ground black pepper

1. In a saucepan, combine lentils, water, bouquet garni, carrot, and whole garlic cloves. Bring to a boil then reduce heat and simmer for 20–30 minutes, until lentils are just tender but still firm. Drain lentils and discard bouquet garni, carrot, and garlic.
2. To make dressing, mince lemon zest and combine with lemon juice, mustard, salt, and thyme. Slowly whisk in olive oil to emulsify. Season vinaigrette with pepper to taste.
3. Place warm lentils in a bowl and toss with vinaigrette. Stir in red pepper and green onions. Crumble goat cheese over salad and toss just to mix. The cheese should melt slightly but stay intact. Serve salad warm over mixed greens. Serves 4 to 6.

COWBOY CAESAR SALAD WITH SPICY CILANTRO MAYONNAISE

This recipe gives a piquant western twist to traditional green goddess salad dressing. Serve it over mixed salad greens like this, or try it with cabbage and carrot coleslaw.

1 head romaine lettuce, washed and torn into bite-sized pieces
1 cup (250 mL) homemade croutons, seasoned with cumin and
    oregano (see tip, following page)
1/2 cup (125 mL) aged white Cheddar cheese from Sylvan Star, or
    Parmesan, freshly grated

Spicy Cilantro Mayonnaise
1 bunch cilantro, washed, with stems removed
    (about 1 cup/250 mL)
2 tablespoons (25 mL) each: garlic and jalapeño pepper,
    both chopped
2 tablespoons (25 mL) each: white wine vinegar and
    Dijon mustard
1/2 teaspoon (2 mL) salt
1 1/2 cups (375 mL) mayonnaise, regular or low-fat
1/2 cup (125 mL) plain yogurt or sour cream

1. For dressing, combine all ingredients in a food processor and purée.
2. Transfer to a clean jar or covered container and refrigerate. Makes 2 cups.
3. Meanwhile, place lettuce in a large bowl. Toss with just enough dressing to coat. Add croutons and grated cheese and toss again. Serve immediately. Serves 4 to 6.

> ### TIP
> To make croutons, cut French, Italian, or sourdough bread into 1-inch (2.5 cm) cubes, making about 2 cups. Place in a large bowl and drizzle with 2–3 tablespoons (25–45 mL) canola or olive oil. Season with 1/2 teaspoon (2 mL) each of ground cumin and oregano, and one clove of garlic, minced. Toss to coat with oil and flavourings, then toast croutons on a cookie sheet, in a preheated 400°F (200°C) oven, for 10–15 minutes until golden and crisp. Season with salt and set aside to cool. Store covered.

MIXED GREENS WITH WARM BLUE CHEESE VINAIGRETTE AND PICKLED RED GRAPES

Serve this salad in winter months, topped with a Canadian blue cheese like Ermite from Quebec.

6–8 cups (1.5–2 L) mixed salad greens
1/3 cup (75 mL) olive oil
2 tablespoons (25 mL) red wine vinegar
1 tablespoon (15 mL) Dijon mustard
salt and freshly ground black pepper
1 cup (250 mL) blue cheese, crumbled

Pickled Grapes
2 pounds (1 kg) seedless red grapes
2 cups (500 mL) raspberry wine vinegar, or 1 cup (250 mL) each:
   red and white wine vinegar
1 cup (250 mL) dry red wine
1 cup (250 mL) brown sugar
4 whole cloves
1 cinnamon stick
6 cardamom seeds

1. To make pickled grapes, wash and dry grapes and place in a large, clean jar. Combine remaining ingredients in a saucepan and heat, stirring to dissolve sugar. Cool slightly, then pour over grapes. Cover jar tightly and refrigerate. Marinate grapes for at least two days, inverting jar occasionally. Pickled grapes will keep for 10 days in the refrigerator.
2. For the salad, divide greens among four plates. Whisk together olive oil and vinegar with mustard and salt and pepper to taste. Warm vinaigrette over medium heat in a sauté pan.
3. When vinaigrette is warm but not boiling, add blue cheese and mix. The cheese should not completely melt into the dressing, but should just begin to soften.
4. Drizzle warm dressing and softened cheese over salads. Scatter some of the pickled grapes over each salad and serve immediately. Serves 6.

SMOKED SALMON SALAD IN A PARMESAN CUP

Cunningham's Scotch Cold Smoking in Pincher Creek is the place to get locally cold–smoked salmon and trout. Serve smoked fish in this elegant salad, from Chef Chris Gaudet.

4 cups (1 L) freshly grated Parmesan cheese
1 cup (250 mL) balsamic vinegar
1 bunch green onions
1/2 cup (125 mL) canola oil
salt
1 pound (500 g) thinly sliced smoked Atlantic salmon or rainbow trout
8 cups (2 L) mesclun salad mix or other mixed baby greens

1. To make Parmesan cups, divide cheese into six portions and use one portion to completely cover the bottom of a 6-inch (15 cm), nonstick sauté pan. Over medium heat, let Parmesan melt and start to brown slightly—this will take about 2 minutes. Loosen the melted cheese patty with a spatula and flip out of the pan onto an upturned old-fashioned glass or other similarly shaped bowl or glass. Form the cheese lightly around the glass with your hands before it hardens to create a cup. Set aside to cool. Repeat with remaining cheese to create six Parmesan cups.

2. Meanwhile, place balsamic vinegar in a small pot over medium heat. Bring to a boil and simmer to reduce to a thick reduction, the consistency of light molasses. Set aside. The reduction will thicken as it cools.

3. To make green onion oil, wash and trim green onions and cut them into 2-inch (5 cm) pieces. Purée onions in a blender or food processor while slowly adding canola oil through the feed tube. Process until mixture is smooth. Strain oil and season with salt to taste. Cover and refrigerate.

4. To assemble salads, overlap pieces of smoked salmon or trout like flower petals inside each Parmesan cup. Gather salad leaves into bundles and use to fill the centre of each cup. Place salads on individual serving plates and drizzle with green onion oil and balsamic reduction. Serves 6.

Turkey, Black Bean, and Rice Salad

This is the perfect salad to make after Christmas, for a New Year's buffet table, or after Thanksgiving as a take-along lunch. If you don't have leftover turkey, deli turkey or smoked turkey make great alternatives, or you can substitute poached or roasted chicken.

2 cups (500 mL) water
1 cup (250 mL) Texmati or other long-grain,
    scented rice (see tip, below)
1 tablespoon (15 mL) olive oil
1 teaspoon (5 mL) salt
1/2 cup (125 mL) light mayonnaise
2 cloves garlic, minced
1/2 cup (125 mL) salsa
1 pound (500 g) cooked turkey, cut into small cubes
1/4 cup (50 mL) chopped fresh cilantro
2 cups (500 mL) cooked black beans, or 1 can (19 oz/540 mL)
    black beans, rinsed and drained
6 green onions, chopped
1 4-ounce (114 mL) can diced green chiles
romaine or spinach leaves

1. Bring water to a boil. Add rice, olive oil, and salt. Cover tightly and simmer on low heat for 30 minutes. Remove from heat and let stand, covered, for 10 minutes. Fluff rice with a fork and cool, then chill.
2. Combine mayonnaise, garlic, and salsa in blender or food processor and purée until smooth. Stir into rice to combine well.
3. Add chopped turkey, cilantro, black beans, green onions, and chiles to rice mixture and toss gently. Chill until serving time.
4. To present salad, line a bowl or platter with romaine or spinach leaves and pile salad on top. Serves 4 to 6.

> **TIP**
> Texmati is a nutty brown basmati rice grown in Texas. Feel free to substitute any fragrant basmati or scented Thai rice in this dish, or use a blend of brown and wild rice from the Lundberg company in California.

Roasted Beet and Grapefruit Salad

Roasting beets brings out their flavours and concentrates the sugars. Once roasted and cooled, it's easy to slip off the skins and use them in any dish.

4 medium beets (red, golden, or striped)
salt and freshly ground black pepper
2 tablespoons (25 mL) balsamic vinegar
1 tablespoon (15 mL) cold-pressed canola oil or extra-virgin olive oil
1 large pink grapefruit, peeled and sectioned
2 tablespoons (25 mL) sushi vinegar or fruit vinegar
1/2 cup (125 mL) cold-pressed canola oil
1/2 teaspoon (2 mL) salt
2 cups (500 mL) watercress leaves
freshly ground black pepper

1. Wash beets well and remove tops, leaving about 1 inch (2.5 cm) of stem. Place beets in a shallow baking dish and cover with foil (or wrap beets loosely in foil), and bake in a preheated 400°F (200°C) oven for 45 minutes. Remove the beets from the oven. When they are cool enough to handle, trim tops and bottoms and slip off skins.
2. Cut the beets into wedges, place in a bowl, and season with salt and pepper. Drizzle with the balsamic vinegar and 1 tablespoon (15 mL) of canola or olive oil, toss to coat, and set aside.
3. Using a citrus zester or sharp knife, remove some of the zest from the grapefruit. Remove the coloured skin only, not the bitter white pith. Mince zest and set aside.
4. To section the grapefruit, cut both ends off, exposing the flesh. Cut the peel away in sections. Using a sharp knife, cut between the membranes to release the fruit sections. Do this over a bowl to capture any juice. Squeeze the remaining membrane to release the rest of the juice. You should have about 2 tablespoons (25 mL).
5. Combine vinegar, grapefruit juice, and 1/2 teaspoon (2 mL) of minced grapefruit zest and slowly whisk in 1/2 cup (125 mL) of canola oil. Season with salt.
6. Arrange washed greens on four salad plates and place beet and grapefruit wedges alongside greens. Drizzle salads with vinaigrette and grind a little black pepper over them. Serves 4.

CARROT SLAW

Crunchy jicama, a Mexican vegetable, makes this south-of-the-border slaw especially refreshing, but you can use turnips or shredded raw kohlrabi, too. Make it when you're serving burgers or fried chicken for a picnic-style supper.

1 pound (500 g) sweet garden carrots, peeled and grated
3 green onions, chopped
1 jicama or white turnip, grated
2 tablespoons (25 mL) chopped fresh cilantro
1 teaspoon (5 mL) ground cumin

Dressing
2 tablespoons (25 mL) fresh lime or lemon juice
1/4 cup (50 mL) olive oil
1/2 teaspoon (2 mL) chili powder
1/2 teaspoon (2 mL) hot sauce
salt and freshly ground black pepper to taste

1. Combine carrots, onion, jicama or turnip, cilantro, and cumin in a bowl.
2. Whisk together dressing ingredients and add to vegetables, tossing to combine. Serves 4 to 6.

BARLEY SALAD WITH RED ONION, AVOCADO, AND ORANGE VINAIGRETTE

You can add cooked, chopped chicken to this portable salad and serve it over mixed baby greens for a complete meal.

1 cup (250 mL) pearl barley
2 1/2 cups (625 mL) chicken stock
2 avocados, peeled and diced
1 tablespoon (15 mL) fresh lemon or lime juice
1/2 cup (125 mL) finely chopped red onion
1/2 red bell pepper, seeded and chopped
1 orange, zest removed and reserved, flesh chopped
1/4 cup (50 mL) chopped fresh parsley or cilantro

Dressing
2/3 cup (150 mL) orange juice
1/4 cup (50 mL) white wine vinegar
1/4 cup (50 mL) olive oil
2 green onions, minced
1/2 teaspoon (2 mL) ground cumin
1 clove garlic, minced
1 teaspoon (5 mL) honey
1/4 teaspoon (1 mL) hot chili sauce, or more to taste
salt and freshly ground black pepper

1. Combine dressing ingredients in blender or food processor and whirl until smooth. Pour dressing into a jar and refrigerate (shake dressing well before adding to salad).
2. Place barley in a dry saucepan and toast it over medium-high heat, stirring continuously, until fragrant and barely golden, about 5 minutes.
3. Add stock and bring to a boil. Cover and simmer for 45 minutes, until barley is tender. Drain and fluff with a fork. Toss warm barley with dressing and refrigerate to chill. This may be done the night before.
4. Peel and dice avocados (see tip next page) and toss with lemon or lime juice to prevent discolouration. Just before serving, combine barley with red onion, red pepper, avocado, orange pieces, 1 teaspoon (5 mL) of finely minced reserved orange zest, and parsley or cilantro. Toss gently. Serves 6 to 8.

POTATO SALAD WITH WARM MUSTARD DRESSING

This potato salad can be served warm in the fall with grilled chicken and apple sausages, or alongside a baked ham. Use a waxy red potato when you make any potato salad—they hold their shape and toothsome texture, while others fall apart in the pot.

6 slices smoky bacon, chopped
1/2 cup (125 mL) finely sliced red onion
2 cloves garlic, minced
1/4 cup (50 mL) olive oil
2 tablespoons (25 mL) cider vinegar
2 tablespoons (25 mL) grainy Brassica mustard
freshly ground black pepper
2 teaspoons (10 mL) minced fresh rosemary
2 pounds (1 kg) baby red potatoes, halved or quartered if large

1. Sauté bacon until crisp. Remove from pan and drain off all but 1 tablespoon (15 mL) of fat. Set bacon aside.
2. Sauté onion in bacon fat until starting to become translucent. Add garlic and cook for 1 minute. Set aside.
3. Whisk together olive oil, cider vinegar, mustard, a generous amount of black pepper, and rosemary in a large bowl.
4. Cook potatoes in boiling water until just barely cooked. Drain well and add to dressing. Toss potatoes to coat well, then stir in sautéed onion mixture and reserved crispy bacon. Serve warm. Serves 4 to 6.

Soups and Chowders

CORN, BEANS, AND SQUASH: THE THREE SISTERS OF SOUP

Near Canmore, en route to Banff as you enter the Rocky Mountains, there are three mountains called the Three Sisters. But if you look back in Native lore, "three sisters" refers to the three vegetables they cultivated in a symbiotic trio—beans wrapping their way to the sky up tall corn stalks, and big

squash leaves shading the ground, conserving the water and choking out the weeds. These weren't the prairie nomadic Natives, but they may have been their trading partners, tribes living to the south and the east, where it was practical to put down roots and grow crops.

Corn was perhaps the most important native North American food, used in flours, grits, masa,

and hominy from Santa Fe to southern Ontario. The original Native corn was harvested when dry, then ground into meal or flour, or soaked and boiled with unslaked lime to remove the outer hull.

The corn we eat today is sweet corn, and it keeps getting sweeter all the time. Alberta-grown varieties like 'Peaches and Cream', 'Sheba', and 'Krispy King' are so sweet you can eat them without even cooking.

In Taber, Alberta, the little town that bills itself as the Corn Capital of Canada, the annual corn harvest is a time for feverish work and serious celebration. On the farms all around Taber, the harvesters begin work in the cool midnight hours and keep working until midday, filling massive grain trucks and wagons with cobs plucked from the tall stalks by special harvesting machinery.

At farms like Gary Valgardson's, one of the largest in the area, an army of seasonal Mexican workers bustles around in a massive steel building, packing the harvest for shipping. As each huge wagonload of corn is brought into the bay, they pull down the hinged sides and count cobs into big, green net bags. Five dozen cobs are packed in each bag, ready to be picked up by entrepreneurs who sell them at farmer's markets or roadside stands to the city dwellers who greedily await their arrival every summer.

Meanwhile, back in Taber, pretty young girls defy the blistering August heat in formal gowns, vying for the chance to wear the coveted Corn Queen crown. Kids are selling corn on every corner, and locals gather at the town's central park to see who can chow down on the most corn in five minutes to win the annual Corn Bust contest.

The Taber Corn Festival is one place where it's polite to pick your teeth in public, the main consumable being freshly shucked and boiled corn on the cob. Every nonprofit group in town has a corn booth, their big cauldrons of boiling water at the ready and volunteer shuckers forming little assembly lines to strip the green husks and corn silk from warm cobs that were in the field only hours before. Some people use insulated rubber ice-fishing gloves to reach into the boiling water and retrieve your freshly cooked cob. Others impale it on a stick so you can dunk it in a vat of melted butter that drips down your arm as you crunch along its length.

There's no question that this is some of the best corn you will ever eat—so juicy that it snaps and spurts with every bite. It's a bargain, too. At about $1–$2 a dozen, it's no wonder that Albertans gorge on this golden treat every August when the Taber corn harvest begins. It's such an event that the Taber corn-growers, who claim that the special soil and heat in this corn belt make their corn the best, issue certificates of authentication to corn vendors to prevent the practice of palming off foreign corn as the real thing.

Beans are an equally important crop in southern Alberta. This is obvious when you pull into Bow Island, where a giant concrete mascot—a cartoon character dubbed Pinto MacBean, complete with cowboy hat and six-shooter—towers over the road into town. Bow Island is the home of Agricore's bean processing plant, where this local commodity is gathered before being shipped around the world. Canadians eat beans, too, but 98 percent of the annual crop is exported.

Not particularly glamorous, but infinitely nourishing, beans and lentils are cheap, portable, and long-lasting, forming the backbone of peasant cuisines from Mexico to Milan, Kenya to Kashmir. It's not surprising that beans were a staple in prairie households, where fresh food was seasonal at best, and dried foods provided sustenance during the long, cold winters.

Cowboys are particularly famous for surviving on beans. Chuckwagon cooks always carried dried beans on cattle drives, and often served them morning and night, their love of legumes earning some the nickname "bean master." Beans were sometimes cooked overnight, buried in a Dutch oven or sealed pail with coals, so that they would be ready for breakfast. And cowboys had lots of fun coming up with names for their staple food: "prairie strawberries," "whistle berries," or "deceitful beans—'cause they talk behind yore back."

While beans and legumes, from soybeans to favas and chickpeas, are grown all over the world, some have a strictly North American heritage. Black beans, pinto beans, kidney beans, navy beans, cranberry beans, and heirloom varieties like tongues of fire, Anasazi, and rattlesnake beans are all indigenous to the New World.

At the Bow Island Bean Plant, five main varieties are stacked in three-storey piles like edible pyramids. Blacks, speckled pintos, Great Northern white beans, burgundy kidney beans, and pink beans pour through augers into huge iron tote boxes, labelled and stacked to the ceiling in massive steel buildings that are half a block long. Later they will tumble over a gravity table, where lighter, small, or damaged beans float off on a layer of air, separated from the best beans to be shipped off for animal feed. The beans are then sorted and graded, rushing by electric eyes that can spot a bad bean in a blink and keep it out of the mix.

Beans that came into the building in trucks leave in 50-kilogram bags en route to places like Australia, China, Japan, South America, Africa, Turkey, and Greece. Red beans go to Latin America, pink to American canners for pork and beans, pintos to Mexico for refried beans, small red beans to Caribbean countries for traditional dishes like beans and rice, and white and red kidney and black beans to Canada and the United States for soups, baked beans, and bowls of red (Texas talk for chili).

Squash, the third sibling in our story, is also an ideal Alberta vegetable—prolific, easy to grow, and simple to store in a root cellar. Even Native growers baked their squash and sweetened it with maple syrup the way we like to eat it today. The shells of squash and other gourds were used as bowls and ladles, and it's not surprising that the vegetable that provided the original soup tureen is so popular as a base for hearty soups.

Today, squash is grown throughout Alberta—from fields of big pumpkins in Smoky Lake, where an annual fall contest sees world-record giants weighing in at more than 275 kilograms, to summer squash like zucchini and white cousa, or butternuts, acorn, and other winter squash in every exotic shade of orange. It's that deep colour that signals the healthful qualities of squash, rich in beta-carotene and other vitamins.

All squash is indigenous to the Americas and comes from the Cucurbitaceae family, although many squashes of different species share the same common name. Summer squash—big green 'Milano' zucchini, white cousa, scalloped pattypan, and slim yellow gold fingers—are harvested when young and are available in local markets from July to September. Later, winter squash like sweet buttercup, acorn, delicata, and grey-mottled kabocha are available, their thick skins making them such good keepers that local producers can store and sell them well into February. Fine-fleshed and colourful winter squashes are good choices for baking, roasting, and "pumpkin" pies. Tiny 'Golden Nugget' pumpkins make perfect individual containers for fall soups. And spaghetti squash separates into crisp noodle-like strands that make the perfect base for sauces. Like summer squash, winter squash can also be sliced and served raw with other crudites.

ROASTED GARLIC AND CORN SOUP

Don't worry about the whole head of garlic in this delicious soup. Roasting tames the strong flavour and gives the garlic a sweet, nutty edge that works well with the bit of spiciness from the chipotle chile. Use fresh sweet corn kernels in season for a spectacular summer soup.

1 whole head garlic, roasted
2 tablespoons (25 mL) canola oil
1 medium onion, chopped
1 tablespoon (15 mL) ground cumin
1 teaspoon (5 mL) ground coriander
3 cups (750 mL) corn kernels, fresh or frozen, divided
1 stalk celery, diced
2 red bell peppers, roasted, peeled, and diced (see tip, page 10)
1/2 teaspoon (2 mL) chipotle chile in adobo
4 cups (1 L) chicken stock
2 tablespoons (25 mL) chopped fresh cilantro
salt
juice of 1 lime

FRUGAL FRUIT

Beans offer cheap protein with lots of fibre and little fat. Traditionally, beans are eaten with rice or other grains, the complement of amino acids in these ingredients combining to form a protein as nourishing as that found in a steak dinner.

Dried beans should be soaked overnight before cooking. This speeds up the cooking process and drains away some of the starches that can lead to indigestion later. You can also quick-soak beans. Cover them with twice their volume of cold water, bring to a boil, remove from heat, and let stand for 1 hour before draining. A pressure cooker is also a great tool for cooking dried beans. Beans can be pressure soaked in 1 minute, and cooked in about one-third of the time of conventional cooking, usually in less than 15 minutes.

Always wait until beans are cooked before adding salt. Salt inhibits the absorption of water and can lead to a pot of beans that never properly hydrates and softens.

1. To roast garlic, cut 1/4 inch (5 mm) off the whole head so the cloves are just showing. Drizzle a little canola oil over garlic, wrap it loosely in foil and bake in a preheated 400°F (200°C) oven for 45 minutes or until soft. Set aside to cool.

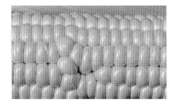

2. Heat oil and sauté onion until tender. Add cumin, coriander, 2 cups (500 mL) corn, and celery. Continue to sauté for 5 minutes. Add half of the roasted peppers and the chipotle chile. Squeeze roasted garlic out of the head into the pot, add stock, and bring to a boil. Cover, reduce heat, and simmer for 20 minutes.

3. Purée soup in blender or food processor, or use an immersible blender, then return to pot.

4. Reheat soup and add reserved corn and roasted peppers. Heat through until corn is tender. Stir in cilantro and season to taste with salt and lime juice. Serves 6.

CHOWDER OF WILD ALBERTA MUSHROOMS WITH MIXED PRAIRIE BEANS

Many years ago, David MacGillivray, a true blue Albertan and former chef at the Jasper Park Lodge, shared this hearty signature soup from the mountain resort with me. It's a rich combination of homegrown ingredients that's perfect after a day of alpine hiking or skiing.

1/2 cup (125 mL) butter
2 cloves garlic, chopped
4 shallots, finely diced
1/2 cup (125 mL) all-purpose flour
8 cups (2 L) chicken stock, heated to boiling
1 ounce (30 g) dried porcini mushrooms, crumbled to a powder
1/4 cup (50 mL) canola oil
3/4 cup (175 mL) each: sliced shiitake, oyster, and chanterelle mushrooms, or equal amounts of brown or button mushrooms
1/2 cup (125 mL) dried morels, soaked in water to soften and sliced

2/3 cup (150 mL) dry white wine
1/2 cup (125 mL) wild rice
1 medium potato, peeled and diced
1/2 cup (125 mL) each: cooked black and white beans
3 tablespoons (45 mL) fireweed honey
1 teaspoon (5 mL) minced fresh rosemary
1 cup (250 mL) whipping cream
1 cup (250 mL) milk
salt and freshly ground black pepper

1. In a soup pot, melt butter and sauté garlic and shallots until translucent, about 5 minutes. Add flour and cook over medium heat for 5 minutes, stirring constantly, until it begins to brown.
2. Slowly add hot chicken stock, whisking constantly to avoid any lumps. Reduce heat to medium-low and stir in powdered porcini mushrooms.
3. In another pan, heat canola oil over high heat and sauté oyster, shiitake, and chanterelle mushrooms until softened. Drain excess oil and add morels. Add white wine to mushrooms to deglaze pan, and cook for 3 minutes longer over medium-high heat. Add mushrooms and wild rice to soup pot, reduce heat, and simmer soup for 45 minutes.
4. Add potato and cooked beans and simmer for 15 minutes. Stir in fireweed honey, rosemary, whipping cream, and milk, and heat through for only about 10 minutes longer. Season with salt and freshly ground black pepper. Serves 10.

GOLDEN PRAIRIE SQUASH BISQUE

*Thick, sweet, and colourful, serve this creamy soup at the beginning
of a fall supper or Thanksgiving meal to pique the palate.*

1 tablespoon (15 mL) butter
1 tablespoon (15 mL) canola oil
1 large onion, chopped
2 cups (500 mL) peeled and diced tart
   green apples (like Granny Smith)
2 cups (500 mL) peeled and diced
   acorn, butternut, or other winter
   squash
2 cups (500 mL) peeled and diced
   orange-fleshed sweet potato

CORN 101

Corn starts to lose its sweetness the minute it's picked—sugars turn to starches, giving old corn that unappealing bland flavour. Taber corn producers say the best way to tell if corn is sweet is to take a bite of a raw cob. If it's not sweet when it's raw, it won't be sweet after it's cooked. Fresh corn has green husks, golden silk, and plump, juicy kernels. Store corn unhusked in the refrigerator, but if you don't plan to eat it within two days, blanch it in boiling water for 1–2 minutes. This will arrest the sugar conversion process and you can keep the corn in a sealed bag for three additional days.

Even at the Taber Corn Festival, there's no consensus on how to cook corn. Some locals simply boil it, others add salt and/or sugar to the water, while some steam it in the microwave or grill it on the barbecue. Here's some basic advice:

• Bring a pot of water to a rolling boil, add the clean cobs, and return the water to boiling. Cover the pot and remove from heat, then wait 5–10 minutes. Some people add 1 tablespoon (15 mL) sugar and/or 1 teaspoon (5 mL) salt to the water.

• Microwave corn, in the husk or wrapped in plastic wrap, on high for 3–5 minutes per cob.

• To grill, pull back the husks, discard the silk, and pull the leaves back in place. Tie with string or strips of husk. Fill the kitchen sink with cold water and soak cobs for 10 minutes. Grill the soaked cobs 15–20 minutes, until the husks are charred and the corn is steamed.

• You can freeze corn on or off the cob. Blanch cobs in boiling water for 7–11 minutes depending on the size of cob, and chill in ice water before freezing. Alternatively, cut the kernels off the cobs and cover with a mixture of 1 cup (250 mL) water, 1 tablespoon (15 mL) sugar, and 1 teaspoon (5 mL) salt before freezing (you can reheat the corn in this mixture).

1 small Yukon Gold potato, peeled and chopped
1 tablespoon (15 mL) chopped fresh ginger
5 cups (1.25 L) chicken or vegetable stock
1 teaspoon (5 mL) chopped fresh thyme
1/2 teaspoon (2 mL) celery salt
1/4 teaspoon (1 mL) cayenne pepper
1/4 cup (50 mL) rye whisky
1 tablespoon (15 mL) maple syrup
1 cup (250 mL) evaporated milk
salt and white pepper
chopped green onion, unpeeled green apple, sliced thinly and
    tossed with lemon juice, for garnish

1. Melt butter with oil and sauté onions until beginning to brown. Add apple and cook for 10 minutes, or until tender.
2. Stir in squash, sweet potato, Yukon Gold potato, ginger, stock, thyme, celery salt, and cayenne pepper. Cover and bring to a boil. Reduce heat and simmer for 35–40 minutes, until squash is cooked and breaking up.
3. Pureé soup in batches in food processor until smooth, or use an immersible blender to purée. Return to pot. Stir in whisky, maple syrup, and evaporated milk. Season with salt and white pepper to taste, and heat through. Serve soup garnished with chopped green onion and slices of green apple. Serves 6 to 8.

> **TIP**
> To cut a winter squash, place a heavy knife or cleaver along the length of the squash and tap the back of the blade, where it joins the handle, with a wooden meat mallet until the squash is cleaved in half. Scrape out the seeds and stringy bits with a spoon. Bake squash halves, rubbed with oil or butter and seasoned, in a shallow pan with a little water.

SOUTHWESTERN CORN AND SAUSAGE SOUP

I like to use Spolumbo's apple and chicken sausage in this soup. Yukon Gold potatoes are great for thick soups like this one—the buttery flesh breaks down slightly and acts as a natural thickener.

1 large onion, chopped
3 cloves garlic, minced
1 tablespoon (15 mL) olive oil
1 pound (500 g) fresh chicken or turkey sausage
2 large Yukon Gold potatoes, peeled and cubed
2 cups (500 mL) water or chicken stock
1 stalk celery, chopped
1/2 green pepper, seeded and diced
2 jalapeño peppers, chopped
1 14-ounce (398 mL) can creamed corn
1 cup (250 mL) fresh or frozen corn kernels
1/4 teaspoon (1 mL) crushed red chilies
1/2 teaspoon (2 mL) black pepper
1 teaspoon (5 mL) dried oregano
1 bay leaf
2 cups (500 mL) buttermilk
2 tablespoons (25 mL) chopped fresh cilantro
3 green onions, chopped

1. In a soup pot, sauté onion and garlic in olive oil until tender. Remove sausage from its casing and crumble into pot. Cook until browned.
2. Add potatoes and water or stock, bring to a boil, then reduce heat and simmer for 10 minutes.
3. Stir in celery, green pepper, jalapeño pepper, creamed corn, corn kernels, crushed red chilies, black pepper, oregano, and bay leaf and simmer for 20 minutes over low heat until all vegetables are tender. Stir in buttermilk and heat through. Add cilantro and green onions and serve immediately. Serves 6.

BLACK BEAN SOUP

At the bean plant in Bow Island, dried black beans are piled in towering pyramids three storeys high. But all it takes is a couple of cups to make this classic, earthy soup.

2 cups (500 mL) black beans
2 tablespoons (25 mL) butter or olive oil
2 onions, finely chopped
3 cloves garlic, minced
2 stalks celery, chopped
2 carrots, chopped
1/4 cup (50 mL) all-purpose flour
1 pound (500 g) spicy pork sausage, such as chorizo,
    preferably smoked
1 chipotle chile in adobo, chopped
8 cups (2 L) cold water
2 bay leaves
salt and freshly ground black pepper to taste
1 tablespoon (15 mL) chili powder
1 teaspoon (5 mL) each: ground cumin, oregano, and thyme
1/2 teaspoon (2 mL) ground cinnamon
1/2 teaspoon (2 mL) fennel seeds
1/4 cup (50 mL) Madeira or sweet sherry
1 large red bell pepper, finely chopped
1/4 cup (50 mL) chopped fresh parsley
hot sauce

1. Cover beans with cold water and set aside to soak overnight, or use quick-soak method (page 29).
2. Place soaked beans in a clean pot and cover with water. Bring to a boil, reduce heat to medium-low and simmer, uncovered, for 1 hour. Drain beans.
3. In a large stock pot, melt butter or heat olive oil and sauté onions, garlic, celery, and carrots until beginning to turn colour. Add flour and stir well, cooking to brown slightly. Add the whole pork sausage, chipotle chile, and water, and bring to a boil. Stir in bay leaves, salt, pepper, chili powder, cumin, oregano, thyme, cinnamon, and fennel seeds. Simmer, covered, for 30 minutes.
4. Add cooked and drained beans to broth and continue to simmer for 45 minutes. Remove bay leaves. Using a food processor or hand blender, purée one-third of the soup. Return to pot.
5. Remove sausage, chop, and return to soup. Stir in Madeira, red pepper, parsley, and hot sauce to taste. Thin with water if necessary and heat through. Serves 12.

PRAIRIE FISH CHOWDER

When I was a kid, fresh fish was almost nonexistent, except for the perch and pickerel caught in local prairie lakes in the summer. But a block of frozen fish fillets—usually cod or halibut—could easily be transformed into a creamy fish soup, reminiscent of the best East Coast chowders.

4 slices smoky bacon, chopped
1 large onion, finely chopped
4 cups (1 L) peeled and cubed potatoes
2 tablespoons (15 mL) all-purpose flour
2 cups (500 mL) fish stock or water
1/2 teaspoon (2 mL) salt
1/4 teaspoon (1 mL) freshly ground black pepper
2 pounds (500 g) fresh or frozen fish fillets, bones removed,
    cut into small cubes
2 cups (500 mL) milk
1 cup (250 mL) evaporated milk or half-and-half cream
2 tablespoons (25 mL) chopped fresh parsley

1. Cook bacon slowly in a large soup pot until crisp. Remove bacon from pan and allow to cool. Crumble and set aside.
2. Add onion to fat in pan and sauté until tender. Add potatoes and sauté a few minutes longer.
3. Stir in flour and mix well. Slowly add stock or water, and season with salt and pepper to taste. Bring to a boil, then cover and simmer for 10 minutes, or until potatoes are cooked.
4. Add fish and simmer 10 minutes longer. Stir in milk and evaporated milk or cream and heat through but don't boil. Serve soup sprinkled with reserved bacon and parsley. Serves 6 to 8.

Gingery Carrot and Golden Lentil Soup

Golden lentils (CDC Gold) are white with a bright yellow interior. They cook in about 30 minutes without presoaking and make a colourful addition to soups, stews, and salads. This simple combination is low in fat and equally alluring served hot or cold.

2 tablespoons (25 mL) butter or olive oil
1 onion, chopped
1 pound (500 g) carrots, peeled and shredded or chopped
1 tablespoon (15 mL) minced ginger
3 tablespoons (45 mL) all-purpose flour
8 cups (2 L) chicken stock
3/4 cup (175 mL) golden or red lentils
bay leaf
1 teaspoon (5 mL) granulated sugar
salt and freshly ground black pepper
1/2 teaspoon (2 mL) curry powder, or to taste
2 tablespoons (25 mL) chopped fresh cilantro or parsley

1. Heat butter or oil and sauté onion, carrots, and ginger, covered, until soft and starting to brown, about 10–15 minutes. Stir flour into vegetables and cook 1 minute.
2. Add stock, lentils, bay leaf, sugar, salt, and pepper. Simmer until vegetables are very soft and lentils are tender, about 45 minutes.
3. Discard bay leaf and serve. If a smoother soup is desired, purée with immersible blender; alternatively, purée in food processor or blender, return to pot and reheat. Season with curry powder to taste and garnish each serving with cilantro. Serves 4 to 6.

BLACK AMBER ALE SOUP

Klaus Wockinger, a longtime Calgary chef who is in charge of the casual restaurant at Big Rock Brewery, shared this recipe for a simple, creamy soup flavoured with Big Rock's dark Black Amber Ale.

1 small onion, chopped
1 medium carrot, chopped
1 stalk celery, chopped
1/3 cup (75 mL) butter
1/2 cup (125 mL) all-purpose flour
4 cups (1 L) chicken stock
1 cup (250 mL) whipping cream
1 cup (250 mL) Black Amber Ale, or substitute
   your favourite dark beer
salt and freshly ground black pepper

1. In a food processor, combine onion, carrot, and celery and process until finely chopped.
2. Heat butter in a large saucepan over medium-high heat. Add minced vegetables and sauté for 1–2 minutes. Stir in flour and cook for another minute or two.
3. Slowly whisk in stock and bring to a boil, stirring constantly. Reduce heat to low and simmer for 30 minutes.
4. Add cream and beer and heat through. Season with salt and pepper to taste. Serves 4 to 6.

Klaus Wockinger

POLISH SAUSAGE AND SOUR CABBAGE SOUP

With its flavours of home-made sauerkraut and garlic sausage, this soup reminds me of my own prairie roots. Serve this rich, hearty meal-in-a-bowl with a loaf of good caraway rye bread.

1 pound (500 g) sauerkraut made with wine
   (either homemade or a jar of the milder European
   sauerkraut, not the canned brands)
6 cups (1.5 L) water
2 teaspoons (10 mL) caraway seed
2 teaspoons (10 mL) salt
1 tablespoon (15 mL) Vegeta (a vegetable-based seasoning
   available at European delis and specialty stores), optional
2–3 bay leaves
2 large potatoes, peeled and cut into small cubes
1/4 pound (125 g) double-smoked bacon, chopped
1 small onion, chopped
1 tablespoon (15 mL) sweet Hungarian paprika
2 tablespoons (25 mL) all-purpose flour
1/2 pound (250 g) smoked Polish sausage or other garlic sausage
1/2 cup (125 mL) whipping cream
2 tablespoons (25 mL) chopped fresh parsley

1. Combine sauerkraut, water, and caraway seed with salt, Vegeta, and bay leaves. Bring to a boil, then reduce heat and simmer 1 hour.
2. Boil potatoes separately for 20–30 minutes. Drain.
3. Sauté bacon until beginning to render its fat, and add onions. Sauté until onions are light golden in colour, then add paprika and flour, cooking together to make a roux. Add this mixture to the soup and boil for 10–15 minutes.
4. Cube sausage and add to soup along with cooked potatoes. Stir in cream and heat through. Soup should have a thick, chowder-like texture. Serve soup in shallow, wide-rimmed bowls dusted with paprika and sprinkled with chopped fresh parsley. Serves 4.

CREAMY TOMATO SOUP WITH BASIL POTATO DUMPLINGS

The addition of sundried tomato chunks and fresh basil dumplings makes this comforting tomato soup far superior to the canned versions of our youth.

3 tablespoons (45 mL) butter
3 tablespoons (45 mL) all-purpose flour
1 10-ounce (284 mL) can beef broth, undiluted
1/4 cup (50 mL) white wine
1 5 1/2-ounce (156 mL) can tomato paste
1/3 cup (75 mL) sundried tomatoes in oil, drained and chopped
1 tablespoon (15 mL) minced garlic
3 cups (750 mL) 2 percent milk
salt and freshly ground black pepper

Basil Dumplings
1 pound (500 g) Yukon Gold potatoes, peeled and boiled
2 egg yolks
1/2 cup (125 mL) all-purpose flour
1/4 cup (50 mL) minced fresh basil, plus additional chopped
   fresh basil for garnish
pinch each of salt and pepper

1. Melt butter in a saucepan and stir in flour. Cook for 1 minute.
2. Slowly add beef broth, whisking to prevent lumps. Whisk in wine, tomato paste, sundried tomatoes, and garlic. Bring to a boil and simmer until thick, about 5–10 minutes.
3. Stir in milk and heat through. Season to taste with salt and pepper.
4. To make dumplings, mash potatoes, then stir in egg yolks, flour, basil and seasonings. The dough should be quite firm. Add more flour if necessary.
5. Roll the dough into a rope and cut into 1/2-inch (1.5 cm) dumplings. Cook dumplings in a large pot of boiling water until they are tender and float to the top, about 3–4 minutes. Remove with a slotted spoon and drain.
6. To serve, ladle soup into bowls and place several dumplings in the centre of each bowl. Garnish each serving with additional chopped fresh basil. Serves 4.

ROASTED ROOTS SOUP WITH POPPED WILD RICE

Roasting the root vegetables before making this soup is like roasting bones before making stock—the dry heat caramelizes the sugars in the vegetables and concentrates the flavours so the soup tastes rich and delicious. The popped wild rice adds a colourful and crunchy garnish and also makes an unusual cocktail snack.

1 large potato and 1 sweet potato, peeled and cubed
3 carrots, cut up
2 parsnips, peeled and chopped
2 large onions, chopped
1 medium acorn squash, peeled and cubed
2 large red bell peppers, seeded and quartered
6 cloves garlic, peeled
2 tablespoons (25 mL) olive oil
3 cups (750 mL) chicken or vegetable stock
1/2 teaspoon (2 mL) ground sage
1/2 teaspoon (2 mL) marjoram
salt and freshly ground black pepper

Popped Wild Rice
1 cup (250 mL) vegetable oil
1/2 cup (125 mL) wild rice

1. Combine cubed potato, sweet potato, carrots, parsnips, onions, squash, red peppers, and garlic in a bowl. Toss with olive oil to coat. Spread in a single layer in one or two shallow baking pans.

2. Roast vegetables in a preheated 375°F (190°C) oven for 1 hour, or until soft and nicely caramelized. Stir vegetables occasionally.

3. Remove skin from roasted peppers and discard. Place all vegetables in food processor and purée until smooth, adding a little of the stock if necessary. Place purée in a pot and add remaining stock, sage, marjoram, salt, and pepper. Bring to a boil and simmer for 20 minutes to combine flavours.

4. To make the popped wild rice garnish, heat vegetable oil in a wok or deep pot over high heat, watching carefully, until it is almost smoking. Put about 2–3 tablespoons (25–45 mL) of wild rice into a wire mesh strainer and lower it carefully into the hot fat. The rice will pop and triple in size. When it's popped and browned, remove from

oil, shake off excess fat, and place in a bowl. Salt to taste while still warm. Repeat with remaining rice.

5. Ladle soup into individual shallow bowls and garnish with popped wild rice. Serves 8.

TOMATO CHICKPEA SOUP WITH BARLEY

Southern Alberta farmers are finding their climate is perfect for growing field peas and all kinds of beans, including chickpeas, or garbanzo beans, the classic legumes of Italian and other Mediterranean cuisines. Top each bowl of soup with curls of Parmesan cheese or aged Gouda from Sylvan Star Dairy.

1 cup (250 mL) finely chopped lean back bacon or ham
1 medium onion, chopped
1 large carrot, chopped
2 stalks celery, chopped
2 cloves garlic, minced
1/4 cup (50 mL) olive oil
1 14-ounce (398 mL) can tomatoes, puréed
1 19-ounce (540 mL) can chickpeas, drained and rinsed
5 cups (1.25 L) chicken broth
1/2 cup (125 mL) pearl barley or small pasta like orzo
2 teaspoons (10 mL) chopped fresh rosemary,
   plus additional sprigs for garnish
salt and freshly ground black pepper to taste
pinch of cayenne pepper
fresh Sylvan Star aged Gouda or Parmesan cheese, at room
   temperature

1. Place ham, onion, carrot, celery, and garlic in food processor and chop finely. Heat olive oil in a soup pot and sauté chopped vegetable mixture until tender and fragrant, about 10 minutes.

2. Add tomatoes to pot with chickpeas and chicken broth. Bring to a boil, then reduce heat and simmer for 40 minutes.

3. Add barley and rosemary, and cook until barley is tender, about 15–20 minutes. Season to taste with salt, black pepper, and cayenne pepper. Ladle soup into bowls. Using a potato peeler, slice thin curls from the block of Parmesan to sprinkle over each serving. Garnish with additional fresh rosemary. Serves 6.

Beet and Cabbage Borscht

Borscht is a classic Ukrainian soup and the perfect way to utilize root vegetables stored in the cold room during the winter. Some versions of this beet soup start with beef or pork soup bones or spare ribs to make a meat broth base. This one is vegetarian.

3 medium beets, scrubbed but unpeeled
2/3 cup (175 mL) cubed carrots
1 medium onion, finely chopped
2 cloves garlic, minced
2 cups (500 mL) finely shredded green or purple cabbage
1 large Yukon Gold potato, peeled and cubed
1 14-ounce (398 mL) can tomatoes, puréed
8 cups (2 L) water (or beef bouillon)
1 cup (250 mL) cooked small white beans
3 tablespoons (45 mL) fresh lemon juice, or red wine vinegar
1 tablespoon (15 mL) granulated sugar

1/2 teaspoon (2 mL) paprika
2 tablespoons (25 mL) all-purpose flour
salt and freshly ground black pepper
1/2 cup (125 mL) whipping cream or sour cream
2 tablespoons (25 mL) chopped fresh dill weed

1. Combine beets, carrots, onion, garlic, cabbage, potato, tomatoes, and water or bouillon in a soup pot. Bring to a boil over high heat, then reduce heat to low, cover, and simmer for 1 hour.

2. Remove beets from soup, peel, and chop or grate back into the soup. Add white beans, lemon juice, sugar, and paprika and simmer for 10 minutes.

3. In a bowl, whisk together flour, salt, pepper, and cream or sour cream. Whisk this mixture into soup to thicken. Heat through but do not boil or the soup will curdle. Stir in fresh dill and serve immediately. Serves 6 to 8.

My Minestrone with Ham and White Beans

This recipe makes a big pot of homey vegetable soup, inspired by Italian minestrone but with the addition of barley or brown rice instead of the usual pasta.

2 tablespoons (25 mL) olive oil
1 large onion, chopped
1 cup (250 mL) chopped cooked ham, or substitute
   4–5 slices of double-smoked bacon, chopped
1 cup (250 mL) chopped carrots
2 cups (500 mL) peeled and chopped potatoes
2 cloves garlic, minced
1 cup (250 mL) chopped celery
4 large tomatoes, chopped (fresh or canned)
6 cups (1.5 L) chicken broth
1 ham bone
1 bay leaf
1/2 cup (125 mL) pot barley or brown rice
1 1/2 cups (375 mL) cooked white beans, or 1 19-ounce
   (540 mL) can white beans, drained and rinsed

1 cup (250 mL) frozen peas, thawed (optional)
salt and freshly ground black pepper
2 tablespoons (25 mL) basil pesto or to taste
hot sauce (optional)

1. In a large stock pot or Dutch oven, heat olive oil and sauté onion until it starts to brown (if using bacon instead of ham, cook it with the onions). Add ham, chopped carrots, potatoes, garlic, and celery and continue to sauté until vegetables are fragrant and beginning to get tender, about 5–10 minutes.
2. Add tomatoes and cook 2 minutes. Add broth, ham bone, and bay leaf. Bring to a boil, cover partially, reduce heat to medium-low, and simmer for 1 hour.
3. Stir in barley or rice, beans, and peas, if using, and return the soup to boiling. Cover and simmer at low heat for 30 minutes longer, until barley or rice is tender. Season soup with salt and pepper to taste, and stir in pesto (or place a little dollop in each bowl of soup when serving). Season with hot sauce to taste. Serves 8.

CREAMY ONION SOUP WITH GOAT CHEESE CROUTONS

This is an alternative to the classic onion soup made with beef broth. Serve it to start an elegant meal, topped with a crisp crouton with bubbly goat cheese on top, or a few big curls of aged Sylvan Star Gouda cheese.

3 pounds (1.5 kg) yellow or white onions, sliced
3 tablespoons (45 mL) butter
2 cloves garlic, minced
1 cup (250 mL) white wine
4 cups (1 L) chicken or vegetable stock
1 cup (250 mL) half-and-half cream
1 tablespoon (15 mL) cornstarch
1/2 teaspoon (2 mL) turmeric
salt and freshly ground black pepper
2 tablespoons (25 mL) chopped green onion or fresh parsley

Croutons
8 1/2-inch (1.5 cm) slices baguette
2 tablespoons (25 mL) olive oil
1 clove garlic, minced
4 ounces (125 g) goat cheese (soft or sliceable)

1. Cook onions with butter over medium heat until soft and golden brown. This will take about 30–40 minutes as onions must be caramelized. Keep heat low to avoid burning. Stir in garlic and wine and simmer until wine is reduced by half.
2. Add stock and simmer, uncovered, for 20 minutes.
3. Combine cream, cornstarch, and turmeric and gradually stir into hot soup, simmering until thickened slightly. Season with salt and pepper.
4. To make the croutons, combine olive oil and garlic and let stand for 10 minutes to infuse. Brush bread slices on both sides with a little of the garlic oil and place on a baking sheet. Toast the bread for 5 minutes in a preheated 400°F (200°C) oven until crisp and beginning to brown. Top each toast with some of the goat cheese and broil until bubbly, about 2 minutes.
5. Ladle hot onion soup into eight individual bowls and top each with a hot cheese crouton. Sprinkle with chopped green onion or parsley and serve immediately. Serves 8.

HUNGARIAN MUSHROOM SOUP

The recipe for this creamy mushroom soup with the eastern European flavours of dill and paprika comes from the Sonoma Café in Calgary. You can use any kind of fresh mushrooms, although a few shiitake or portobellos will add depth to the flavour.

3/4 cup (175 mL) chopped onions
3 tablespoons (45 mL) butter
2 teaspoons (10 mL) sweet Hungarian paprika
2 teaspoons (10 mL) dill weed
1 teaspoon (5 mL) kosher salt
1 teaspoon (5 mL) freshly ground black pepper
1/4 cup (50 mL) all-purpose flour
1 cup (250 mL) milk
1 cup (250 mL) chicken stock
1 cup (250 mL) water
2 cups (500 mL) sliced mushrooms
1 tablespoon (15 mL) soy sauce
1 tablespoon (15 mL) fresh lemon juice
1/4 cup (50 mL) crème fraîche or sour cream
1 1/2 tablespoons (20 mL) chopped parsley

1. Sauté onion in butter for 5 minutes. Add paprika, dill weed, salt, and pepper. Cook until tender.
2. Sift in flour and stir to create a roux. Slowly add milk, stock, and water, stirring. Bring to a boil.
3. Add mushrooms, then reduce heat and simmer for 20 minutes. Remove from heat and add soy sauce, lemon juice, crème fraîche or sour cream, and parsley. Season to taste and heat through. Serves 4.

Beef and Other Red Meat

RED MEAT ON THE RANGE

"Alberta beef" is the phrase that slips off the lips of almost anyone thinking about food in this province. While bison was the original red meat of the plains, today it's beef. Nearly two of every three farms in Alberta raise cattle, and we are famous for our barley-fed beef, meat with that pure white marbling you don't find in American corn-fed beef. The beef producers' popular poster, with its crew of dusty, motley cowboys, says it all: "If it ain't Alberta, it ain't beef."

But there's more than one way to put a steak on a plate. There is a new era of beef production beginning on the Alberta range, spearheaded by a new breed of beef producer, aiming for a unique piece of the economic pie. Francis and Bonnie Gardner are devoted to the ideal of preserving the wild, rough fescue grasslands along the southern Alberta foothills, where generations of their family have farmed. On their Mt. Sentinel Ranch—8,200 acres of some of the most stunning foothills ranchland you'll find south of Calgary—the Gardners and a group of like-minded area ranchers have formed a company to raise and market certified organic beef.

It's just an extension of the natural foothills ecosystem, says Gardner, surveying the steep, rolling grassland from his historic 1920s ranch house. Where his contented cattle roam, there are also wild cougars, coyotes, lynx, wolves, and bear. "For centuries, the buffalo wintered on this rough fescue grass, which keeps 7 percent of its protein in winter," he says. "This is a very rare area—the biggest bio-region in Alberta that hasn't been broken up. The producers of the Diamond Willow are a bunch

of ranchers on the eastern slopes who are putting the natural system to work. The land is organic anyway—the beef is a natural spin-off of a natural piece of ground."

Diamond Willow organic beef is sold across the country, popular today because it comes with a guarantee that no antibiotics, growth hormones, or genetically-modified organisms were used in its production. The ranchers raise the beef on organic grass and finish it on organic grain in a feedlot.

Other modern-day ranchers, like John Cross, a fourth-generation Alberta cattle producer, take that ideal a step further. He is raising beef fed exclusively on the grasses of the open range. Cross studied the art of grass management and low-stress handling techniques from another Alberta grass feeder, Dylan Biggs, who markets 100 percent grass-fed beef under the family's TK Ranch label. Biggs has made a career out of being kind to his cattle and teaches others in the business how to handle the big animals without resorting to cattle prods, noisy yelping, and other scare tactics. It's amazing to watch him quietly coax a massive bull into a trailer, simply by walking alongside the animal's flank and talking. It makes the cattle calmer, he says, and the result is a more tender product on the plate. Chefs looking for high-quality regional foods are taking note.

Not only are Biggs' animals humanely handled, they're grazed exclusively on wild fescue pasture, the same way all cattle were raised only a few generations ago. Grass-fed beef is produced without the growth hormones and antibiotics that some consumers want to avoid, and grown without grain. According to some research, that gives this meat another advantage: it's high in

John Cross

conservation. Cross, the grandson of well-known Calgary businessman and pioneer A.E. Cross, takes a holistic approach to ranching on his A7 Ranch, where his partner also raises organic vegetables and free-range chickens. With miles of portable electric fences, Cross divides his 3,000-acre ranch into mini-pastures and moves his cattle from one patch of fresh grass to another every two to five days. This gives the wild fescue, timothy, and brome grasses sixty or more days to regenerate between grazing, says Cross, preserving the prairie while feeding the animals in a purely natural way. "What I'm trying to sell is healthy land, clean water, clean air, and clean and healthy food products," he says. "Because the grass plants are only exposed to animals for a short period, they stay healthy. The alternative is using fossil fuels and chemicals and that doesn't fit my values."

healthy Omega-3 fatty acids, the essential fatty acids that health-conscious consumers seek out from other sources, like wild fish and flax seed. Grass is part of these animals' natural diet while grain is not. When cattle are fed grain, the percentage of Omega-3 and Omega-6 fatty acids in their meat is thrown out of balance. That unnatural balance is reflected in today's North American diet, which is too high in Omega 6s and too low in Omega 3s. Cattle fed on grass alone have two to three times the levels of heart-healthy Omega 3s in their meat than conventional, grain-fed beef. Although grain feeders would argue that the meat is not as consistently tender as their grain-fed beef, grass feeders say their beef is leaner, with a more robust, beefy flavour.

Producing food for the growing niche market of health-conscious and environmentally sensitive consumers is important to ranchers like Gardner, Cross, and Biggs, but it's more than money that lures these beef producers out of the huge conventional cattle business. All of these ranchers are driven by principles of grassland management and

It is the preservation of the open rangeland that drives Francis Gardner, too. "People have a way of turning the world to their use and that cannot go on forever," says Gardner, who received the Alberta Cattleman's Association's first environmental stewardship award in 1992 for his environmental ranching ethic, and is a founding member of a nonprofit society dedicated to protecting ranchland from subdivision and development. "The land is self-sustaining and self-renewing if we allow it."

While the ranchers producing organic, natural, and grass-fed beef are careful not to claim that their meat is healthier than conventionally raised beef, they say it gives consumers another choice. But it is still an extremely small part of Alberta's beef production. Most of the over 5.1 million head of cattle on Alberta farms are raised conventionally, grazed as calves on pasture and finished on grain in one of the province's 4,000 feedlots, some of which handle up to 40,000 animals at a time.

Pork production is also a major industry in Alberta, with farmers raising nearly 1.8 million hogs every year. Some producers, like the Price family of Acme, are taking pork into gourmet territory. Stan and Flo Price and their seven children have built the local gourmet food store chain, Sunterra Food Markets, on the base of their innovative pig breeding program. After breeding a leaner, more flavourful hog, they wanted to bring the meat directly to market and their retail stores were born. Today the family produces both the pork and the beef that is sold in their stores and processes their own animals at their Trochu plant. Their food markets, which offer fresh foods and in-store chefs and bakeries, are located in both Edmonton and Calgary.

Another great pork product is the gourmet sausage made by Spolumbo's Fine Foods in Calgary. Three ex-Calgary Stampeder football players—Tom and Tony Spoletini and Mike Palumbo—have joined forces to create their own line of lean pork and poultry sausages. The sausages are made without additives, preservatives, or fillers, from 100 percent pork butt or boneless, skinless chicken thighs.

(L-R) Mike Palumbo, Tony & Tom Spoletini

From their original mild and spicy Italian sausage (a classic family recipe) to great new combinations like whisky fennel sausage, chorizo sausage, maple syrup breakfast sausage, and chicken and apple sausage, the Spolumbo's team has nearly thirty different gourmet sausages in their lineup. They also make several lean sausages with turkey. I like to grill any of their sausages, or remove them from their casings and use them instead of ground meat in pasta sauces, soups, and bean or lentil dishes for fast flavour.

Alberta lamb is a premium product, full-flavoured but mild, and far superior to imports. Sheep were first introduced to Alberta one hundred years ago and played an important part in opening the West. In fact, it was 1884 when the British American Ranche at Cochrane received the first huge herd of sheep to arrive in

COOKING ALBERTA BEEF

While it's important to cook hamburgers until they're no longer pink and have reached an internal temperature of 160°F (70°C), any other cut of beef is juiciest and easiest to digest if it's never cooked past medium rare. To cook a tender roast, sear the meat in a pan or very hot oven to start, then roast at a lower temperature until cooked to an internal temperature of 140–150°F (60–65°C) (for rare to medium-rare meat). As a general rule, cook for about 10–15 minutes per pound. Always roast tender cuts uncovered. Allow roasts to rest on the carving board, loosely covered with foil, for 20 minutes to prevent loss of juices when carving.

Less tender cuts of beef, usually labelled "braising" roasts or steaks, need to be cooked slowly in a covered, moist environment. To extract more flavour and colour, always brown braising roasts in a hot pan on all sides before adding liquid. Pressure cooking is a wonderful way to quickly cook and tenderize tougher braising cuts and stew meat. Don't miss out on non-prime beef cuts like meaty short ribs and flank steak. They're inexpensive and, when properly cooked, actually have more rich, beefy flavour than the more tender cuts.

Grass feeders recommend you cook their leaner grass-fed beef low and slow, but don't overcook it. Some assume that grass-fed beef won't be tender, but that's not the case. Marbled fat is not the only guarantee of tenderness; it is also dependent on breed, handling of animals, and cooking. Find a producer you like and learn to cook a steak properly.

Any Alberta steakhouse chef knows you can quickly judge a steak's readiness by how it feels. Chefs use a "touch test" to determine when your steak is cooked to medium-rare perfection. Here's a trick to help you learn how a well-cooked steak should feel. Relax your hand and touch the fleshy pad at the base of your thumb. It feels soft, like a rare piece of steak. Touch your thumb and index finger together and press the base of your thumb again. It's a little firmer, like a steak that's medium rare. There's no need to go on (steakhouse chefs say beef should never be cooked beyond medium rare), but if you must, touch your middle finger to your thumb. It feels like a steak cooked to medium. When you touch your fourth finger, it's as firm as a steak that's well done. And what you get when your thumb and baby finger meet is a bouncy spot the consistency of overdone shoe leather—not the way to treat prime Alberta beef!

COOKING ALBERTA PORK

While pork is marketed as "the other white meat," in terms of cuts and cooking techniques it fits in the red meat category. Boneless pork loin roasts are lean and extremely easy to carve and serve. Pork tenderloin is as fast and easy to grill as chicken breasts; serve it sliced over greens or in stir fries. Pork shoulder is the best cut to rub with spices and slow smoke in your smoker, and it also makes a tender addition to traditional stews and chilies. Baby back ribs are the top choice to grill alongside barbecued chicken. And what would a prairie breakfast be without good double-smoked bacon or pork sausages?

Pork matches well with fruit sauces and sweet glazes. To prevent burning, you should only glaze pork with sugary sauces during the last 20 minutes of cooking. Fresh herbs like thyme and rosemary, mustard sauces, and garlic are also perfect with pork.

All pork (except ground pork) should be cooked to medium, when internal juices run clear. Start with a room temperature pork roast, place it on a rack, and roast, uncovered, in a preheated 325°F (160°C) oven for about 25 minutes per pound, to an internal temperature of 160°F (70°C), using a meat thermometer to gauge internal temperature. Cover roast with foil and allow to stand for 15 minutes before carving.

Don't preboil baby back ribs before grilling, but make sure that you pull off the paper skin on the back of the rack before marinating or seasoning. Use a paper towel to help you grab and pull away the skin.

Alberta—8,000 Merinos driven across the border from Montana. By 1921, Mormon farmers, many around Raymond and Magrath, were raising most of the province's 432,000 head of sheep.

Today, as fine lamb once more gains popularity among discriminating diners, sheep production is on the rise. Breeds like shaggy Columbia, black-faced Suffolk, and stocky North Country Cheviot are raised for their wool, meat, and milk. At Pasu Farm, a charming country restaurant just a 45-minute drive northwest of Calgary near Carstairs, Patrick de Rosemond tends his sheep and his stoves. A sheep farmer and chef, de Rosemond and his wife, Sue, are wonderful hosts, serving lamb and other fine gourmet cuisine in the vaulted dining room and gift store on their farm. While de Rosemond can cook you almost anything decadent (his creamy mushroom soup and desserts are legendary), he also offers items like stuffed roast leg of lamb à la Languedoc and classic French-style rack of lamb. His South African roots come through in dishes like Grilled Lamb Chops in Yogurt Marinade (page 53).

Alberta lamb is a seasonal product, expensive but of the highest quality. Look for it in the spring and summer, and roast or grill lamb loins, legs, and chops to medium rare. Lamb shoulder is delicious trimmed and stewed with red wine, served in classic Irish stew, or cooked in curries. Lamb shank is also a wonderful cut when braised slowly with vegetables and wine.

BEEF BURGERS WITH COWBOY COFFEE BARBECUE BASTE

On a summer day nothing beats a good, homemade hamburger, hot off the grill. Make sure to cook all ground meats until well done.

1 1/2 pounds (750 g) lean ground beef
1 egg
1/2 cup (125 mL) dry breadcrumbs or cracker crumbs
freshly ground black pepper
1/4 cup (50 mL) coffee barbecue baste (see recipe, below)
1 small onion, finely minced
1 clove garlic, minced
1/4 teaspoon (1 mL) dried thyme
whole-wheat buns
lettuce, tomato slices, cheese slices, white onion slices, ketchup, mustard, relish, mayonnaise, and horseradish

Coffee Barbecue Baste

1/2 cup (125 mL) ketchup
1/4 cup (50 mL) strong black coffee
2 tablespoons (25 mL) brown sugar
2 tablespoons (25 mL) cider vinegar
1 tablespoon (15 mL) Worcestershire sauce
1 teaspoon (5 mL) canola oil
1/2 teaspoon (2 mL) canned chipotle chile in adobo
  or Asian chili paste

1. Whisk together barbecue baste ingredients, reserving 1/4 cup (50 mL) for hamburger patty mixture.
2. Combine all burger ingredients except buns and condiments, mixing with your hands to combine well. Add more breadcrumbs if mixture seems too wet.
3. Form into eight large patties. Don't make them too thick as they will shrink in to the middle and thicken as they cook.
4. Grill over medium-hot coals or on medium heat on gas grill for 7 minutes. Turn and brush heavily with barbecue baste. Cook 7 minutes longer, brushing again with baste, until burgers are no longer pink in the centre.
5. Serve burgers on buns with lettuce, tomato, cheese, onions, and condiments. Makes 8 burgers.

CLASSIC ALBERTA PRIME RIB ROAST

Prime rib roast, or standing ribs as it's sometimes called, is the ultimate Sunday roast. Order your roast from the butcher, a rib for every two people you plan to serve.

1 6-pound (2.5–3 kg) prime rib or ribeye roast
2 tablespoons (25 mL) butter, softened
1 tablespoon (15 mL) Dijon mustard
1 tablespoon (15 mL) Worcestershire sauce
1/4 teaspoon (1 mL) salt, plus additional salt to taste for gravy
1 tablespoon (15 mL) coarsely-cracked black peppercorns
3–4 tablespoons (45–50 mL) all-purpose flour
1/2 cup (125 mL) red wine
1/2 cup (125 mL) beef stock
1 cup (250 mL) water

1. Combine butter with mustard, Worcestershire sauce, salt, and peppercorns. Rub this mixture over the meat and let stand at room temperature for 30 minutes.
2. Place meat in a shallow roasting pan, fat side up, and roast in a preheated 450°F (230°C) oven for 30 minutes.
3. Reduce heat to 300°F (150°C) and continue to roast until internal temperature is 125–130°F (50–55°C) for medium rare, or 150°F (65°C) for well done, about 15 minutes per pound. Remove roast from oven, set on a platter, and tent with foil to keep warm while it rests.
4. Set roasting pan over medium-high heat on top of stove and blend flour into the drippings, stirring until smooth and brown.
5. Slowly add red wine, beef stock, and water (or 2 cups/500 mL water), stirring constantly, and bring to a boil. Stir until mixture is smooth and thickened. Season gravy with salt to taste and serve with roast and mashed potatoes. To carve prime rib roast, lay it on its side and slice along ribs to separate the meat from the bone. Then slice the meat toward the bone—the slices will come away from the bone as you carve. A boneless ribeye can simply be sliced across the grain. Serves 10 to 12.

GRILLED BEEF FLANK STEAK SERVED WITH HEIRLOOM TOMATOES THREE WAYS

Michael Allemeier, former chef at Calgary's Teatro restaurant, marinates this flavourful steak in the refrigerator for several days before cooking to infuse flavours, then cooks it quickly over high heat. His method of immersing the spiced beef in canola oil allows it to age and tenderize for up to a week in a safe environment, away from air and oxidation.

2 1/4 pounds (1.2 kg) beef flank steak
2 cups (500 mL) canola oil
6 tablespoons (75 mL) paprika
1/2 cup (125 mL) coarsely chopped fresh thyme
1 tablespoon (15mL) freshly ground black pepper

1. Mix paprika, thyme, and black pepper in a large bowl. Rub this spice mixture onto the steaks and place them in a container that has a sealing lid. Pour in canola oil, seal container, and refrigerate for at least three and up to six days.

2. Remove steaks from oil and leave at room temperature for 30 minutes. The barbecue must be very hot. If you are cooking the steak indoors, use a very hot, heavy frying pan. You will also need a good exhaust fan, as the steaks will smoke.

3. Cook steaks for 3–4 minutes on each side, depending on the thickness of the steaks, remembering to keep them rare. If flank steak is cooked past rare, it will be tough.

4. Place steaks on a cutting board, tent with foil to keep warm, and let them rest for 5–10 minutes. Using a sharp knife, thinly slice steaks across the grain into long, thin pieces. Serve at once with one or all of Paul Hotchkiss's heirloom tomato dishes (page 104). Serves 6.

STEAK IN WILD MUSHROOM SAUCE

Most cowboys cooked their steaks in a heavy, cast-iron frying pan with little more than salt and fried onions for seasoning. But expensive beef filet or striploin calls for a dash of elegance. This easy recipe makes a fried steak like no other.

1 2-pound (1-kg) beef tenderloin, cut into 8 filets,
    or 8 4–5-ounce (125–150 g) striploins
4 tablespoons (50 mL) olive oil
4 cups (1 L) fresh wild mushrooms (preferably morel, shiitake,
    oyster, and brown), thickly sliced
1 small onion, minced
2 cloves garlic, minced
1/2 cup (125 mL) Cabernet Sauvignon or other good,
    full-bodied red wine
1/2 teaspoon (2 mL) dried sage leaves
1/4 cup (50 mL) whipping cream
salt and freshly ground black pepper

1. Heat oil in a large, heavy skillet until almost smoking. Add steaks to hot pan and sauté 1 minute per side. Remove steaks from pan and set aside, covered, to stay warm.

2. Add mushrooms, onion, and garlic to pan and cook for 5 minutes over medium-high heat until starting to brown.

3. Add wine and sage to pan and boil for 5 minutes, until reduced by half.

4. Add cream to sauce and return steaks to pan. Simmer 5 minutes longer, turning meat once. Remove steaks and arrange two on each plate.

5. Turn heat under pan to high and reduce sauce until thick enough to coat a spoon. Season with salt and pepper to taste. Pour sauce over steaks and serve with garlic mashed potatoes or wild rice. Serves 4.

BEEF SHORT RIBS IN PORT AND ALE SAUCE

The Belvedere may be one of Calgary's most chic spots to dine, but its former Chef Alan Groom had no problem getting his patrons to order rustic short ribs, braised to tender perfection for up to six hours. Ask your butcher for short ribs on the bone—they give the most flavour and body to the sauce. Fleur de sel is a coarse French sea salt, which Groom uses for a final garnish.

1 tablespoon (15 mL) vegetable oil
12 beef short ribs on the bone, trimmed of visible fat
   (about 4 pounds/2 kg)
2 onions, chopped
1 carrot, chopped
1 stalk celery, chopped
2 teaspoons (10 mL) minced garlic
1 teaspoon (5 mL) crushed juniper berry
2 cups (500 mL) dark ale
1/2 cup (125 mL) port
1/4 cup (50 mL) light soy sauce
1/4 cup (50 mL) brown sugar
1 teaspoon (5 mL) ground cumin
1 cup (250 mL) veal stock or water
1/2 cup (125 mL) orange juice
1 small orange, zest removed and reserved
salt and freshly ground black pepper to taste
fleur de sel

1. Heat the oil in a sauté pan over medium-high heat and sear the ribs, meat side down, until brown. Place in a large, covered casserole dish.
2. Add onion, carrot, and celery to hot pan and sauté until beginning to brown. Add garlic and juniper berry and cook for 1 minute longer. Remove vegetables from pan and add to casserole. Deglaze pan with ale, port, and soy sauce, stirring to incorporate any browned bits. Pour liquid over ribs and vegetables in casserole dish.
3. Add sugar, cumin, stock or water, orange juice, halved orange, and salt and pepper to ribs. Place covered casserole dish in a preheated 325°F (160°C) oven and bake for 4–6 hours, until ribs are tender. Remove ribs from sauce. If you desire a smooth sauce, strain, pressing cooked vegetables through a sieve.
4. Boil to reduce sauce until it reaches a nice, thick consistency. Arrange ribs on individual plates with mashed potatoes and cabbage. Drizzle with some of the reduced sauce and garnish with minced orange zest and fleur de sel. Serves 4 to 6.

POT ROASTED BEEF BRISKET

Serve this tender braised beef with mashed potatoes or dumplings and Cabbage with Grainy Mustard and Currants (page 115) or broad egg noodles.

1 2–3 pound (1–1.5 kg) beef brisket or flank steak
1/2 cup (125 mL) all-purpose flour
1/2 teaspoon (2 mL) each: salt and freshly ground black pepper
3 tablespoons (45 mL) olive oil
2 large carrots, cut into small cubes
1 large onion, chopped
1 small rutabaga, cut into small cubes
2 cups (500 mL) beef broth
butter/flour paste consisting of equal portions of butter
    mixed with all-purpose flour (optional)

1. Combine flour with salt and pepper and coat beef heavily with mixture on both sides.
2. Heat oil in a Dutch oven over high heat, until almost beginning to smoke. Add beef to pan, sear 2 minutes, then turn and brown second side. Reduce heat to medium and continue to brown the meat for 15 minutes, turning as necessary, until beef is deep brown and crusted. Remove from pan and set aside.
3. Add vegetables to pan and return heat to medium-high. Sauté vegetables until tender and beginning to brown, about 10 minutes. Stir 5 minutes longer to lightly caramelize carrots and rutabaga. Set browned beef on top of vegetables and pour beef broth over top.
4. Cover Dutch oven and place in a preheated 275°F (140°C) oven. Braise beef and vegetables until very tender, about 2–3 hours. Remove beef from pan and place on a warm platter. Cover with foil to keep warm. Strain cooking liquid through a coarse sieve, pressing vegetables through and into the gravy, or use an immersible blender, blender, or food processor to pureé vegetables with cooking juices. Reheat gravy and thicken with a little butter/flour paste if necessary. Slice beef and serve with pan gravy. Serves 4 to 6.

CALGARY GINGER BEEF

Cowboys never ate ginger beef in the old west, but they certainly do today. This recipe is from the Ginger Beef Peking House. You may not think that this dish is indigenous, but, according to Chinese chefs in Alberta, it was created right here in Canada for beef-loving Alberta palates and cannot be found on menus in China!

1 pound (500 g) top beef sirloin or brisket, cut into
    thin julienne strips
1 egg, beaten (use only half an egg in the batter)
1/2 cup (125 mL) cornstarch
2 tablespoons (25 mL) all-purpose flour
3/4 cup (175 mL) water
1/4 cup (50 mL) vegetable oil
4 cups (1 L) canola oil for deep-frying
slivered green onion, carrot and green pepper

Sauce
3/4 cup (175 mL) chicken stock
1/2 cup (125 mL) regular soy sauce
2 tablespoons (25 mL) mushroom soy sauce
2 tablespoons (25 mL) white vinegar
3/4 cup (175 mL) granulated sugar
1 teaspoon (5 mL) sesame oil
2 teaspoons (10 mL) Chinese cooking wine
1/2 teaspoon (2 mL) minced fresh ginger
1/2 teaspoon (2 mL) minced fresh garlic
1/2 teaspoon (2 mL) crushed red chilies
2 teaspoons (10 mL) cornstarch mixed with
2 teaspoons (10 mL) cold water (optional)

1. Combine beef with half of the beaten egg, cornstarch, flour, water, and vegetable oil and mix with your hands in a big bowl until everything is well coated with batter.
2. Carefully heat the canola oil to 380°F (190°C) in a wok or deep fryer, watching constantly to prevent flare-ups.
3. When oil is hot, deep-fry beef in small batches for about 5 minutes. Using a large skimmer spoon, lift beef from the oil and shake well to remove excess oil. Set aside in a paper-lined strainer to drain further.

4. Make sauce by combining all ingredients in a wok and bringing to a boil. Boil for 2 minutes. Thicken with cornstarch solution, if desired. Keep sauce hot in wok.
5. Meanwhile, deep-fry beef a second time, until well browned. Drain well and toss with hot sauce in the wok.
6. Serve ginger beef immediately, garnished with slivers of green onion, carrot, and pepper. Serves 4 to 6.

GRILLED STEAK FAJITAS

This is the perfect food to serve for a casual summer party. Create a fresh and colourful salsa bar for your buffet table, and make some spicy rice to serve on the side or wrap up with the grilled meat and vegetables in tortillas.

1 1/2 pounds (750 g) round or flank steak
2 red bell peppers, seeded and sliced into strips
1 green pepper, seeded and sliced into strips
1 yellow pepper, seeded and sliced into strips
1 white onion, peeled and cut into slivers
2 ripe tomatoes, chopped
1 ripe avocado, peeled and chopped
1/2 cup (125 mL) crumbled blue cheese or goat cheese
12 flour tortillas, warmed

Marinade
3 tablespoons (45 mL) canola oil
juice of 2 limes (about 1/4 cup/50 mL)
1 small hot pepper, minced
1 clove garlic, minced
1 green onion, minced
2 tablespoons (25 mL) tequila
1/2 teaspoon (2 mL) ground cumin
1/4 cup (50 mL) chopped cilantro

1. Combine marinade ingredients in a food processor and whirl smooth. Place half of marinade in a bowl with peppers and onions and toss to coat. Put remaining marinade in a zippered plastic bag with steak. Set both aside at room temperature to marinate for 30 minutes.
2. Meanwhile, chop tomato and avocado. Crumble blue cheese. Set aside.

3. Heat barbecue grill to high heat. Using a perforated barbecue grill pan, stir-fry peppers and onions in batches on grill until starting to char. This will take 10–15 minutes. Grill steak for 6–8 minutes per side, then set aside for 10 minutes to allow juices to set.
4. Carve steak into thin strips across the grain. Pile steak in the centre of a serving platter and surround with grilled vegetables.
5. Serve with warm tortillas, tomatoes, avocado, and blue cheese. Let diners assemble their own fajitas, piling the tortillas with steak and vegetables, then sprinkling with tomatoes, avocado, and cheese, and rolling them up. Makes 12 fajitas, serves 6.

BEEF AND BIG ROCK

In these parts, Calgary's famous brewery, Big Rock, is synonymous with beer. I use their dark Traditional Ale in this recipe, but you can substitute your own favourite dark ale. This stew is even better the next day when the flavours have melded and softened.

2 tablespoons (25 mL) vegetable oil
2 pounds (1 kg) round steak, cubed
3 large white onions, thinly sliced
2 cloves garlic, minced
2–3 tablespoons (25–45 mL) all-purpose flour
1/2 teaspoon (2 mL) salt
1/2 teaspoon (2 mL) freshly ground black pepper
1 teaspoon (5 mL) chopped fresh thyme
1 bay leaf, crumbled
1 bottle (341 mL) dark ale
3 tablespoons (45 mL) dark brown sugar
2 tablespoons (25 mL) tomato paste
1 pound (500 g) whole baby potatoes (halved if larger potatoes are used), steamed
1/4 cup (50 mL) chopped fresh parsley

1. Heat oil in a Dutch oven over medium-high heat and sear beef in batches until nicely browned. Set beef aside. Add onion and garlic and cook 10–15 minutes longer, until onions are browned. Return beef to pot.

2. Stir flour into pan juices, season with salt, pepper, thyme, and bay leaf. Add ale, sugar, and tomato paste and stir well.

3. Bring stew to a simmer on top of stove, then cover and bake in a preheated 325°F (160°C) oven for 2 hours. Remove from oven, uncover, and simmer on top of stove for a few minutes to thicken the sauce, if necessary. Stir in steamed potatoes (or serve them around the stew) and sprinkle with parsley. Serves 6.

SPICED SHEPHERD'S PIE WITH ROOT VEGETABLE MASH

This updated version of a prairie classic, shepherd's pie, is inspired by a South African ground meat pie called bobotie, which is topped with a milk and egg custard, instead of potatoes. In this unique and colourful version, the sweet, richly spiced ground beef filling is covered with a mixed prairie mash of gold and sweet potatoes, parsnips, and carrots.

1 tablespoon (15 mL) curry powder
1/4 teaspoon (1 mL) cayenne pepper
1 teaspoon (5 mL) turmeric
1 teaspoon (5 mL) salt
1/2 teaspoon (2 mL) freshly ground black pepper
1 tablespoon (15 mL) canola oil
2 medium onions, chopped
1 tablespoon (15 mL) minced fresh ginger
1 green apple, finely chopped or shredded
1 pound (500 g) lean ground beef or lamb
1 tablespoon (15 mL) fresh lemon juice
1/4 cup (50 mL) dried cranberries, or chopped
    sundried tomatoes
2 tablespoons (25 mL) mango chutney
2 tablespoons (25 mL) Worcestershire sauce
3 tablespoons (45 mL) ketchup or tomato sauce
1/2 cup (125 mL) fresh bread crumbs
1 egg, beaten

Topping
3 large Yukon Gold potatoes, peeled and cubed
1 medium sweet potato, peeled and cubed
2 carrots, peeled and cubed
2 parsnips, peeled and cubed
1/4 cup (50 mL) butter
4 green onions, minced
1 tablespoon (15 mL) minced fresh ginger
1/4 cup (50 mL) milk or whipping cream
salt and freshly ground black pepper

1. Combine curry powder, cayenne pepper, turmeric, salt, and pepper. Heat canola oil over medium heat and sauté spices for 30 seconds until fragrant. Add onion, ginger, and apple and sauté until tender and beginning to brown.

2. Add ground beef to pan and cook until browned. Drain any excess oil. Remove from heat and cool slightly. Stir in remaining ingredients and spread in a shallow baking dish.

3. Meanwhile, combine potatoes, sweet potato, carrot, and parsnip in a saucepan. Cover with water, bring to a boil, and simmer until tender, about 20–30 minutes. Drain well and mash together until fairly smooth (the mash can be a bit rustic and chunky).

4. Sauté green onions and ginger in butter for 2–3 minutes. Stir into mashed vegetables with milk, salt, and pepper. Pile on top of filling in baking dish and smooth top.

5. Bake in preheated 350°F (180°C) oven for 45 minutes or until filling is hot and topping is golden brown. Cool slightly before cutting into squares to serve. Serves 4 to 6.

PORK TENDERLOIN WITH SWEET SASKATOON HORSERADISH GLAZE

Lean pork tenderloin is wonderful when quickly grilled with a sweet and spicy glaze. For an elegant meal, serve it with sautéed purple cabbage and wild rice.

1/2 cup (125 mL) Saskatoon berry syrup, or substitute dark Alberta honey or other fruit syrup
1 tablespoon (15 mL) prepared horseradish
1 clove garlic, minced
1 teaspoon (5 mL) Dijon mustard
1 teaspoon (5 mL) chili powder
1 tablespoon (15 mL) olive oil
2 1-pound (500 g) pork tenderloins
1/4 cup (50 mL) fresh saskatoon berries (optional)

1. Combine ingredients, except pork and fresh saskatoons, in food processor and whirl until smooth. Place pork in a shallow pan and pour half of the glaze over it. Cover and marinate in refrigerator for 1–2 hours.
2. Remove pork from marinade. Heat barbecue to high, and quickly sear tenderloins on all sides. This will take 2–3 minutes. Turn off one burner, reduce heat to medium, and place pork over unlit burner to grill with indirect heat until just cooked through and still pink inside, about 30–40 minutes, brushing with reserved marinade every 10 minutes to glaze.
3. Remove pork tenderloins from grill and let rest, covered, for 5 minutes before slicing into 1–1 1/2-inch (3–4 cm) pieces. Reheat remaining marinade to boiling and drizzle a little over pork, then scatter fresh saskatoons over top. Serves 4.

SAUSAGE AND PINTO BEAN CHILI

Chili is part of prairie cooking. Some versions have only beans, some include ground or cubed pork and beef, while this updated chili is made with sweet and spicy Italian sausage. Serve it with Corn Sticks (page 125) for a complete meal.

2 cups (500 mL) dried pinto beans
1/2 pound (250 g) each: mild and spicy Italian sausage
2 medium onions, chopped
1/2 cup (125 mL) white wine
1/4 cup (50 mL) molasses
1/4 cup (50 mL) maple syrup
1/2 cup (125 mL) tomato sauce
1 tablespoon (15 mL) dry mustard
1 tablespoon (15 mL) Worcestershire sauce
4 cloves garlic, minced
2 teaspoons (10 mL) chili powder
1/4 cup (50 mL) rye whisky or rum
1 teaspoon (5 mL) salt
1 cup (250 mL) tomato juice
1–2 cups (250–500 mL) water

1. Wash beans well and place in a pot of water to soak overnight, or use the quick-soak method (page 29).
2. Remove sausage from casings and brown in a large Dutch oven. Add onions and continue to cook until they are beginning to brown. Add wine and boil for 5 minutes, scraping up any browned bits. Stir in remaining ingredients and drained beans, along with about 1 cup (250 mL) of water. Bring to a boil.
3. Cover pot and place in a preheated 250°F (120°C) oven. Bake beans for 3 hours, adding up to 1 cup (250 mL) additional water during cooking period if mixture becomes too dry. Serves 6 to 8.

LAMB CHOPS IN ROCKY MOUNTAIN MINT SAUCE

Mint has long been the classic herb to pair with lamb. In this recipe, the usual sweet mint sauce is replaced with a savoury mint-infused marinade that's also delicious drizzled over the new spring vegetables served on the side.

6 cloves garlic
1 teaspoon (5 mL) hot sauce
1/4 teaspoon (1 mL) each: salt and pepper
1/4 cup (50 mL) fresh lemon juice
2 tablespoons (25 mL) coarse-grained mustard
1 tablespoon (15 mL) olive oil
1 bunch fresh mint, stems discarded
8 Alberta lamb chops, each 1 inch (2.5 cm) thick

1. Combine garlic, hot sauce, salt, pepper, lemon juice, mustard, olive oil, and mint leaves in food processor and blend until minced. Reserve half of sauce, covered, in the refrigerator.
2. Rub chops on both sides with remaining 1/4 cup (50 mL) mint sauce and marinate at room temperature for 30 minutes.
3. Heat 1 tablespoon (15 mL) olive oil in a heavy pan until very hot. Sear chops until brown on one side, about 5 minutes, then turn and cook 5 minutes more. (Alternatively, grill chops about 5 minutes per side to medium rare).
4. Serve lamb chops immediately with steamed new potatoes and mint sauce on the side. Serves 4.

GRILLED LAMB CHOPS IN YOGURT MARINADE

Patrick de Rosemond of Pasu Farm likes to season lamb with garlic, freshly squeezed lemon juice, fresh rosemary, olive oil, salt, and white pepper. This recipe is a favourite barbecue recipe in de Rosemond's native South Africa.

8 large Alberta lamb chops, at least 1 inch (2.5 cm) thick
1 cup (250 mL) plain yogurt
4 tablespoons (50 mL) fresh lemon juice
2 tablespoons (25 mL) orange juice
zest of half a lemon, finely chopped
1 teaspoon (5 mL) coarsely ground black pepper
2 tablespoons (25 mL) chopped fresh mint
1 tablespoon (15 mL) chopped fresh rosemary
1 teaspoon (5 mL) salt
2 tablespoons (25 mL) olive oil

1. Trim and score fat on chops. Combine remaining ingredients, add chops, and marinate in refrigerator for 4–8 hours. Before cooking, remove lamb from marinade and bring to room temperature.
2. Barbecue chops over hot coals or high heat on a gas barbecue to sear, then move to a moderately hot section of the grill to finish cooking.
3. Cook about 5 minutes per side in total, depending on thickness of chops. Baste with reserved marinade after turning. Do not over-cook—the lamb should remain pink in the centre. Serves 4.

SPICY RACK OF RIBS WITH SECRET SAUCE

Baby back ribs are expensive but worth the treat, especially when you're grilling. While cheaper pork ribs benefit from a brief blanching to precook, baby backs just need to be marinated and grilled. Look for the best deals on pork ribs at Asian markets. A good side of ribs should weigh in at close to 2 pounds (1 kg).

2–3 sides baby back ribs

Secret Sauce
1 tablespoon (15 mL) canola oil
1 onion, minced
2 cloves garlic, minced
1 tablespoon (15 mL) minced fresh ginger
1 14-ounce (398 mL) can tomato sauce
1/2 cup (125 mL) chili sauce
2 tablespoons (25 mL) cider vinegar
1/2 cup (125 mL) strong brewed coffee
1/2 cup (125 mL) maple syrup
2 tablespoons (25 mL) blackstrap molasses
1 tablespoon (15 mL) Worcestershire sauce
2 chipotle chiles in adobo, minced
1 teaspoon (5 mL) minced orange zest
1/4 teaspoon (1 mL) ground cinnamon
salt and freshly ground black pepper

1. For sauce, combine all ingredients in a saucepan and simmer for 15 minutes at medium-low heat. Cool and purée in a blender or food processor. Pour into a jar and refrigerate.
2. Remove membrane from the back of the rack of ribs. Using a knife, free a corner of the membrane then grasp it tightly (a paper towel makes this easier) and pull the skin away in one piece.
3. Coat ribs on both sides in barbecue sauce. Marinate in the refrigerator for at least 1 hour or up to 8 hours.
4. Heat barbecue to medium-low (300–325°F/150–160°C), brush grill with oil, and place ribs on grill, meaty side down. With barbecue lid down, cook ribs for about 1 hour, frequently turning and basting with extra sauce. Watch to make sure barbecue temperature stays at an even 300–325°F (150–160°C). Stop basting about 15 minutes before ribs are done. They are cooked when the meat pulls away from the ends of the bones. To serve, cut each side of ribs into 3 or 4 sections. Serves 4.

GRILLED SPOLUMBO'S SAUSAGE ON CRUSTY BUNS WITH BEER-BRAISED ONIONS AND PEPPERS

This is one of my favourite ways to cook the classic spicy or fennel-scented mild Italian sausages made at Spolumbo's Deli in Calgary. Although these sausages need no embellishments, a little sweet onion and bell pepper, braised in beer to sweet, caramelized perfection, really gilds the lily.

2 red bell peppers, slivered
2 large sweet red or white onions
1/4 cup (50 mL) good-quality virgin olive oil
1 clove garlic, minced
1 tablespoon (15 mL) granulated sugar
1/2 cup (125 mL) dark beer, like Big Rock Traditional Ale
salt and freshly ground black pepper to taste
6 good-quality fresh sausages, like Spolumbo's
6 crusty panini buns

1. Cut peppers lengthwise, remove stems and seeds, and slice into long slivers. Cut onions in half and slice thinly.
2. In a large sauté pan, heat olive oil over medium heat and cook onions and peppers slowly until onions are golden and caramelized. This will take at least 30 minutes. Stir in garlic, sugar, and beer and simmer until most of the liquid is gone and onions and peppers are thick and jammy. Season with salt and pepper to taste and set aside.
3. Grill sausages over medium heat for 10 minutes, until nicely browned and cooked through. Pile some of the caramelized pepper and onion mixture on each bun and top with a grilled sausage. Serves 6.

BRAISED LAMB SHOULDER WITH WHITE BEANS

Slowly cooked shoulder of lamb makes a wonderful wintertime stew to enjoy after skating or skiing. This is the perfect dish to make a day ahead and reheat—it actually gets better! Chill it and skim off any excess fat before reheating.

1 cup (250 mL) dried white beans
1 large head garlic
1 tablespoon (15 mL) olive oil
1 3-pound (1.5 kg) boneless shoulder of lamb
1 onion, chopped
3 carrots, chopped
2 stalks celery, diced
1/2 cup (125 mL) dry red wine
1/2 cup (125 mL) beef stock
1 28-ounce (796 mL) can tomatoes, puréed
2 tablespoons (25 mL) chopped fresh rosemary, or
   2 teaspoons (10 mL) dried rosemary
1 bay leaf
salt and freshly ground black pepper

1. Cover beans with cold water and set aside to soak overnight, or use quick-soak method (page 29).
2. To cook, drain beans, add water to cover by about 4 inches (10 cm), and simmer for 1–2 hours, or until tender.
3. To roast garlic, cut off the top 1/4 inch (5 mm) of the bulb to expose the tops of the cloves, place cloves on foil and drizzle with 1/2 teaspoon (2 mL) of olive oil. Wrap loosely with foil and bake in a preheated 400°F (200°C) for 40 minutes. Cool.
4. Cut lamb shoulder into large serving pieces, removing any excess fat. Brown lamb pieces in a Dutch oven in olive oil over medium-high heat, then remove from pan and set aside. In same pot, sauté onion, carrots, and celery until soft. Add wine and boil until reduced by half, about 5 minutes. Stir in beef stock, puréed tomatoes, rosemary, and bay leaf.
5. Peel roasted garlic, squeezing cooked cloves from the skins. Add to pan with reserved meat. Bring to a boil.
6. Cover pan and place in preheated 325°F (160°C) oven. Bake for about 2 hours, until meat is almost tender. Drain cooked beans and add to pot. Cover and bake 30 minutes longer. Season with salt and pepper to taste and serve with mashed potatoes. Serves 4 to 6.

POLENTA TAMALE TORTE

Mexican tamales are made of steamed masa or corn dough filled with chicken, pork, or beans and wrapped in corn husks or banana leaves for steaming. This layered pie gives you all the flavour of a great tamale. Masa harina is dried masa or corn flour, used for making tortillas and tamales.

Polenta Layer
4 cups (1.25 L) water
1 tablespoon (15 mL) salt
1 cup (250 mL) coarsely ground polenta or cornmeal
1/2 teaspoon (2 mL) freshly ground black pepper
2 tablespoons (25 mL) butter
1/2 cup (125 mL) good-quality grated Parmesan cheese

Filling
1 pound (500 g) ground pork
1/2 onion, quartered
3 cloves garlic, unpeeled
4 Roma tomatoes
1 teaspoon (5 mL) ground cinnamon
1/2 teaspoon (2 mL) dried oregano
1/2 teaspoon (2 mL) freshly ground black pepper
1 cup (250 mL) chicken broth
1 tablespoon (15 mL) olive oil
1/4 cup (50 mL) chopped black olives
2 tablespoons (25 mL) chopped raisins
1 jalapeño, minced
1 chipotle chile in adobo, or 1 teaspoon (5 mL) Asian chili paste
2 tablespoons (25 mL) chopped fresh parsley

1. Sauté pork until browned well. Drain in a colander and rinse with hot water to remove excess fat. Set aside.
2. Heat a cast-iron pan over medium-high heat and roast onion, whole garlic cloves, and tomatoes until blackened. Peel garlic and tomatoes and place in food processor with onion, cinnamon, oregano, pepper, and broth. Process until smooth.
3. Heat oil over medium-high heat. Add sauce and stir for 5–10 minutes, until starting to cook down. Add black olives, raisins, jalapeño, chipotle, and reserved pork and simmer until thick, about 20 minutes. Remove from heat. Stir in parsley.
4. For polenta, pour 3 cups (750 mL) cold water into a heavy pot, add salt, and gradually whisk in cornmeal. Bring to a boil, stirring, and cook until thick, about 10 minutes. Add another cup of water and continue to cook until tender, about 15 minutes. Polenta should be soft and creamy with no hard grains; add more water only if necessary. Stir in pepper, butter, and half of the cheese.
5. Pour half of the polenta into a greased 10-inch (25 cm) springform pan. Top with pork filling and remaining polenta. Smooth the top. Cover pan with foil and bake in preheated 350°F (180°C) oven for 30 minutes until pie is set. Uncover, sprinkle with remaining cheese, and bake 10 minutes longer or until golden on top. Cool slightly before cutting into wedges to serve. Serve warm or cold. Serves 6 to 8.

PULLED PORK BUTT WITH MUSTARD SAUCE

In Alberta there is a growing interest in the skill of slow-smoking food. There's even an annual slow-barbecue competition where teams vie for the chance to qualify for big American barbecue championships in places like Texas and Kansas City.

1 3-pound (1.5 kg) pork butt or shoulder, bone in
   (leg is too lean for this process)
1/4 cup (50 mL) regular ballpark mustard such as French's
   (don't use fancy Dijon, it doesn't contain enough sugar)

Dry Rub
1 tablespoon (15 mL) salt
1/4 cup (50 mL) granulated sugar
2 tablespoons (25 mL) each: brown sugar, ground cumin, ground ginger, chili powder, black pepper, and granulated garlic
1/4 cup (50 mL) Hungarian paprika (or other good-quality sweet paprika)
1 tablespoon (15 mL) dry mustard

Mustard Sauce

1 tablespoon (15 mL) mayonnaise
1/4 cup (50 mL) mustard
1 tablespoon (15 mL) ketchup
2 tablespoons (25 mL) honey
1 tablespoon (15 mL) cider vinegar
1 teaspoon (5 mL) Tabasco sauce
1 clove garlic, pressed

1. Rub pork with mustard to coat. Combine dry rub ingredients and massage generously into pork. Leave the pork at room temperature for 10 minutes to allow rub to get tacky. The salt will draw some of the moisture out of the meat, forming a crust as it cooks that will seal in the juices.

2. Place pork in a smoker, or barbecue indirectly, setting meat on grill away from coals or over unlit gas burner. Keep heat constant and low (about 200–225°F/95–110°C) and cook pork until meat can be easily pulled apart with two forks. This will take 6–8 hours. Cook to an internal temperature of 180°F (85°C); pork should be tender and falling apart.

3. Combine sauce ingredients in a saucepan over medium heat and whisk until warm and well-combined. Pull pork apart into shreds and serve on crusty buns. Drizzle sauce over pulled pork sandwiches. In the American South, they add a spoonful of creamy coleslaw to each pulled pork sandwich before serving. Serves 6.

TIP

For best results, get a good home smoker or use a charcoal-fired Weber kettle barbecue. This recipe can also be attempted on a gas barbecue (one with at least two burners), although it can be difficult to maintain a low enough temperature for true slow-smoke cooking. Pork is safe to eat at an internal temperature of 165°F (75°C), when it will be sliceable, but for pulled pork you must cook the meat to the "falling apart" stage. You can also try this dry rub on meaty pork ribs. Smoke baby back ribs for about 3 hours at 200°F (95°C).

LEG OF PORK ROASTED WITH POTATOES, ONIONS, AND RUTABAGAS

Take a boneless pork leg roast, season it with garlic, herbs, and chiles, and surround it with caramelized root vegetables.

1 4-pound (2 kg) pork leg roast, boned and rolled
2 tablespoons (25 mL) minced fresh rosemary
3 cloves garlic, minced
2 teaspoons (10 mL) salt
1/4 teaspoon (1 mL) freshly ground black pepper
1/2 teaspoon (2 mL) ground sage
1 dried chili pepper, crumbled
3 tablespoons (45 mL) olive oil, divided
1 cup (250 mL) white wine
16 small white onions, peeled, or 1 large onion, cut into wedges
16 baby potatoes, scrubbed but not peeled
1 medium rutabaga, peeled and cubed
extra wine, water, or chicken broth to deglaze pan

1. Mince rosemary, garlic, and salt together until fine. Combine with pepper, sage, chili pepper, and 1 teaspoon (5 mL) of olive oil to form a paste. Using a long, thin-bladed knife, cut twelve slits into roast and press some of the seasoning mixture into each slit. Rub any excess seasoning over roast and let stand at room temperature for 30 minutes.

2. Heat remaining oil in a heavy roasting pan at medium-high. When oil is hot, brown roast on all sides. Turn fat side up, pour in wine.

3. Cover pan and roast in preheated 325°F (160°C) oven for 1 hour. Remove lid and place onions, potatoes, and rutabaga around roast. Stir vegetables to coat them in pan drippings. Return roast to oven, uncovered, and cook for 1 additional hour, until meat reaches an internal temperature of 160°F (70°C). Use a meat thermometer to make sure it is cooked to a juicy medium, not well done. Add more wine or water if pan gets dry during roasting.

4. Remove roast and vegetables from pan. Place roast on a platter, tent with foil, let rest for 15 minutes. Deglaze pan with a little water, wine, or broth, stirring up any brown bits to make a light sauce. Slice roast and serve surrounded by roasted vegetables and drizzled with the jus. Serves 6.

LAMB STEW WITH RED WINE GRAVY

Cooked to tender perfection and dotted with pungent black olives, lamb stew makes an elegant alternative to the usual beef stew. Serve with plenty of garlic mashed potatoes or polenta to soak up the rich sauce.

4 pounds (2 kg) lamb shoulder, cut into large cubes and
    trimmed of excess fat
1/3 cup (75 mL) all-purpose flour
salt and freshly ground black pepper
2 tablespoons (25 mL) olive oil
2 thick slices double-smoked bacon, cut into matchstick pieces
25 small boiling onions, blanched and peeled
1 stalk celery, chopped
6 cloves garlic, whole
2 medium carrots, cut into chunks
1 cup (250 mL) good-quality, air-cured black olives
2 cups (500 mL) beef broth
2 cups (500 mL) red wine

Marinade
2 onions, finely chopped
1 stalk celery, finely chopped
1 carrot, finely chopped
8 cloves garlic, halved
2 tablespoons (25 mL) olive oil
2 bay leaves
1 tablespoon (15 mL) chopped fresh rosemary
1 sprig fresh thyme
1 bottle (750 mL) dry red wine

1. To prepare marinade, sauté onions, celery, carrot, and garlic in olive oil until vegetables are soft and starting to brown. Add bay leaves and herbs and cook 2 minutes longer. Add wine and bring to a boil. Simmer 20 minutes. Chill. When marinade is cold, add lamb and marinate overnight in the refrigerator.

2. The next day, remove lamb and strain marinade, reserving liquid and discarding herbs and vegetables. Place flour, salt, and pepper in a bag and toss lamb in flour to coat. Heat 2 tablespoons (25 mL) olive oil in large sauté pan and brown meat in batches. As it's browned, remove lamb to a large covered casserole. Add bacon to pan and cook until fat is rendered and bacon is nearly crisp. Remove bacon with a slotted spoon and add to casserole.

3. In bacon fat remaining in pan, sauté blanched and peeled onions until they begin to caramelize. Remove with a slotted spoon and add to casserole. Lightly sauté celery, garlic, and carrots in same pan, until starting to brown. Deglaze with reserved marinade, boiling until liquid is reduced by half.

4. Pour marinade and vegetable mixture over stew in casserole. Stir in olives. Add beef broth and red wine, cover casserole, and cook in a preheated 350°F (180°C) oven for 2–3 hours, or until meat is very tender and sauce is thick. Thicken as necessary with a little flour and butter roux or cornstarch solution before serving. Serves 8.

TIP

The easiest way to thicken a sauce is to reduce it—that is, to simmer it uncovered over low heat until enough liquid evaporates to achieve the proper thickness. Reductions of stocks are healthy and trendy, a way to concentrate flavours without adding traditional high-fat thickeners like egg yolks and cream. But don't season the liquid until the sauce is reduced, and expect this to take some time.

A roux is a thickener used at the beginning of the sauce-making process. Flour is blended with fat (butter or oil) and cooked over low heat. Cook the roux for 5 minutes for white sauces, longer if you want it to brown and add colour to the finished sauce. At the end of cooking, a paste or cornstarch solution will quickly thicken the liquid. A cornstarch solution of 1 tablespoon (25 mL) of cornstarch and 1–2 tablespoons (15–25 mL) of cold water will thicken 1 1/2–2 cups (375–500 mL) of liquid and result in the kind of translucent sauces common in Asian cooking. Flour paste made of all-purpose flour and cold water or stock is a bit trickier, as it can turn a sauce lumpy. Add some of the hot liquid to the paste and whisk, then whisk the entire amount into the sauce. Simmer the sauce until it thickens.

Wild Game

BISON: THE ORIGINAL ALBERTA GAME

Maurice Moore turns his red pick-up off a muddy road and we bump down into a hilly pasture where a bison herd grazes in the spring sunshine. The spruce and aspen forest has been cleared from his central Alberta farmland, but it's only the big shaggy cows and their brindled calves that move easily through this rough and rolling landscape. We are out of our element. The bison are at home on this range and they are ultimately in control.

Maurice Moore

That's exactly what raising bison is all about, explains Moore, who, with his wife, Pat, runs Triple 7 Bison Ranch near Rimbey. "Buffalo are a wild animal, but we're raising them under farm conditions," he says. "You can't walk up and pet them. And you don't drive them, you lead them." That is evident this day. As Moore steps out of his truck and toward the herd, the animals move a safe distance away. A few stalwarts stand and curiously face a photographer, but none approach the strangers. It's not easy to get close to any of these huge animals and almost impossible to cut one out from the herd, the place where bison fight fiercely to stay. In fact, most bison ranchers concede that you can do little more than "chase a bison any-where it wants to go."

When it comes to raising wild game in Alberta, bison (or buffalo as they were misnamed by early explorers) are the most popular candidates. The provincial government also licenses game farms to raise white-tailed deer, elk, and moose, but bison are closely related to cattle, and that gives both ranchers and consumers closer ties to the big beasts.

Nearly all existing bison are raised in captivity today, but they survive much as they did in the past, with little intervention from people. They browse on almost any pasture and require less protein than cattle in their diets to thrive. Most are vaccinated when young and resist handling thereafter. They don't need drugs—most seem to resist the illnesses that affect cattle—and that's what makes their meat so desirable to consumers. It is clean and lean, free of antibiotics, growth hormones, and other agricultural chemicals.

Moore's herd is small, only 48 cows, but all of his five brothers, and some of their children, are now raising bison. In Canada today, there are more than 100,000 animals and the business is expanding by 30 percent every year. Nearly half of these animals are raised in Alberta, although there are bison producers across the country. But that's still only a tiny part of the red meat business. Even in fifty years, says Moore, bison production will likely never reach more than 10 percent of beef production. "We just can't over-produce," he says. "Bison will always be a specialty product."

Moore is the president of Canadian Rangeland Beef and Bison Inc., a processing and marketing company formed by eighteen Alberta producers that sells bison and natural beef, much of it to a growing European market. Canadian Rangeland buys bison from Alberta producers and creates products like bison burgers, pure bison hot dogs, and seasoned steaks. It's a way to get readily available less-than-prime cuts to consumers, since prime cuts are in great demand by high-end restaurants around the world. "We are trying to make people in Alberta more aware of bison meat," says Moore of the company. In 2000, Canadian Rangeland was the country's largest bison processor, handling 2,800 animals or over 800,000 kilograms of bison meat.

Like elk and deer, the other large ruminants of the prairie region, bison are survivors. Bison descend from the ancient wisent, an animal that may have arrived here from Mongolia 700,000 years ago, and archaeologists have uncovered bison skulls that are 30,000 years old. Bison are huge and hardy. Their big, shaggy heads and humps lend an almost prehistoric look to the animals. Some bulls reach over 1,100 kilograms, making them the largest land mammal in North America to survive the Ice Age.

Millions of bison once roamed the continent from Great Slave Lake to Texas. Now the only truly wild herds in Canada are confined in Wood Buffalo National Park, north of Great Slave Lake. They are the free-ranging wood bison, a subspecies of the more common plains bison. At Elk Island Park, east of Edmonton, there are captive but separate populations of both types of bison.

Nomadic prairie Native people once used every part of the bison to sustain life. Meat was sliced and dried for jerky or pemmican, hides became clothing and tipis, some lashed together with sinews and sewn with bone needles. While prairie Natives also consumed wild plants and berries, bison meat was their mainstay; in fact, the Blackfoot word for bison is "nitani-waksim," which means "real food."

While Native tribes were known to routinely kill large numbers of bison, often by stampeding them over a cliff, they took only what they needed and never came close to endangering the wild populations. However, the first non-Natives to arrive in western Canada wanted only the tongues and hides. It was that insatiable early demand for buffalo robes and tongues that all but wiped out the wild bison of the North American plains. Some estimates suggest there were more than 60 million bison roaming the prairies in 1800. Less than one hundred years later, the wild animals were almost extinct, with fewer than 1,000 preserved by ranchers, conservationists, and zoos.

The stories and photographs documenting the demise of the wild bison are horrific. By 1878 nearly all of the animals had been shot, many from moving tourist trains. Native hunters delivered hides to traders, too, receiving three cups of coffee or ten cups of sugar for a single buffalo robe. But it was white hunters, who were known to shoot up to one hundred animals a day, who quickly decimated the population.

It's estimated that 3.7 million bison were killed between 1872 and 1874 alone, only 150,000 of those by Natives. A decade later, entrepreneurs found there was money in the bleached bones that were left behind on the prairies, and they gathered them and packed them in massive forty-foot piles along railway sidings, to be shipped to American fertilizer factories. By 1897 even the bones were gone.

Native people revered the bison, and, after the last animal was exterminated, created a Ghost Dance ceremony, praying that the bison might reappear. Whenever a rare white calf is born, Native people still come to honour it, believing the white buffalo is a spiritual sign of new beginnings and hope.

It's perhaps ironic that the hope for renewed bison populations has come in the form of commercial production for slaughter, but interest in the new clean and lean meat has quickly increased the numbers of these majestic animals. They are especially popular on farms where grain or cattle production is not viable, and offer health-conscious consumers a safe and natural protein that is similar to beef in flavour. The lean purplish-red meat is not marbled like beef and has less fat and cholesterol per gram than other meats, even turkey. A government study found the average 3-ounce serving of bison has 93 calories, 1.8 g of fat, and 43 mg of cholesterol, compared with 125 calories, 3 g of fat, and 59 mg of cholesterol for 3 ounces of turkey, and 183 calories, 8.7 g of fat, and 55 mg of cholesterol for 3 ounces of beef. Canada has developed the only federally regulated grading system for grading bison, with requirements for Canada Grade A animals being youth, firm, fine-grained meat, and at least 1 mm of white back fat.

Some bison producers, like Moore and his partners, are now finishing their pastured bison on grain in special feedlots designed to confine the big animals with more space than conventional feedlots. They are processing the massive chuck or shoulder and hump into ready-to-cook steaks that have been marinated with papain, a tenderizer extracted from papaya seeds. While this process does remove the products from the truly "natural" realm, Moore says the meat is free from hormones, antibiotics, and other agricultural inputs.

There is a strong demand for hormone-free bison and beef in Europe, California, New York, and Boston. Top American food magazines like *Gourmet* and *Saveur* have featured bison in their pages, and top restaurants like New York's Tribeca Grill and Washington's Red Sage have bison on the menu. Here in Alberta, bison is at the forefront of the trend to serve regional cuisine in the best and most creative restaurants, because it is truly an indigenous ingredient.

As Moore notes, bison will never again be North Americans' primary food source. There is still far more demand than supply, and there will never be enough produced to make it common in every supermarket in the country. But it can be an alternative to other red meat, and we will continue to have more opportunities to try it.

Another game farm success story involves the wild boar, or *Sus scrofa*, in the family Suidae, the wild predecessor of the farmyard sow. The Hagman family's company, Hog Wild Specialties, in Mayerthorpe, Alberta, is providing wild boar meat and specialty products like prosciutto, sausage, and paté to top chefs across the province. Despite the fact that they are essentially wild animals, the wild boar raised

COOKING BISON AND GAME

Bison is expensive, averaging about $20 per pound for top rib eye or strip loin cuts, so treat it with care. While bison is similar to beef in flavour, it is a denser meat that requires a different style of cooking. Bison has 30 percent less water per gram than beef, so it's easy to dry it out by overcooking. Because it has less fat and little or no marbling, bison cooks more quickly than beef and it should never be cooked past medium rare.

Tender cuts like tenderloin or steaks don't need marinating, but may be marinated up to 24 hours. On the grill, cook steaks over high heat, about 3 minutes per side. Thicker steaks that need slightly longer cooking should be moved to a cooler part of the grill to finish cooking after they have been seared. Loin or rib roasts can be dry roasted at 275°F (140°C) to an internal temperature of 130–160°F (55–70°C). Less tender cuts (sirloin tip, cross rib, inside round) can be successfully pot roasted or braised. Brown these cuts for 30 minutes at 500°F (260°C), then reduce heat to 275°F (140°C), add liquid, cover pan and braise to medium rare (145°F/63°C). Bison also makes a delectable stew, cooked slowly in red wine and stock, or ground and made into patties for the grill.

It's a similar story when it comes to cooking venison, caribou, and other wild meats. The lean nature of all wild game means roasts should be barded (topped with sliced bacon or other fat) for cooking, or braised with stock or wine, and tender cuts should be cooked quickly. Don't cook venison or caribou past rare—use a meat thermometer and remove from heat when you reach an internal temperature of 120–130°F (50–55°C). The meat will continue cooking as it rests and will be rare and juicy, not dry and leathery. Farmed game is generally milder in flavour than wild meat, but the flavour can still be assertive and pairs well with marinades made with red wine, fruit vinegars, peppercorns, juniper berries, and fresh herbs. Even wild boar, while similar to domestic pork, is far leaner with a more pronounced flavour. Marinating wild, hunted game for 24 hours can eliminate any "gamey" taste.

native Europe. The red meat is dark and lean—100 g of wild boar shoulder has 160 calories and 2.8 g of fat, less than chicken breast or venison, and considerably less than domestic pork, which weighs in at 219 calories and 10.6 g of fat for a similar serving.

While you will find some Alberta-raised game on top menus, prices are high, and most restaurants are forced to charge more than $30 per plate for caribou, wild boar, or venison. Much of the venison served in Canada still comes from New Zealand, the world's largest producer, and some wild boar, quail, pheasant, and partridge comes from farms in British Columbia, Ontario, and Quebec. In Alberta, breeding stock for some species is so valuable (more than $10,000 for a bred doe, or $20,000 for a productive elk cow) that it's still impractical to slaughter the animals for meat.

Look for bison and game in specialty groceries and better butcher shops. Canmore's Valbella Meats specializes in patés, cold cuts, and sausages made with wild game, from buffalo prosciutto to wild boar paté and venison smokies. In most of the following recipes, a similar cut of beef may be substituted for the bison or game.

Chef Glen Manzer

in Alberta are considered domestic farm animals. Most of them are not full-blooded wild boar, but animals with some domestic pig in their genetic background. Still, the tusked wild pigs are rugged and hard to handle, preferring open pasture to the confinement of a typical pig barn.

The famous Serrano ham of Spain is made from the meat of black wild boar, which feed on wild chestnuts in the deciduous forests of their

WILD BOAR COUNTRY LOAF WITH OAT CRACKERS

Some farmers are raising the long-tusked wild boar on the Alberta prairie, a lean ingredient for this hearty pork loaf. Served cold with salad and bread, it makes a lovely first course or a picnic or pub-type lunch, and will keep for several days in the refrigerator. Make it at least a day before serving to allow it to chill well. The oat crackers are traditional Scottish fare—try them for breakfast with jam or butter, or serve them with cheese.

1 pound (500 g) lean, double-smoked bacon or capicollo, thinly sliced
1 large onion, quartered
2 cloves garlic
1/4 cup (50 mL) brandy or sherry
1/4 cup (50 mL) minced fresh parsley
1/2 teaspoon (2 mL) each: dried thyme, marjoram, and sage
1/2 teaspoon (2 mL) salt

1/2 teaspoon (2 mL) peppercorns, coarsely cracked
1 pound (500 g) ground wild boar or lean ground pork
1 pound (500 g) ground turkey
1 small egg
1/2 cup (125 mL) pine nuts or chopped walnuts, toasted until light brown
gherkins, pickled beets, cranberry chutney, and assorted mustards

Oat Crackers
3 cups (750 mL) quick-cooking oatmeal
1/2 teaspoon (2 mL) salt
1/4 teaspoon (1 mL) baking soda
3 tablespoons (45 mL) unsalted butter, melted
1/2 cup (125 mL) hot water

1. For wild boar loaf, place bacon in food processor, reserving eight strips. Add onion, garlic, and garlic, and brandy and process until smooth. Mix in herbs, salt, and peppercorns.

2. Mix ground wild boar or pork, ground turkey, and egg with your hands until well combined. Add onion/bacon mixture and fold in toasted nuts.

3. Line a 9 x 5-inch (2 L) loaf pan or terrine mould with reserved bacon strips, letting ends hang over edges of loaf pan. Place meat mixture in pan and press firmly. Fold overhanging bacon over meat. Cover with foil or lid and place in a roasting pan. Add 2 inches (5 cm) of hot water to roasting pan. Bake in a preheated 350°F (180°C) oven for 1 hour and 45 minutes.

4. Remove from oven, cool to room temperature, and drain excess fat. Wrap in foil, top with a board and a weight (like a heavy can), and refrigerate overnight. The loaf is best if refrigerated for 2 days before serving.

5. To make oat crackers, combine oatmeal, salt, and baking soda in a bowl. Pour in melted butter and then stir in enough water to make a stiff dough. You may have to wait a few minutes for the oats to absorb the water to check the consistency.

6. Turn dough onto a floured surface and quickly knead for 30 seconds. Roll out on a sheet of plastic or wax paper to a 1/4-inch (5 mm) thickness, then cut out crackers with a 3-inch (8 cm) cookie cutter or water glass.

7. Use a spatula to transfer crackers to a lightly greased baking sheet lined with parchment paper and bake in a preheated 350°F (180°C) oven for 30 minutes, or until crackers begin to brown. Cool on a rack and store in an airtight tin.

8. Serve wild boar loaf from the loaf pan or unmould onto a plate. Slice and serve with oat crackers or bread, garnished with gherkins, pickled beets, or cranberry chutney, and assorted gourmet mustards as a starter or pub-style lunch. The wild boar loaf will keep for up to five days in the refrigerator. Serves 8.

HOME-MADE STOCK

If you want to make the best-tasting soups, stews, and sauces, home-made stocks are far superior to canned products. It's easy to make stock from scratch, especially if you get into the habit of saving clean vegetable scraps like celery tops, mushroom stems, carrot peelings, and other vegetable trimmings in your freezer. Add a bag for chicken scraps and bones, and another for red meat trimmings and you'll soon have a cache for making fine stocks.

Brown meat stocks need browning for depth of colour and flavour. Start with 4 pounds (2 kg) of beef or pork bones (or even game trimmings) that have been browned in a 400°F (200°C) oven, then combine in the stock pot with some peppercorns, sprigs of fresh parsley and thyme, diced carrot, celery, onion, turnip, tomatoes, and 12 cups (3 L) cold water. Bring to a boil slowly, reduce heat, and simmer for a few hours, skimming anything that rises to the top. Season with salt after stock is strained, degreased, and cooled.

For light chicken, vegetable, and fish stocks there's no need to brown ingredients first. Use bones, coarsely chopped celery, onions, carrots, parsnips (for chicken soup), and a bay leaf, a few whole peppercorns, and some fresh parsley in the stock pot. Cover with 8–12 cups of cold water and bring to a boil. Skim off the foam that rises to the top, then reduce heat and simmer, partly covered, for 2–3 hours. Cool, degrease, and season.

Fish stock, or fumet, is usually made with any kind of white fish bones and trim, lobster or shrimp shells, and crab carcasses (don't use salmon scraps). Fish heads are usually available from the fish market. Season the stock with peppercorns, carrots, celery, and onion, and use some white wine or lemon juice along with the water. Fish fumet cooks quickly—it only takes 15–20 minutes to make a good fish stock. Strain before using. Vegetable stock can be similarly made, with sautéed onions, carrots, turnips, parsnips, mushrooms, tomatoes, or other vegetables, and enough cold water to cover. Bring to a boil, partly cover, and simmer for 2 hours, then strain and chill. To make stocks quickly in a

VENISON LOIN ROAST WITH SASKATOON BERRY SAUCE

This is adapted from a recipe developed by Canmore chef Hubert Aumeier, the originator of Alberta's Rocky Mountain Cuisine. Hubert cooks the roast in a salt crust to keep it tender. In this home-style version, the venison loin is quickly seared and finished in the oven, then served with his savoury, berry-infused game sauce. Saskatoons are the prairie berry of choice, but wild blueberries work well, too.

2 pounds (1 kg) venison loin, all silver skin removed
1 tablespoon (15 mL) olive oil
salt and freshly ground black pepper
clarified butter or olive oil
1 handful pine or spruce needles
12 juniper berries

Sauce
3 tablespoons (45 mL) butter, divided
  (1 tablespoon/25 mL should be cold)
1 shallot, minced
4 black peppercorns, crushed
1 crushed juniper berry
1 cup (250 mL) dry red wine
1 cup (250 mL) brown venison or beef stock (see tip, at left)
1/4 cup (50 mL) saskatoon berries, crushed or puréed
saskatoon liqueur or port (optional)
salt and freshly ground black pepper
1/2 cup (125 mL) whole saskatoon berries

1. Rub venison loins with 1 tablespoon (15 mL) of olive oil and season with salt and pepper. In an ovenproof sauté pan or roasting pan, heat a little more olive oil or clarified butter over medium-high heat and sear venison to brown on all sides.

2. Add pine or spruce needles and juniper berries to the pan and place meat on top. Put pan into a preheated 425°F (220°C) oven and cook for 10–12 minutes, until roast is cooked to medium rare.

3. Remove meat from pan and set aside on a cutting board, covered loosely with foil, to rest for 5 minutes. Remove spruce needles and juniper berries from pan and discard.

4. To make sauce, heat 2 tablespoons (25 mL) of butter in a pan and sauté shallots, black peppercorns, and juniper berry for 3 minutes, until shallots are beginning to brown. Add red wine and venison stock and boil vigorously, until reduced to about 1/2 cup (125 mL).

Add berry purée and cook a few minutes longer. Strain and set aside. Just before serving, reheat sauce and whisk in 1 tablespoon (15 mL) of cold butter. Season with salt and pepper, and a splash of liqueur or port, if using. Add whole berries and heat through.

5. To serve, slice loins into medallions and arrange on individual plates in a pool of sauce. Serves 6 to 8.

WILD BOAR STEW WITH RYE WHISKY

David Garcelon, the executive chef at the Jasper Park Lodge, shared this recipe for a tender stew created from another Alberta product, wild boar. The rye whisky gives it a real prairie punch.

1 tablespoon (15 mL) vegetable oil
1 pound (500 g) wild boar meat, cut into 1-inch (2.5 cm) cubes, or substitute pork leg or shoulder
1 purple-top turnip, in small dice
1 carrot, in small dice
1 small rutabaga, in small dice
1 medium onion, in small dice
6 cloves garlic, minced
1/2 cup (125 mL) butter
1/2 cup (125 mL) all-purpose flour
1/2 cup (125 mL) Canadian Club rye whisky
8 cups (2 L) brown stock
2 bay leaves and 10 peppercorns tied into cheesecloth (sachet)
2 sprigs fresh rosemary, finely chopped
salt and freshly ground black pepper

1. Heat oil in a large saucepan over medium-high heat and brown meat on all sides. Remove from pan and set aside.
2. Sauté root vegetables, onions, and garlic in oil until nicely browned. Remove from heat.
3. Using the same pan, melt butter and whisk in flour to make a roux. Continue cooking roux over medium heat until lightly browned.
4. Heat whisky and brown stock together in a separate pot and bring to a boil. Slowly add hot liquid to roux, whisking constantly to avoid leaving lumps in the sauce.
5. Add browned meat and vegetables to sauce. Add sachet and simmer stew, covered, over low heat for approximately 2 hours, or until meat is very tender.
6. Skim all fat off stew, add rosemary, and adjust seasoning to taste with salt and pepper. Serve with buttermilk biscuits and butter flavoured with fireweed honey, if desired. Serves 6.

pressure cooker, start with raw or browned meat or poultry bones, fish bones, and/or clean vegetable scraps or chopped carrots, celery, onions, and herbs. Cover with about 8 cups (2 L) of water, bring up to full pressure and cook for 15–30 minutes. Release pressure, strain, and skim excess fat.

Sometimes recipes call for demi-glace, which is a brown stock that has been cooked down slowly until it becomes almost solid. Demi-glace is gold to the chef—a little adds body and intense flavour to any soup or sauce—and you can freeze it.

GRILLED BISON ON MIXED GREENS WITH SASKATOON BERRY DRESSING

Bison steak is rich, ultra-lean, tender, and expensive. Serving grilled bison steak over fresh greens is a good way to stretch this rare, premium product. If you can't find saskatoon berries, substitute blueberries in the dressing.

1 pound (500 g) bison medallion (tenderloin steak) or strip loin
2 teaspoons (10 mL) black peppercorns, coarsely crushed

Dressing
1 tablespoon (15 mL) balsamic vinegar
1/4 cup (50 mL) canola oil
1/4 teaspoon (1 mL) Asian chili sauce
1 shallot, minced
1/4 cup (50 mL) saskatoon berries
2 teaspoons (15 mL) saskatoon berry jam or jelly
2 tablespoons (25 mL) water (optional)

Salad
8 cups (2 L) mixed salad greens and herbs
   (try including unusual leaves
   like arugula and mint with baby lettuces)
2 green onions, chopped
1 cup (250 mL) currant, cherry, or other miniature tomatoes,
   whole or halved
1 tablespoon (15 mL) cold-pressed canola oil or extra-virgin olive oil

1. Combine dressing ingredients in a blender or food processor and whirl until smooth. Add up to 2 tablespoons (25 mL) water if dressing is too thick.
2. Place bison steak in a zippered plastic bag with 3 tablespoons (45 mL) of dressing and marinate in refrigerator for at least 2 hours. Chill remaining dressing separately.
3. Wash salad greens and herbs well. Spin in a salad spinner to remove excess moisture and wrap loosely in a paper towel. Place greens in a plastic bag and refrigerate until ready to serve.
4. Remove steak from marinade and bring to room temperature. Place crushed peppercorns in a dish and roll meat in pepper to coat on all sides. Heat barbecue to high heat and sear steak for 3 minutes per side. Steak should be seared on the outside but rare on the inside. Set steak on a cutting board for 10 minutes to rest.
5. Toss salad greens with green onions and tomatoes, and enough of the reserved dressing to coat greens lightly. Arrange on four individual salad plates. Slice steak in thin strips across the grain and arrange on top of each salad. Drizzle salads with canola oil or olive oil and serve immediately. Serves 4.

BRAISED BISON WITH MUSHROOM SAGE GRAVY AND WILD RICE FRITTERS

This slow-cooked stew is flavoured with fresh sage.
Serve it over wild rice fritters for a traditional taste.

2 pounds (1 kg) lean bison chuck or round steak, cut into
    2-inch (5 cm) cubes
2 tablespoons (25 mL) canola oil
1 cup (250 mL) chopped onions
2 cloves garlic, minced
2 tablespoons (25 mL) all-purpose flour
1 cup (250 mL) Cabernet Sauvignon wine
1 cup (250 mL) beef stock
1/2 cup (125 mL) dried wild mushrooms, rehydrated in
    1/2 cup (125 mL) hot water
1 tablespoon (15 mL) chopped fresh sage
salt and freshly ground black pepper

Marinade
1 tablespoon (15 mL) balsamic vinegar
1/2 teaspoon (2 mL) freshly ground black pepper
2 teaspoons (10 mL) minced fresh sage

1. Combine marinade ingredients. Add bison and marinate at room temperature for 30 minutes.
2. Heat canola oil in a Dutch oven and brown meat over high heat in batches. Set aside meat as it's cooked.
3. Add onions and garlic to drippings in the pan and sauté 5 minutes, until beginning to brown. Add flour and stir to combine. Slowly stir in wine, stock, and wild mushrooms with their soaking liquid. Return meat to pan and bring to a boil. Cover, reduce heat to low, and simmer for 1–2 hours or until bison is very tender. Stir in fresh sage and season with salt and freshly ground black pepper to taste. Serve with wild rice fritters. See page 111. Serves 4.

GROUND BISON PIE WITH GARLIC POTATO CRUST

This version of classic shepherd's pie includes lean ground bison, smoky roasted tomatoes, and chili peppers.

2 pounds (1 kg) ground bison
1 onion, minced
2 cloves garlic, minced
3 tablespoons (45 mL) soy sauce
1 cup (250 mL) frozen sweet corn
1 cup (250 mL) frozen peas

Sauce
2 pounds (1 kg) Roma tomatoes, halved and seeded
1 jalapeño pepper, halved and seeded
1 red onion, cut into eighths
2 cloves garlic, peeled
2 tablespoons (25 mL) olive oil
salt and freshly ground black pepper

Potato Topping
2 pounds (1 kg) Yukon Gold or other yellow-fleshed potatoes
6 cloves garlic, peeled
3 tablespoons (45 mL) butter
1/2 cup (125 mL) milk or cream
1 cup (250 mL) finely grated Parmesan cheese
freshly ground black pepper

1. For sauce, toss tomatoes, jalapeño, red onion, garlic, and olive oil with salt and pepper. Arrange in a single layer in a roasting pan and roast in preheated 500°F (260°C) oven for 30 minutes, stirring occasionally. Roast until vegetables begin to caramelize and char. Place in a food processor and purée to form a thick sauce. Set aside.

2. Cook ground bison in a sauté pan over medium heat for 10 minutes, or until no longer pink. Add onion and garlic and cook for 5 minutes longer, until meat and onions begin to brown. Stir in soy sauce, corn, peas, and reserved roasted tomato sauce. Spread mixture in a 13 x 9 inch (3.5 L) baking dish.

3. Meanwhile, boil potatoes and whole garlic cloves in salted water until tender. Drain and mash with butter and milk until fairly smooth, although it's fine to leaves some lumps. Stir in Parmesan cheese and season with pepper to taste. Spread potatoes on top of meat mixture and bake in preheated 350°F (180°C) oven for 30–45 minutes, until potatoes are puffed and golden. Set aside to cool for 15 minutes before cutting into squares to serve. Serves 8.

Bison Carpaccio with Cold-Pressed Canola Oil

Fred Zimmerman, the award-winning Alberta chef who led the culinary Team Canada to a gold medal at the Culinary Olympics, devised this wonderful carpaccio of lean bison, drizzled with cold-pressed canola oil. Although served raw, it is first seasoned and seared on the outside, so there is no danger of contamination.

1 2-pound (1 kg) top sirloin bison butt
2 teaspoons (10 mL) each: minced fresh thyme, basil,
    oregano, and rosemary
2 teaspoons (10 mL) black peppercorns, coarsely crushed
7 juniper berries, crushed
2 tablespoons (25 mL) canola oil
salt
cold-pressed canola oil
freshly ground black pepper

1. Separate sirloin into major muscles and trim all fat, sinew, and silver skin. Cut meat into 3-inch (8 cm) square strips with the grain.
2. Mix fresh herbs, peppercorns, and crushed juniper berries and roll meat in mixture to coat all sides. Wrap seasoned meat tightly in plastic wrap and refrigerate for 6–8 hours.
3. Discard plastic wrap. Heat oil in a nonstick pan over high heat. Sear meat quickly on all sides, about 1 minute per side. Cool meat and wrap in plastic.
4. Freeze bison until stiff but not solid. Using a sharp knife, cut very thin slices across the grain. Arrange carpaccio on individual appetizer plates, overlapping pieces in a pattern. Drizzle with cold-pressed canola oil and season with salt and pepper to taste. Serve alone, or use to garnish soups or salads. Serves 12.

Pemmican Patties

These sausage patties are inspired by the traditional Native staple, pemmican, a mixture of ground dried bison meat, fat, and wild berries that kept nomadic tribes alive over harsh prairie winters. While these patties are panfried rather than dried like real pemmican, they'll add some Wild West flavour to your next pancake breakfast or brunch. For a hot appetizer, make the mixture into meatballs, glaze with red currant or cranberry jelly, and serve with toothpicks.

1 pound (500 g) lean ground buffalo, or ground beef
1/2 pound (250 g) ground pork
2 teaspoons (10 mL) freshly ground black pepper
2 teaspoons (10 mL) salt
1 teaspoon (5 mL) crushed allspice berries
2 cups (500 mL) fresh saskatoons, blueberries, or cranberries
    (or a mixture), whole or roughly chopped in food processor
1 cup (250 mL) minced onion
2 tablespoons (25 mL) dried juniper berries, soaked in boiling
    water to soften, then drained
1 cup (250 mL) red currant or cranberry jelly, melted,
    for appetizer meatballs
2 tablespoons (25 mL) chopped fresh parsley

1. Combine all ingredients, except jelly and parsley, and work lightly with your hands to combine.
2. Form into small patties and grill or sauté until browned on the outside and just cooked through, about 4–5 minutes per side. Serve patties as an alternative to breakfast sausages.
3. To make pemmican balls to serve as appetizers, roll pemmican mixture into walnut-sized balls and place in a baking pan. Bake in a preheated oven at 350°F (180°C) for 30–40 minutes, until well browned and cooked through.
4. Drain any accumulated fat and toss meatballs with melted red currant or cranberry jelly, sprinkle with parsley, and serve warm with toothpicks for appetizers. Makes about 16 patties or 40 meatballs.

BRAISED VENISON SHANK WITH CARIBOU MINCEMEAT AND WILD MUSHROOM GRITS

One of Calgary's most popular destination restaurants, the River Café is a casually elegant dining experience in the centre of Prince's Island Park, an urban green space next to the Bow River in the downtown core. The creative chefs at the River Café were leaders in the Alberta regional cuisine movement, working hard to incorporate Alberta's bounty into their menus. The River Café buys local vegetables, wild game, grains, and fruits and, like generations of prairie cooks, the chefs preserve the summer bounty for use over the long winters.

2 tablespoons (25 mL) olive oil
1 tablespoon (15 mL) butter
4 venison shanks, or substitute lamb shanks
salt and freshly ground black pepper
2 yellow onions, rough chop
2 carrots, rough chop
2 celery stalks, rough chop
1 parsnip, rough chop
10 garlic cloves, smashed
2 cups (500 mL) red wine
2 cups (500 mL) venison stock or good beef stock
3 star anise
15 juniper berries, toasted and smashed
6 bay leaves
4 sprigs rosemary
1 small bunch of fresh thyme
1 small bunch of fresh parsley

1   Heat olive oil and butter in a large, deep Dutch oven. Season shanks with salt and pepper. Sear on all sides until well browned, then remove.

2. Stir onions, carrots, celery, parsnip, and garlic into Dutch oven and cook for about 10 minutes until slightly caramelized. Add wine and slightly deglaze the pan, boiling for 2 minutes to reduce slightly.

3. Add stock, star anise, juniper, bay leaves, and herbs. Add shanks and bring mixture to a boil. Cover and braise in a preheated 250°F (120°C) oven for 4 hours. Remove shanks from pan and strain braising liquid, pressing the solids through the strainer into the sauce. Simmer to thicken.

4. Serve with wild mushroom grits, caribou mincemeat, and your favourite winter vegetables on a cold winter night. Serves 4.

Caribou Mincemeat
10 apples, peeled and grated
1 lemon
1 orange
1/4 pound (125 g) venison suet, or beef suet
1 pound (500 g) ground caribou, or ground beef or lamb
3 cups (750 mL) dried currants
1/2 cup (125 mL) dried cherries
1/2 cup (125 mL) dried apricots, chopped
1/2 cup (125 mL) dried cranberries
2 cups (500 mL) good-quality apple juice or apple cider
1/2 cup (125 mL) demerara sugar
1/4 teaspoon (1 mL) ground cinnamon
1/4 teaspoon (1 mL) ground nutmeg
1/4 teaspoon (1 mL) dry mustard
1/4 teaspoon (1 mL) ground coriander
salt and freshly ground black pepper to taste
1/2 cup (125 mL) brandy or maple whisky

1. Peel and core apples. Grate them by hand or in food processor. Use a zester to remove zest from lemon and orange, then peel them and chop the flesh, reserving all juice. Combine all mincemeat ingredients in a heavy-bottomed pot.

2. Simmer for 2 hours over very low heat, stirring occasionally. Be careful not to scorch. Mincemeat should be very thick.

3. Serve warm mincemeat over braised shanks. Cover extra mincemeat and refrigerate or freeze for later use. This is also good to serve as a condiment with braised or grilled bison or lamb. Mincemeat improves if stored in the refrigerator for two weeks before using. If desired, flavour the mincemeat with a little extra brandy just before serving.

Wild Mushroom Grits
4 cups (1 L) chicken stock
1/2 cup (125 mL) whipping cream
3 tablespoons (45 mL) butter
1 cup (250 mL) stone-ground cornmeal or coarse polenta
2 cups (500 mL) fresh chanterelles or other wild mushrooms
2 tablespoons (25 mL) olive oil
3 tablespoons (45 mL) chopped fresh sage
salt and freshly ground black pepper

1. Combine stock, cream, and butter in a pot and bring to a boil. Lower heat and slowly stir in cornmeal, whisking as you go to prevent lumps.
2. Cook over very low heat for 20–25 minutes, stirring frequently to prevent scorching. The cornmeal should be thick and creamy, and begin to come away from the sides of the pot.
3. Meanwhile, cook mushrooms. If using fresh wild mushrooms, immerse quickly in ice-cold water to rinse off any debris, lifting the mushrooms from the water and draining well. Toss mushrooms with olive oil and roast in a preheated 400°F (200°C) oven until tender, about 15 minutes. If mushrooms have been frozen, sauté them slowly until they are tender and cooking juices have been absorbed.
4. Remove polenta from heat. Fold in sage and season to taste with salt and pepper. Stir in mushrooms and serve immediately.

MEDALLIONS OF VENISON WITH CANADIAN RYE WHISKY AND FOREST MUSHROOMS

This is the perfect recipe to serve two in style—say, a home-based anniversary dinner or Valentine's celebration. Venison is expensive, but it is a lovely, lean meat and there is no waste with medallions like this. If you can find some fresh local morel mushrooms in the spring, or chanterelles in the fall, this creamy, whisky-spiked sauce will be even more decadent.

6 venison medallions, cut from the hip, each about 3 inches (8 cm) in diameter
olive oil

Sauce
2 tablespoons (25 mL) butter
4 shallots, minced
2 cloves garlic, minced
1 cup (250 mL) sliced mushrooms (wild mushrooms make this especially tasty, or use cultivated shiitake or portobello mushrooms)
1/4 cup (50 mL) Canadian Club or other rye whisky
3/4 cup (175 mL) whipping cream
salt and freshly ground black pepper to taste

1. Pound medallions until they are all the same thickness.
2. For sauce, melt butter in pan and sauté shallots and garlic over medium-high heat until tender, about 5 minutes. Add mushrooms and sauté 5 minutes longer.
3. Heat whisky in a small pan, add to vegetables, and ignite. Stand back when you do this. Cook until flames die down.
4. Add cream and boil over medium-high heat until sauce is reduced and thick enough to coat a spoon.
5. Meanwhile, panfry venison in a little oil in a nonstick pan over medium-high heat for a total of 3 minutes, turning once. Serve in a pool of mushroom cream sauce accompanied by wild rice and squash. Serves 2.

Venison with Lavender Rub

Lavender's distinctive flavour mixes well with fresh sage and thyme. Use culinary lavender that has not been sprayed or otherwise treated with pesticides.

4 pounds (2 kg) venison loin
2 tablespoons (25 mL) olive oil or clarified butter
2 cups (500 mL) full-bodied red wine (Petit Syrah,
    Zinfandel, or Cabernet Sauvignon)
1 tablespoon (15 mL) dried lavender flowers
1 shallot, chopped
3 tablespoons (45 mL) cold butter, chopped

Marinade
1/2 cup (125 mL) olive oil
1/4 cup (50 mL) each: chopped fresh sage leaves and thyme leaves
1/2 cup (125 mL) chopped fresh parsley
1 yellow onion, minced
4 carrots, peeled and chopped
4 stalks celery, chopped
5 tablespoons (65 mL) dried lavender flowers
salt and freshly ground black pepper

1. For marinade, combine olive oil, sage, thyme, parsley, onion, carrots, celery, lavender, salt, and pepper. Purée in food processor. Rub mixture over all surfaces of meat, cover, and refrigerate for 4–6 hours.
2. Remove venison from marinade, allowing some of the rub to remain on surface of meat. In an ovenproof sauté pan or roasting pan, heat olive oil or clarified butter over high heat and sear venison to brown well on all sides. Put pan into a preheated 425°F (220°C) oven and cook for 10–12 minutes, until roast is cooked to medium rare.
3. Remove meat from pan and set aside on a cutting board, covered loosely with foil, to rest for 10 minutes.
4. Meanwile, add wine, 1 tablespoon (15 mL) lavender, and chopped shallot to the roasting pan. Bring to a rolling boil and cook until liquid reaches a light sauce consistency and is reduced by half. Strain sauce and whisk in butter, a few pieces at a time, to emulsify.
5. Slice loins into medallions, arrange on plates. Serve sauce over medallions. Serves 8.

Wild Boar Prosciutto and Sylvan Star Gouda Frittata

This fritatta from the chefs at the River Café is a wonderful dish to serve for breakfast, lunch, or dinner—especially when you have leftover potatoes in the refrigerator. Try making it with purple-fleshed blue potatoes from growers like Rosemary Wotske and Robert Boshman of Poplar Bluff Farm, wild boar prosciutto ham from Hog Wild, and Sylvan Star's award-winning Gouda.

1 pound (500 g) purple potatoes
8 eggs
1/2 cup (125 mL) whole milk
1 tablespoon (15 mL) unsalted butter
1 cup (250 mL) finely sliced shallots or leeks
1/4 pound (125 g) wild boar prosciutto or regular prosciutto,
    thinly sliced and cut into strips
3 tablespoons (45 mL) each: chopped fresh thyme and oregano
salt and freshly ground black pepper
6 ounces (180 g) Sylvan Star aged Gouda cheese, grated

1. Cook potatoes in boiling salted water until barely cooked, and let cool completely. Use leftover potatoes that have been chilled overnight if possible. Chop potatoes. You should have about 2 cups (500 mL).
2. In a large mixing bowl, whisk together eggs and milk until thoroughly incorporated.
3. In a 10-inch (25 cm) nonstick ovenproof sauté pan, melt butter and sauté potatoes until they begin to brown in the pan. Stir in shallots or leeks and cook until they are limp and brown. Add prosciutto and herbs and stir to combine. Add the egg mixture, season with salt and pepper, and stir for 1 minute.
4. Bake frittata in preheated 350°F (180°C) oven for 10 minutes—it should still be quite loose in the centre. Sprinkle with grated cheese and bake 10–15 minutes longer, until golden brown. Cut into wedges to serve. Serves 4.

Poultry and Eggs

CHICKEN RUN: PULLETS ON PASTURE

It's midsummer and the bugs and butterflies are buzzing around Rosemary Wotske's mixed farm. In one corner of the yard, a circular electric fence creates a wide pen around a low, shady coop. Inside are White Plymouth Rocks and Cornish game hens, scratching and eking out a diet of grass and bugs. Down past the garden, another grassy pen holds her laying hens. The handsome, russet-plumed Rhode Island Reds peck at her rubber boots and strut around foraging until they head inside to deposit their big, brown, free-range eggs in nesting boxes, the kind of eggs that are prized by consumers who love their deep yellow yolks and organic pedigree.

This is what's known as "free-range" or "pastured" poultry. A growing number of Alberta producers let their birds roam freely to feed on grass, clover, and other greens, then supplement their diets with grains. It's an old-fashioned style of poultry production that has gained farmers like Wotske and others new fans among consumers, although they have struggled against conventional egg producers and their marketing boards, who argue that organic, free-range producers must stay small or join their quota system. It's a chicken and egg dilemma. The hands-on, organic growers say their eggs, already expensive at retail, would be priced out of the market by the added cost of quota. Furthermore, they can't produce a free-range egg for the price paid by the marketing board. It's the main reason that conventional egg producers don't switch to the free-range style of farming.

Ron Hamilton has been a leader in the pastured poultry movement in Alberta, raising his organic Cornish Giants in low, moveable pens. Every day he takes a furniture dolly and manually moves each large, bottomless cage a few more feet along his pasture onto clean, fresh grass. The birds are also fed a mixture of organic wheat, oats, barley, oyster shells, and canola meal. He says it makes for healthy birds and tastier fowl.

"You don't concentrate their manure in one spot, like in a barn, and they get plenty of clean air and fresh, green grass."

All this translates into happier, healthier livestock that don't need drugs and antibiotics to thrive. It's a holistic style of farming that is sustainable, not only to the farm families, but to the environment where they work and live. The fresh grass also gives the meat and eggs another added advantage. Like the free-range chickens our grandparents raised and served, the meat and eggs from these pastured birds are high in Omega-3 fatty acids, the essential fatty acids (EFAs) lacking in the average North American diet.

A study funded by the USDA Sustainable Agriculture and Research Education Program (SARE) found that, compared with conventionally-raised broilers, free-range chickens had 21 percent less total fat, 30 percent less saturated fat, and 28 percent fewer calories, along with 50 percent more Vitamin A or beta carotene, and 100 percent more Omega 3s. The SARE study also concluded that free-range eggs contained 40 percent more Vitamin A, 34 percent less cholesterol, and 400 percent more Omega 3s than eggs from caged birds.

But you have to shop wisely when you're buying eggs and poultry labelled "free-range." Words like "free-range" and "free-run"

FLAVOUR FIRST

Chefs and savvy consumers love the great taste of free-range chicken and eggs. The meat has golden yellow fat and a more intense chicken flavour—something that's especially obvious when you simply roast one of these farm fresh birds. Another advantage is size. You are buying a mature bird that's the right size to roast, not a 1.5 kilogram fryer designed to satisfy the fast-food industry. A free-range chicken will cost more, but that reflects the labour-intensive style of farming and slower, hormone-free growth.

The orange-yolked eggs of grass-fed birds are delicious, with no traces of the antibiotics and other medications that can be concentrated in the yolks of conventional eggs. The beta carotene that turns yolks yellow is obtained naturally from grass, although some egg producers use supplements to obtain the deep yellow yolks without grass feeding.

COOKING EGGS

I like my eggs poached or fried sunny side up, on a nice thick piece of buttered wholegrain toast. It's easy to poach eggs in advance and reheat them when you're ready to serve them. Fill a deep sauté pan with water, bring to a simmer, break eggs into a saucer, and slide into boiling water, one at a time. A few drops of lemon juice or vinegar in the water will help keep the whites together. Cook for about 4–5 minutes in total, turning eggs over gently when they look set. Remove poached eggs with a slotted spoon and place in a bowl of ice water to chill. They can be refrigerated this way overnight, then plunged quickly into boiling water for 30 seconds to reheat before serving.

Another easy egg dish to master is the scramble. Heat a little butter in a nonstick pan over low heat. Add beaten eggs to pan, seasoned and flavoured with a little cream if you like, and stir gently until they form big, soft curds. Don't overcook—the eggs should be soft and fluffy. If the heat is too high, your scrambled eggs will be tough and watery.

Rosemary Wotske

are popping up on all kinds of egg cartons and poultry packages. But Wotske says that might only mean the animals were not confined in cages, but still crowded into a barn, or that the barn door opened to an equally crowded pen with no fresh grass. Certified organic growers follow stricter guidelines, but the industry is still struggling with definitions.

True "pastured birds" are raised on grass, regularly moved to fresh pasture, and given feed without antibiotics or hormones. Alexandra Luppold has lots of space for her chickens to roam around the barn on her farm near Nanton, and once they've consumed most of the plants in one spot, she relocates them to another. It's a simple system, but one that requires the commitment to hands-on production methods. If you seek out producers who allow their chickens and turkeys to forage on fresh grass, you will be rewarded with the kind of flavourful meat and eggs that the best chefs are demanding from their local growers.

Hard-cooked eggs are also easy and delicious if you cook them properly. Eggs that are not super fresh are easier to peel. Bring eggs to room temperature, then boil enough water to cover eggs. In a spoon, lower eggs slowly into boiling water. Turn heat down to medium and boil for 8–10 minutes (at 8 minutes the yolk is just set and still creamy; at 10 minutes it is stiffer and better for egg salad). Drain eggs and immediately cover them with ice water to chill for 1–2 minutes, then crack shells and return eggs to cold water for 5 minutes longer. Peel immediately.

When you break a fresh egg, you should find a firm yolk standing tall upon a clear, gelatinous white. Older eggs have flatter yolks and watery whites. White and brown eggs are no different inside; they are simply laid by different kinds of chickens. Keep eggs refrigerated, away from strong-smelling foods, and they will stay fresh for three weeks.

A discussion of prairie poultry wouldn't be complete without a few words about our indigenous turkey. Birds with beautiful plumage and a great heritage, wild turkeys are still found strutting their stuff in the Alberta foothills. It was likely wild turkeys that the Pilgrims and their Native neighbours enjoyed at their first Thanksgiving dinner. These days you can buy wild Alberta turkeys that are produced domestically—go figure.

Turkeys were first raised in pre-Columbian Mexico, and turkey remains prominent in Mexican cuisine. A typical festive meal includes turkey in poblano mole, a braise of turkey with chiles, spices, nuts, and that other New World invention, chocolate. As far back as 500 AD, Anasazi Indians kept turkeys in the pueblos of Arizona and New Mexico, often using their feathers in religious ceremonies.

In Alberta's Peace River country, Jerry Kitt of First Nature Farms has long been raising organic poultry, including domestic and wild turkeys, for the most discerning holiday tables. The Dirt Willy Game Bird Farm near Ardrossan raises wild turkeys as well as other wild game birds for sale to individuals and restaurants. And, of course, ducks and geese, from mallards to the big black and white Canadas, prairie chicken, partridge, pheasant, and quail have long been abundant for westerners who like to hunt their own birds in the wild.

Roasted Chicken Breast with Wild Mushroom Risotto and Sage Pan Gravy

Former Calgary chef Michael Allemeier created this simple but classy chicken dish that anyone can make at home. If fresh mushrooms are not available, use rehydrated dried wild mushrooms. Steam a seasonal green vegetable like green beans, broccoli, or Brussels sprouts to serve alongside chicken.

4 boneless chicken breasts, skin on
salt and freshly ground black pepper
1/4 cup (50 mL) all-purpose flour
2 tablespoons (25 mL) canola oil

Risotto
4 cups (1 L) chicken stock
2 tablespoons (25 mL) butter
1 cup (250 mL) diced onions
1 teaspoon (5 mL) minced garlic
1/4 cup (50 mL) fresh sage, chopped
2 cups (500 mL) wild mushrooms, sliced
2 cups (500 mL) arborio or other short-grained rice
1/2 teaspoon (2 mL) each: salt and freshly ground black pepper
1/2 cup (125 mL) white wine
1 cup (250 mL) whipping cream
1/4 cup (50 mL) grated Parmesan cheese

Gravy
2–3 tablespoons (25–45 mL) all-purpose flour
2 tablespoons (25 mL) chopped fresh sage
1/4 cup (50 mL) dry sherry
1 cup (250 mL) chicken stock

1. For risotto, heat chicken stock in a pot and keep warm. Melt butter in a pan and cook onions, garlic, and sage in butter over medium heat until translucent. Add mushrooms and sauté until lightly browned. Stir in rice and sauté until grains are slightly transparent. Season with salt and pepper, then deglaze pan with wine. Add enough chicken stock to cover rice by 1/2 inch (1.5 cm) and simmer, adding stock when needed to always keep rice covered, until rice is 90 percent cooked (about 20 minutes). Add cream and cheese and finish cooking until still creamy, but thick enough to mound slightly on plate.

2. While risotto is cooking, season chicken breasts with salt and pepper, then dredge in flour to coat, knocking off excess flour. Heat canola oil in a heavy cast-iron frying pan over high heat and sear chicken until lightly browned on both sides. Put pan in a preheated 400°F (200°C) oven and roast chicken for 20 minutes. Remove from oven and let rest 10 minutes. Reserve drippings in pan for gravy.

3. To make gravy, sprinkle flour into drippings remaining in frying pan and cook over medium heat, stirring with a whisk to form a paste. Add sage and sherry and stir until incorporated. Gradually add stock, whisking until well blended and free of lumps. Simmer gravy for 5 minutes to thicken slightly.

4. Slice roasted chicken and arrange on individual plates on top of a mound of risotto with pan gravy drizzled around the outside. Serves 4.

Fried Chicken Salad

Fried chicken is prairie comfort food at its best, but these days it's hard to justify such a high-fat preparation. In this full-meal salad you get healthy greens and your fried chicken fix (hold the fries and gravy) without as much guilt. This is also a fine way to make chicken fingers for appetizers for kids and other true chicken finger fanatics.

3 boneless, skinless chicken breast halves
1/4 cup (50 mL) Dijon mustard
1/2 teaspoon (2 mL) freshly ground black pepper
1/4 teaspoon (1 mL) sweet Hungarian or Spanish paprika
1/4 teaspoon (1 mL) salt
1/4 teaspoon (1 mL) dried thyme leaves
1/4 teaspoon (1 mL) granulated garlic
pinch of cayenne pepper
1 egg
1/4 cup (50 mL) milk or buttermilk
1 cup (250 mL) all-purpose flour or fine dry breadcrumbs
canola or peanut oil for frying
8 cups (2 L) mixed greens

Vinaigrette
2 teaspoons (10 mL) Dijon mustard
1/2 teaspoon (2 mL) each: salt and freshly ground black pepper
2 tablespoons (25 mL) fresh lemon juice
1/2 cup (125 mL) olive oil

1. Mix mustard, pepper, paprika, salt, thyme, granulated garlic, and cayenne pepper in a bowl. Cut chicken breasts into long strips and toss with spices in bowl to coat well. Cover and refrigerate for 1 hour.
2. Whisk together egg and milk or buttermilk. Place flour or breadcrumbs on a plate. Line a baking sheet with waxed paper.
3. Dip chicken strips, one at a time, into egg mixture, shaking off any excess. Roll chicken in flour or breadcrumbs to coat on all sides and set on baking sheet to dry. Chill for 10 minutes.
4. Heat about 1/4-inch (5 mm) of canola or peanut oil in a nonstick frying pan over medium-high heat. Fry chicken pieces until golden on both sides and crisp, about 5–7 minutes. Set aside to drain on paper towels. Keep warm.
5. Whisk together vinaigrette ingredients and toss with salad greens to coat well. Divide greens between four serving plates and top each salad with some of the hot fried chicken. Serves 4.

Cowboy Calzones with Grilled Chicken and Black Beans

In my kitchen the calzone is akin to the stir-fry or the quesadilla—
it's the method that matters, what goes inside is infinitely flexible. Make
these portable turnovers with leftover meats or sliced sausages
and different cheeses and vegetables, from caramelized onions,
olives, and roasted peppers to artichokes.

2 boneless, skinless chicken breast halves
2 tablespoons (25 mL) olive or canola oil, divided
salt and freshly ground black pepper
1/4 cup (50 mL) minced red bell pepper
3 green onions, minced
1/2 cup (125 mL) frozen corn, thawed

1/2 cup (125 mL) cooked black beans
(drained and rinsed well, if canned)
2 cups (500 mL) packed fresh spinach, washed and chopped
1 jalapeño pepper, seeded and minced
1 teaspoon (5 mL) ground cumin
1 teaspoon (5 mL) chili powder
1/4 teaspoon (1 mL) salt
dash cayenne pepper
1/2 cup (125 mL) spicy tomato salsa
1 cup (250 mL) shredded Monterey Jack cheese
1 loaf frozen whole-wheat bread dough, thawed
milk or beaten egg (optional)

1. Rub chicken breasts with 1 tablespoon (15 mL) olive oil, lightly season with salt and pepper, then grill on barbecue at high heat for 4–5 minutes per side, or until just cooked through. Set chicken aside until it cools down enough to handle.
2. Heat 1 tablespoon (15 mL) oil in a medium skillet over medium-high heat. Add red pepper and green onion to the pan and sauté for 5 minutes, until tender.
3. Add corn, black beans, spinach, jalapeño pepper, cumin, chili powder, salt, and cayenne pepper to the pan. Cook for 4 minutes, until spinach is wilted and most of the liquid in the pan has evaporated. Dice cooked chicken and add it to the pan. Set filling aside to cool. Stir in salsa and grated cheese.
4. Divide thawed bread dough into six equal pieces. Roll each piece on a lightly floured surface to form a 6–7-inch (15–18 cm) circle. Moisten dough around edges with cold water, fill with one-sixth of the cooled chicken mixture, fold dough over filling, and press well to seal, folding the edge over once.
5. Place filled calzones on a heavy baking sheet sprayed with cooking spray and heavily sprinkled with cornmeal. Poke each calzone several times with a fork to allow steam to escape while baking and, if desired, brush the tops with a little milk or beaten egg to glaze.
6. Bake filled calzones in a preheated 400°F (200°C) oven for 20–30 minutes, until well browned. Remove from pan and cool on a rack. Serve warm or cool. These turnovers also freeze well. Makes 6.

Classic Chicken Stew

Rich and flavourful, this slow-cooked chicken stew can be made with a cut-up whole chicken, but I like the convenience of skinless, boneless chicken thighs, which offer tender meaty chicken without the excess fat that comes with the skin.

6 slices double-smoked bacon, chopped
3–4 tablespoons (45–55 mL) olive oil, divided
2–3 pounds (1–1.5 kg) boneless, skinless chicken thighs, halved
1/4 cup (50 mL) all-purpose flour, seasoned with 1/2 teaspoon
   (2 mL) each: salt, freshly ground black pepper, and thyme
4 medium carrots, sliced
2 cups (500 mL) small onions, peeled
6 cloves garlic, chopped
3 cups (750 mL) mushrooms, sliced or quartered
2 tablespoons (25 mL) all-purpose flour
2 cups (500 mL) chicken broth
2 cups (500 mL) red wine
1/4 cup (50 mL) brandy or cognac
2 tablespoons (25 mL) tomato paste
1 tablespoon (15 mL) red currant jelly
1 tablespoon (15 mL) brown sugar
1 tablespoon (15 mL) fresh thyme leaves
1 bay leaf
1 teaspoon (5 mL) salt
1/2 teaspoon (2 mL) freshly ground black pepper
6 tablespoons (75 mL) chopped fresh parsley or chives

1. Cook bacon until starting to brown. Remove from pan and reserve.
2. Add 1 tablespoon (15 mL) of oil to bacon drippings in the pan. Toss chicken with seasoned flour and brown in batches in hot fat. Remove from pan and set aside.
3. Add carrots and onions to pan and sauté in remaining oil until beginning to brown. Stir in garlic and mushrooms and cook a few minutes longer, just until they begin to give up their juices.
4. Sprinkle pan with flour, stir well, and slowly add broth, wine, and brandy or cognac. Bring to a boil, scraping up any browned bits. Stir in tomato paste, jelly, sugar, thyme, bay leaf, salt, and pepper.
5. Return chicken to pot with bacon. Cover and bake in preheated 375°F (190°C) oven for 30 minutes. Uncover and bake 30 minutes longer, until stew is thick and chicken is tender. Serve sprinkled with fresh parsley or chives over piles of mashed potatoes. Serves 8.

Smoky Chicken and Roasted Tomato Tortillas with Goat Cheese

Serve this tasty dish on a buffet with a big green salad and lots of hot tortillas for making tacos or wraps.

2 dried chipotle chiles, stems removed, or 2 canned chipotle chiles in adobo

5 ripe plum tomatoes, or 1 14-ounce (398 mL) can tomatoes

4 cloves garlic, unpeeled

2 tablespoons (25 mL) olive oil, divided

6 medium boneless and skinless chicken thighs

4 medium red potatoes, or 3 cups (750 mL) shredded hash brown potatoes

1 medium white onion, thinly sliced

1 teaspoon (5 mL) dried oregano

3/4 teaspoon (4 mL) salt

1/3 cup (75 mL) dry goat or feta cheese, crumbled

1 ripe avocado, diced

flour or corn tortillas for wrapping

1. On an ungreased iron pan or griddle, toast dried chiles over medium-high heat, pressing flat with a spatula for about 30 seconds, until very aromatic. Turn often to prevent burning. Set chiles in a bowl and cover with very hot water to rehydrate for 30 minutes. Drain and discard water. Remove stems and seeds. If using canned chipotle chiles, omit this step.

2. On same iron pan, roast tomatoes and garlic until starting to blacken all over. Peel garlic and purée with tomatoes and chiles in food processor.

3. Heat 1 tablespoon (15 mL) olive oil in a sauté pan over medium-high heat and cook purée for 5 minutes, until it sears and thickens slightly. Nestle chicken thighs in sauce, cover pan, and simmer over medium-low heat for 45 minutes, until chicken is very tender. Remove chicken to a plate, cool slightly, and shred. Return shredded chicken to sauce and keep warm.

4. If using whole potatoes, steam for 10 minutes in skins until partially cooked, then chill and peel. Coarsely shred cold potatoes (or use frozen, shredded hash brown potatoes.)

5. Heat remaining 1 tablespoon (15 mL) oil in a nonstick skillet and cook onions and potatoes together over medium-high heat until well browned. Add sauce with chicken to pan with oregano and bring to a boil. Season with salt to taste.

6. Serve chicken filling in a deep dish, sprinkled with crumbled goat cheese and avocado chunks. Let your guests fill their own warm corn tortillas or make flour tortilla wraps. This is enough filling for 12–15 corn tortillas, or about 6 larger flour tortillas or wraps. Serves 4 to 6.

TIP

Look for good-quality corn tortillas at Latin markets, in the freezer section. To heat corn tortillas for serving, pass them quickly under warm running water. Heat an iron griddle over medium-high heat and place a wet tortilla on the hot, dry pan. Cook until the top looks dry, then flip quickly to cook second side. Keep warm while you cook remaining tortillas. Flour tortillas can be served at room temperature or wrapped in foil and heated in a preheated 250°F (120°C) oven for 10–15 minutes.

Chicken in Creamy Red Sauce with Potato Dumplings

When I was a student in Lethbridge, I often ate in a tiny Hungarian restaurant, run by an elderly couple. Their home-made paprika chicken, goulash, and dumplings sustained me through many lean times. Here's an updated version of that classic Hungarian chicken dish. Serve it over egg noodles, gnocchi, or these tiny potato dumplings.

8 boneless, skinless chicken breasts
salt and freshly ground black pepper
1 tablespoon (15 mL) olive oil
1 medium onion, minced
1 each: red and yellow bell pepper, sliced
1 tablespoon (15 mL) Hungarian paprika
1 teaspoon (5 mL) dried thyme
1 tablespoon (15 mL) cider vinegar
1/2 cup (125 mL) dry white wine
1 10-ounce (284 mL) can chicken broth, undiluted
2 tablespoons (25 mL) tomato paste
1/2 cup (125 mL) sour cream or whipping cream
2 tablespoons (25 mL) Dijon mustard
chopped fresh parsley to garnish

Dumplings
1 cup (250 mL) cold mashed potatoes
2 cups (500 mL) all-purpose flour
1/2 teaspoon (2 mL) salt
1 egg
1 tablespoon (15 mL) butter, melted
3/4–1 cup (175–250 mL) warm water
butter, salt, and freshly ground black pepper

1. Season chicken with salt and pepper on both sides. Heat oil over high heat in a sauté pan and sear chicken to brown on both sides, about 8 minutes in total. Remove chicken from pan and set aside.
2. In same pan, add onion and sliced peppers, and sauté over medium heat until beginning to brown. Stir in paprika and thyme and heat just until fragrant. Add cider vinegar and wine and boil until liquid is reduced by half. Add broth and tomato paste and simmer 2 minutes longer. Stir in sour or whipping cream and mustard and continue to boil until sauce is thick enough to coat the back of a spoon and is reduced to about 1 cup (250 mL).
3. To make dumplings, combine cold mashed potatoes, flour, and salt in a large bowl, working with your hands until crumbly. Whisk together egg, melted butter, and water. Make a well in the centre of the potato/flour mixture and add this liquid, gradually incorporating it with a fork to form a smooth, soft dough. You will want to make a stiffer dough if you are cutting the dumplings, a more liquid dough if you are pressing it into noodles through a ricer or spaetzle machine.
4. Bring a large pot of salted water to a rolling boil and press dough through a large-holed ricer, spaetzle maker, or the holes of a colander into the boiling water, forming small dumplings. Alternatively, divide stiffer dough in four pieces and press each piece onto a floured cutting board with your hand until it's about 1/4 inch (5 mm) thick. With a wet knife, slice dough into slivers and push off board into boiling water. When noodles float, drain and toss with butter, salt, and pepper. Set aside and keep warm.
5. Return chicken to pan and spoon a little sauce over each breast. Cover pan and simmer 3 minutes, just to cook chicken through. Serve on a platter, surrounded by dumplings or noodles, with sauce spooned over top. Sprinkle with parsley to garnish. Serves 8.

Tea-Smoked Chicken with Black Rhubarb and Saskatoon Berry Sauce

Bridge Berry Farms created a Black Rhubarb Juice, a rich, flavourful juice from rhubarb and native black currants that is the perfect base for this elegant sauce. If you must substitute, use port and blueberries.

4 8-ounce (250 g) chicken breasts, bone in and skin on,
   preferably free-range
extra-virgin olive oil
salt and freshly ground black pepper
1 cup (250 mL) tea leaves (use a herbal berry tea, if possible)

Sauce

1/2 cup (125 mL) butter, chilled and divided
2 shallots, minced
1/2 cup (125 mL) chicken stock
1/2 cup (125 mL) Black Rhubarb Juice or port
1 cup (250 mL) saskatoon berries
1 tablespoon (15 mL) blueberry vinegar or red wine vinegar
salt and freshly ground black pepper

1. To make sauce, heat 2 tablespoons (25 mL) butter in a saucepan and sauté shallots for 2–3 minutes, until soft but not brown. Add chicken stock and boil until reduced by half. Add Black Rhubarb Juice, bring to a boil, and continue to simmer, uncovered, for about 15 minutes.
2. Whisk in remaining butter in small chunks so that it melts and emulsifies but doesn't separate from sauce. Stir in saskatoon berries. Season sauce with vinegar, salt, and pepper. Set aside and keep warm.
3. Brush chicken with olive oil. Season with salt and pepper.
4. Soak tea in warm water for 10 minutes and drain. Make a tin-foil packet with tea inside, or spread tea in a disposable foil pie plate and cover with foil. Punch holes in foil to let smoke escape.
5. Heat barbecue over medium-high heat. Turn one gas burner off and place a drip pan under grill on unlit side. Put package of soaked tea leaves under grill and directly over firebricks on hot side of barbecue. If you're using a charcoal barbecue, heat coals and simply sprinkle soaked tea over coals to create smoke while you cook.
6. Start chicken on hot side of barbecue, grilling it skin side down for 6–7 minutes, just until skin starts to brown. Turn and brown underside for a couple of minutes, then move chicken breasts to unlit side of grill. Make sure lid is down on barbecue, but watch chicken carefully, turning and moving it to hotter and cooler parts of grill until it's crisp and golden on the outside and juices run clear. This will take a total of about 25–30 minutes of grilling time.
7. Serve chicken on individual plates with sauce drizzled over and around it. Serves 4.

ROAST CHICKEN WITH GARLIC AND ROSEMARY

The wonderful flavour of this simple chicken dish is achieved by stuffing herbs and garlic under the skin before roasting. Try to find an organic, free-range chicken for roasting—you'll be amazed at the superb taste of grass-fed poultry. Serve with garlic mashed potatoes, or roast some baby potatoes around the chicken.

1 5–6 pound (2.5–3 kg) roasting chicken
8 cloves garlic, minced
2 tablespoons (25 mL) minced fresh rosemary
   (do not substitute dried)
2 tablespoons (25 mL) cold-pressed canola oil, divided
salt and freshly ground black pepper
1 whole lemon, cut into quarters
all-purpose flour
water or chicken stock

1. Wash chicken in cold water and pat dry.
2. Using your fingers and starting around the neck cavity, slowly and carefully pull skin away from breast, working your hands down to pull skin away from thighs and legs.
3. In a small bowl, combine garlic, rosemary, and 1 tablespoon (15 mL) canola oil. Reserve 1 tablespoon (15 mL) of mixture for inside chicken and, using your hands, evenly spread rest of mixture over breast and leg meat, under the skin.
4. Season chicken inside with salt and pepper and rub remaining garlic and rosemary mixture inside cavity. Place a couple of lemon quarters inside chicken and tie legs together. Fold wings under chicken to keep breast skin tight. Rub breast with remaining oil and set chicken on a rack in a roasting pan just large enough to hold it. Squeeze juice from remaining lemon quarters over top.
5. Place chicken in a preheated 450°F (230°C) oven and roast for 30 minutes. Reduce heat to 400°F (200°C) and continue roasting for about 50 minutes, basting occasionally. Chicken is done when juices run clear and leg moves easily in socket.
6. Remove chicken to a platter to rest. Make pan gravy by stirring a few tablespoons of flour into the pan drippings, then thinning with water or chicken stock. Serve chicken and gravy with potatoes. Serves 6.

CHICKEN BREASTS IN CRANBERRY MUSTARD SAUCE

Serve this chicken with mustard sauce over creamy polenta or garlic mashed potatoes, with tender green beans or steamed broccoli on the side.

4 boneless, skinless chicken breasts
1/4 cup (50 mL) all-purpose flour seasoned with 1/2 teaspoon
    (2 mL) each: salt, freshly ground black pepper, and thyme
2 tablespoons (25 mL) canola oil
1/2 cup (125 mL) minced onion
1 clove garlic, minced
1/2 cup (125 mL) white wine
3/4 cup (175 mL) chicken broth
3 tablespoons (45 mL) Dijon mustard
1 teaspoon (5 mL) whole mustard seeds
1 tablespoon (15 mL) honey
1 teaspoon (5 mL) fresh thyme leaves
1 teaspoon (5 mL) cornstarch mixed with 1 teaspoon
    (5 mL) water
1/4 cup (50 mL) dried cranberries

1. Toss chicken breasts in seasoned flour to coat, shaking off any excess. Heat canola oil in a large, nonstick pan over medium-high heat and sauté chicken until browned on both sides, about 8–10 minutes in total. Set aside and keep warm.
2. Add onion to pan and stir until beginning to brown. Add garlic and cook for 1 minute. Stir in wine, stirring up any browned bits, and boil vigorously for 1 minute to reduce by half. Add broth and whisk in mustard, mustard seeds, honey, and thyme. Bring to a boil. Add cornstarch solution and cranberries and continue to cook until sauce is thickened.
3. Return chicken to pan, cover, and heat through for 2–3 minutes. Serves 4.

PRAIRIE PAELLA

Paella is a Spanish rice dish, and Spanish rice has been a home-style prairie staple for decades. While you'll likely see it made with huge shrimp in Spain (and hamburger in Saskatchewan), this updated version combines tender boneless chicken thighs with spicy sausage, prairie beans, and peppers for a delicious one-dish dinner.

1/4 cup (50 mL) canola oil
1 medium onion, chopped
1 large red bell pepper, seeded and chopped
2 pounds (1 kg) boneless, skinless chicken thighs,
    cut into large chunks
1 pound (500 g) spicy pork or chicken sausage, preferably
    Spolumbo's mild or spicy Italian sausage
3 cups (750 mL) white and wild mushrooms
    (portobellos, oyster mushrooms, morels, etc.), sliced
1 28-ounce (796 mL) can Roma tomatoes, puréed in
    a blender or food processor
3 cloves garlic, minced
2 tablespoons (25 mL) chopped fresh rosemary

1 tablespoon (15 mL) chopped fresh sage
2 teaspoons (10 mL) salt
1 teaspoon (5 mL) freshly ground black pepper
1/2 teaspoon (2 mL) ground saffron threads
1/4 teaspoon (1 mL) cayenne pepper or crushed red chilies
2 cups (500 mL) short-grain rice like arborio or sushi rice
6 cups (1.5 L) chicken stock
1 cup (250 mL) chopped green beans
1 14-ounce (398 mL) can chickpeas, drained
chopped fresh parsley
lemon wedges

1. Heat canola oil in a large, heavy sauté pan over medium-high heat and sauté onion and pepper until soft. Remove from pan and set aside. Add chicken to pan and cook until browned. Set aside. Slice sausage and brown in same pan. Set aside with chicken and vegetables.

2. Add mushrooms to pan and sauté for 5 minutes, until soft and most of the liquid is gone. Stir in tomatoes, garlic, and reserved onion and red pepper mixture. Bring to a boil and simmer for 20 minutes. Add rosemary, sage, salt, black pepper, saffron, cayenne pepper, and rice. Stir in chicken stock, chicken, and sausage.

3. Bring to a boil and simmer, uncovered, until chicken and rice are almost cooked, 30–40 minutes longer. Stir in green beans and chickpeas and continue to cook for 10 minutes, until beans are just tender crisp. Serve from pan, garnished with parsley and lemon wedges. Serves 8.

TURKEY AND SQUASH POT PIE WITH WHITE CHEDDAR CRUST

Wondering what to do with leftover turkey? This is the ultimate solution— you'll never know you're eating leftovers. Cooked chicken or even leftover pork roast could stand in for turkey in this comforting dish.

2 1/2 cups (625 mL) water
1 teaspoon (5 mL) salt
2 cups (500 mL) peeled, seeded, and cubed butternut squash
2 tablespoons (25 mL) butter
1 medium onion, slivered
2 tablespoons (25 mL) all-purpose flour
1 cup (250 mL) turkey or chicken broth
2 tablespoons (25 mL) minced fresh sage
1/2 teaspoon (2 mL) freshly ground black pepper
1 cup (250 mL) cooked or canned white beans
1 tablespoon (15 mL) chopped fresh parsley
3 cups (750 mL) cooked, cubed turkey

Crust
1 cup (250 mL) all-purpose flour
1 teaspoon (5 mL) baking powder
1/2 teaspoon (2 mL) salt
2 tablespoons (25 mL) cold butter
1 1/2 cups (375 mL) shredded old Cheddar cheese
2/3 cup (150 mL) skim milk
cayenne pepper or paprika

1. Boil squash cubes in salted water until just tender, about 8 minutes. Remove with a slotted spoon to a casserole dish, reserving 1 cup (250 mL) cooking liquid.

2. In a saucepan, melt butter and sauté onion for 5 minutes, until soft. Stir in flour and cook for 1 minute. Slowly add broth and 1 cup (250 mL) of reserved cooking liquid. Bring to a boil. Stir in sage and pepper and simmer until thick, about 10 minutes.

3. Stir in drained beans (rinse beans if canned), parsley, and cooked turkey. Pour over squash in dish. Adjust seasoning to taste.

4. For crust, combine flour, baking powder, and salt in a bowl. Using your hands or a pastry blender, blend in butter until crumbly. Stir in cheese and enough milk to form a sticky dough. Drop by tablespoonfuls over turkey mixture in baking dish.

5. Bake pot pie in a preheated 400°F (200°C) oven for 25–30 minutes, until crust is golden. Dust with cayenne pepper or paprika before serving. Serves 6.

Braised Turkey in Mole Sauce

This is my pared-down version of the classic Mexican mole poblano. Don't be put off by the small amount of chocolate in this spicy sauce—it adds a rich colour and a depth of flavour to the mole that make it authentic.

4 dried ancho chiles
1 chipotle chile in adobo
3 large ripe tomatoes, peeled and chopped
1 medium yellow onion, chopped
2 cloves garlic, peeled and chopped
1 teaspoon (5 mL) dried oregano, crumbled
1/4 teaspoon (1 mL) ground cumin
bouquet garni of 6 whole allspice berries, 1 stick cinnamon,
   3 cloves, and 4 whole peppercorns, wrapped in cheesecloth
1 cup (250 mL) water
1/4 cup (50 mL) pine nuts or blanched almonds
1/4 cup (50 mL) sesame seeds
1/4 cup (50 mL) chopped pitted prunes or raisins
2 cups (500 mL) homemade chicken or turkey broth
2 ounces (100 g) Mexican chocolate or semi-sweet
   Callebaut chocolate, chopped
2 tablespoons (25 mL) cornmeal
salt and freshly ground black pepper
2–3 pounds (1–1.5 kg) turkey drumsticks and thighs, skin removed

1. In a hot cast-iron skillet, dry roast ancho chiles, pressing with a spatula until softened. Turn often so they don't burn. Remove from heat and place in a bowl with 2 cups (500 mL) of very hot water. Soak 15 minutes, then remove stems and seeds.

2. Put chiles, tomatoes, onion, garlic, oregano, cumin, and bouquet garni in a pot with 1 cup (250 mL) water, bring to a boil, then reduce heat to medium-low and simmer for 30 minutes. Remove from heat, discard bouquet garni, and purée sauce in blender or food processor until smooth.

3. In a nonstick pan, toast pine nuts or almonds until golden, then set aside to cool. Toast sesame seeds in same pan. Cool. Grind nuts and sesame seeds in the blender to a smooth paste, then add prunes or raisins and continue to grind until smooth again.

4. In a large Dutch oven, combine nut paste, chile purée, and chicken broth, and bring to a boil. Stir in chocolate until melted. Stir in cornmeal and season sauce with salt and pepper to taste. Add turkey to the sauce, cover, and braise on low heat or in a preheated 300°F (150°C) oven for 2–3 hours, until turkey is very tender. Remove meat from the bones, discard bones, and shred turkey back into the sauce. Add a little more cornmeal to thicken mole, if necessary.

5. Serve over rice, or roll up in flour tortillas with shredded lettuce, fresh tomato and sliced avocado. Serves 6.

Vegetable Pancakes with Cold-Smoked Salmon, Poached Free-Range Eggs, and Tomato Hollandaise

An Alberta version of that Jewish holiday favourite, potato latkes, these decadent pancakes are perfect for a Christmas morning brunch. If you don't have time to make the pancakes, use a traditional split and toasted English muffin for the base.

8 poached eggs (see tip, page 74)
1/4 pound (125 g) cold-smoked salmon or trout, thinly sliced
dill sprigs
cayenne pepper

Vegetable Pancakes
2 cups (500 mL) grated peeled Yukon Gold potatoes
1/3 cup (75 mL) grated unpeeled zucchini
1/3 cup (75 mL) grated peeled carrot
1/4 cup (50 mL) grated onion
1 teaspoon (5 mL) chopped fresh dill

1/2 teaspoon (2 mL) salt
freshly ground black pepper
2 tablespoons (25 mL) all-purpose flour
6 tablespoons (75 mL) canola oil

Tomato Hollandaise
1/2–3/4 cup (125–175 mL) butter
3 egg yolks
4 teaspoons (20 mL) fresh lemon juice
pinch of salt
1 tablespoon (15 mL) tomato paste

1. Blanch potatoes in boiling water for 1 minute. Drain but don't rinse. Place zucchini in a colander and sprinkle with salt. Let stand 10 minutes to allow the moisture to leach out, then rinse and wrap in a clean kitchen towel. Squeeze to remove any additional water from zucchini.

2. Mix potatoes with zucchini, carrot, onion, dill, salt, and pepper. Stir in flour and let stand 10 minutes.

3. Heat canola oil in a nonstick frying pan over medium-high heat. For each pancake, spoon in 2 tablespoons (25 mL) of vegetable batter, flatten, and fry until golden on both sides, about 6–8 minutes in total. Drain on paper towels. Makes 8–12 pancakes.

4. To make hollandaise sauce, melt butter in a measuring cup in the microwave and keep hot. Place egg yolks, lemon juice, and salt in a blender and cover. With machine running, slowly add melted butter in a thin stream through opening in lid. When sauce is thick, turn off blender, add tomato paste, and whirl until well combined.

5. Place two or three pancakes on each serving plate, and top with slices of smoked salmon and hot poached eggs. Drizzle tomato hollandaise over top, dust with cayenne pepper, and garnish with a sprig of dill. Serve immediately. Serves 4.

TURKEY WITH WHOLEGRAIN STUFFING AND RICH RED WINE GRAVY

The turkey is native to North America and became popular around the world after its discovery by early European explorers. The Dirt Willy Game Bird Farm is a good source for wild turkey. This complicated recipe is worth the effort for a special occasion or holiday. For a really impressive bird, marinate turkey in red wine for 24 hours before stuffing and roasting.

1 15-pound (7.5 kg) turkey, preferably free-range
5–6 bay leaves
6 cloves garlic, unpeeled
6 sprigs fresh parsley
1 tablespoon (15 mL) dried thyme, or 6 sprigs fresh thyme

Wholegrain Stuffing
3 tablespoons (45 mL) butter, divided
1 tablespoon (15 mL) olive oil
1/2 cup (125 mL) wild rice
1/2 cup (125 mL) wheat berries
1/2 cup (125 mL) wholegrain rye
3 cups (750 mL) chicken stock
1 cup (250 mL) dry white wine
1 teaspoon (5 mL) salt
1 medium onion, chopped
1 cup (250 mL) mushrooms, chopped, preferably a mixture of wild and cultivated
1 turkey liver, minced
1 tablespoon (15 mL) dried thyme
2 eggs, beaten
1/2 cup (125 mL) medium-dry sherry
salt and freshly ground black pepper

Red Wine Gravy
turkey neck and gizzard
1 tablespoon (15 mL) olive oil
1 onion, quartered
1 carrot, halved
1 celery stalk, halved

2 sprigs fresh thyme

2 cloves garlic, sliced

2 cups (500 mL) dry red wine

6 cups (1.5 L) chicken stock

1/4 cup (50 mL) cognac

1/4 cup (50 mL) orange liqueur

1 tablespoon (15 mL) brown sugar

juice of 1 orange

**2 tablespoons (25 mL) cornstarch mixed with 2 tablespoons
(25 mL) cold water**

salt and freshly ground black pepper

1. For stuffing, heat 2 tablespoons (25 mL) butter with olive oil in a saucepan and sauté wild rice, wheat berries, and rye over medium heat until starting to brown. Add chicken stock, wine, and salt. Bring to a boil, cover, and simmer on medium-low heat for 50–60 minutes until grains are tender. Cool.

2. In another pan, sauté onion in remaining butter until tender. Add mushrooms and sauté a few minutes more. Add liver and thyme and sauté until no longer pink. Combine this with cooked grains. Mix beaten egg and sherry together and add to stuffing. Season with salt and pepper. Cool mixture and stuff into bird.

3. Rub stuffed turkey with a little olive oil. Place breast side up on a rack in a preheated 475°F (240°C) oven and roast 15–20 minutes. Reduce heat to 325°F (160°C). Scatter bay leaves, garlic, parsley, and thyme around the pan and roast 2–3 hours more, until a meat thermometer inserted in the thigh registers 180–185°F (80–85°C). Baste turkey with pan juices during cooking, and cover with a tent of foil part way through if it is getting too brown.

4. While the turkey roasts, make the gravy. Sauté turkey neck and gizzard in olive oil with onion, carrot, and celery over medium-high heat until browned. Add thyme, garlic, red wine, and chicken stock, and bring to a boil. Simmer for 2 hours, covered, while turkey cooks. Strain and skim fat.

5. Return liquid to saucepan and add cognac, orange liqueur, brown sugar, and fresh orange juice. Boil for 10 minutes to reduce slightly. Stir in the cornstarch solution and simmer until the gravy is the proper consistency. Season to taste with salt and pepper, and keep warm.

6. When turkey is done, remove to platter to rest for 15 minutes before carving. Remove stuffing. Tent with foil to keep warm.

7. Skim excess fat from turkey roasting pan, and deglaze with a few ounces of red wine or stock, scraping up any browned bits. Strain this dark brown concentrate into the gravy, pressing garlic cloves with a spoon to release roasted garlic purée into the gravy. Carve turkey and serve with stuffing and red wine gravy. Serves 8 to 10.

Fish

CALL OF THE WILD TROUT

On a white and grey winter day on the Alberta prairie, the socked-in slate sky meets the stark white landscape with nothing but charcoal clumps of leafless cottonwoods to break the visual monotony. Snowy roadways meld into deep ditches and pallid stubble fields, but there is one flash of natural colour in this black and white world. It's the red and blue-green glint of a silvery rainbow trout, twisting and fighting as it's pulled from a hole in a frozen pond.

It's not exactly fishing season in Alberta, but on this particular family farm, February is the perfect time to hook a trout. In fact, at Dan and Peg Radomske's Valley Springs Trout Farm in the central part of the province, friends have gathered to help Dan harvest the current crop of fish he's been raising naturally all year in a series of spring-fed outdoor ponds.

Like many small farmers, the Radomskes are looking for new ways to boost their farm income. By producing an essentially wild-fed fish in captivity, they are feeding a growing demand for high-quality regional food products and making money to complement their purebred cattle business.

On this chilly Sunday afternoon, Dexter Dersch, a family friend, is perched on an upturned plastic pail on one of Radomske's frozen trout ponds, dangling a baited line into a 6-inch hole. Every 30 seconds or so, he yanks another fish out of the dark depths, carefully removing the barbless hook and depositing the live fish into a nearby holding pond. This is the system the Radomskes have developed to corral the 0.5- to 1-kilogram fish they sell directly from the farm, or to discerning city stores looking for a real taste of Alberta. No other trout farmers let their fish fend for themselves on freshwater shrimp and bugs, growing to brilliant pink perfection for a full summer and fall before they're individually hooked and sold for fine eating—whole, hot-smoked for flaking into dips and spreads, and in delicate 15-cm steaks.

On the gourmet end of the local trout business is former Calgary chef Chris Gaudet. With his family, Gaudet runs Classic Smokers, producing wonderful cold-smoked trout and salmon and custom gravlax for the restaurant trade. Top restaurants that focus on local ingredients and regional cuisine, and all of the Canadian Pacific Hotels, are using Gaudet's products.

Chris Gaudet

Imagine a tender slice of marinated trout gravlax, infused with sweet maple whisky and wild sage, or a cold-smoked Atlantic salmon encrusted with mixed peppercorns, shot with tequila and lime, or fragrant with essence of real oranges.

The shelves in this pristine little plant are lined with fish marinating in plastic tubs, the custom brines flavoured with whisky, tequila, and pure citrus oils. The fish are brined for up to four days, and smoked, hanging like fly paper as they're bathed in the tendrils of cool alder and maple smoke that rise around them in the big stainless steel smokers.

Unlike some commercial smokers, the Gaudets don't inject their fish with brine—it's marinated the old-fashioned way, which takes more time but produces flavourful and delicate smoked fish.

The trout come from Lake Diefenbaker in Saskatchewan, arriving on Monday and smoked by Wednesday. The smoked fillets are sliced paper thin, cryovac packed, and sent out fresh or frozen to discerning customers across the country.

Trout is one of the true bounties of Alberta's mountain, prairie, and woodland landscape, but wild trout is a sport fisher's game, not a species that's fished commercially. Almost every weekend, I lose my husband to his favourite fishing haunts—those rushing rivers and gurgling mountain streams that challenge anyone who's hooked on fly fishing and the restful wilderness experience that this kind of sport brings. Still, there are no wild rainbows in my freezer. Most sports fishers follow the conservationist catch-and-release practice of hooking their prey on barbless hooks, then carefully sending them back into the wild to catch another day.

Fly fishing is now one of the province's hottest tourist draws. Fans of this popular sport arrive in droves every summer and fall to fish the famous Bow River, one of the world's top trophy trout streams. Rivers like the Oldman, Crowsnest, Highwood, Raven, and Red Deer lure keen fishers, their colourful and descriptive names reminding us of the First Nations people who discovered these wild waterways that flow out of the Rocky Mountains and join into major rivers that meander east into Hudson Bay.

But fishing has not always been popular with all Albertans. Some of the earliest Native tribes were averse to eating fish. Although the Blackfoot made their winter camps beside mighty Alberta rivers like the Bow and the Oldman, they relied on the plains bison as their major source of food, only stooping to fishing if they were starving. However, rival tribes like the Stoneys, who lived in the higher ground of the foothills and mountains, were keen fishers. Using snares, nooses of carefully braided sinews, they trapped and flipped their catches of trout and whitefish out of the clear pools of chilly mountain streams. It was Stoney women who began the tradition of smoking these fish, a tradition that continues to be popular today.

The sport of fly fishing, luring fish to bite dry and wet imitation flies, was imported from England and Scotland in the 1880s with the first ranchers. Down on the Bar U and Waldron ranches, some of these early cowboys spent their leisure time in traditional British fashion, playing polo and angling for trout with flies they created with bits of fur and feathers. It may have been their passionate letters home, describing the fine fishing for trout and Rocky Mountain whitefish, that drew the first holiday anglers to Alberta. Travelling by train and guided into the mountains on horseback, fishing tourists from wealthy families in London, New York, and Boston came for a wilderness experience of unsurpassed hunting and fishing.

From rainbows and brown trout to Rocky Mountain whitefish, walleye, pickerel, and northern pike, anglers around the world know that this part of western Canada is home to some of the best sport fishing anywhere. Today the wild fishery is so popular that conservation has become necessary to maintain fishing stocks, and catch-and-release rules or strict catch limits apply in most streams and lakes. While there still is a commercial fishery in Alberta—mainly for lake whitefish and pickerel (also called walleye)—most sport fishers protect the resource by sending their fiesty catches back into the wild after the fight.

Many stretches of popular waterways are now 100 percent catch-and-release, and certain species, like the endangered bull trout, are off limits everywhere. Still, there's nothing like the flavour of a freshly caught trout, split, floured, and fried in browned butter over a campfire, and regulations allow some fish to be taken, depending on the variety and the season.

From the more than forty trout farms across the province, country residents can buy "fingerlings"—tiny rainbow and brook trout—to stock their own ponds and dugouts, and there are U-fish spots where you likely won't get skunked on a family fishing trip. Or, if you've got a hankering for trout but no wish to fish it, there are always farms like the Radomskes' and others that produce fish for the table.

You can buy wild fish like whitefish and pickerel at specialty fish shops, and farmed Alberta salmon and arctic char are available in supermarkets. In Calgary, Classic Smokers is creating new products with its farmed Alberta salmon and trout, from rainbow trout gravlax flavoured with dill, Pernod, and orange rind, to delicately cold-smoked trout and lox, which it ships frozen on dry ice, for next day delivery in Calgary and Edmonton. Allen's Trout Farm near Calgary will deliver live fish, up to 1.5 kilograms, to customers anywhere in the province.

LAKE TROUT FILLETS ON ROASTED ROOT VEGETABLES

Try this elegant and easy dish with thick fillets of lake trout, bass, or salmon. Serve it in the fall or winter, atop a pile of fluffy garlic mashed potatoes or potato, parsnip, and green cabbage purée.

1 large red bell pepper, cut into 1/4-inch (5 mm) dice
1 medium rutabaga or turnip, peeled and cut into
   1/4-inch (5 mm) dice
1 medium zucchini, cut into 1/4-inch (5 mm) dice
2 medium beets, peeled and cut into 1/4-inch (5 mm) dice
1 large fennel bulb, cut into 1/4-inch (5 mm) dice
1 large red onion, cut into 1/4-inch (5 mm) dice
3 cloves garlic, minced
1 tablespoon (15 mL) chopped fresh thyme leaves
1 tablespoon (15 mL) cold-pressed canola or olive oil
6 1–2-inch (2.5–5 cm) boneless lake trout fillets, about 5 ounces (150 g) each, or substitute skinless sea bass or salmon pieces
salt and freshly ground black pepper
cornstarch

FISH PRIMER

While everyone knows a wild fish tastes wonderful, the reality is that much of the fresh fish we eat today is farmed. Even in Alberta, home to some of the world's wildest trophy trout streams, trout, salmon, and exotic fish like tilapia are being raised in artificial environments. Farm-raised rainbows usually weigh less than 500 grams and can be cooked whole for an individual serving. This delicate fish is best poached, baked, fried, or grilled.

While nothing compares with a freshly caught fish, pulled from an icy brook and ferried quickly to a hot pan, today's prairie dwellers are more likely to buy their fish at the market. Fresh fish is often available but frozen fish can be as good or better. A fish that is properly flash-frozen at sea is often tastier than a "fresh" one that has spent several days in transit. When you are buying fish, ask if it is fresh or previously frozen. Never buy fish that smells "fishy," and if you want the best fish, buy it from a reputable fish market or specialty store that keeps the fish on ice, not wrapped in plastic. Never buy a fish that has not been gutted, and look for fish with clear flesh. Mottled or bloody flesh may be an indication that the fish has not been bled or otherwise properly treated.

It is also useful to ask how the fish was caught. Some West Coast fishers are now offering salmon and tuna that are "long-lined." This is an expensive method of fishing, trolling for fish individually on long lines rather than scooping them indiscriminately in massive drift nets. While the fish cost more, they are usually handled carefully to reduce stress-induced damage, and are much tastier. This style of fishing is cleaner and better for the environment, too, which is especially relevant as wild fish stocks continue to dramatically dwindle.

When buying canned salmon or tuna, you can also look for higher-end products made with long-lined fish and canned using the old-fashioned cold-pack method. Once you taste this kind of canned fish, you will never go back to regular commercial products that are cooked, then canned. While cold-packing preserves the fish's healthy oils and flavourful juices, the cheaper hot-pack method cooks them away. There's no comparison in taste.

COLD-SMOKED vs. HOT-SMOKED

Smoked native fish taste wonderful, whether they are prepared commercially or in a home smoker. However, there is a distinct difference between cold-smoked and hot-smoked fish. Before either process, the fish is cured or brined with a dry rub or wet brine that is high in salt. In the cold-smoking process, the fish is smoked over an indirect heat source, and the temperature of the fish never rises above 85°F (30°C). The result is a still-raw product, but one that is ready-to-eat, with a smooth, moist, and silky texture. This process is used for lox and cold-smoked salmon. Hot-smoked fish is cooked over hotter smoke at temperatures reaching 140°F (60°C) and higher. This kind of fish is sometimes described as "kippered" and has a drier, flaky texture. Hard-smoked salmon, smoked longer at a higher temperature, is often called salmon jerky or Indian candy, and is heavily salted and glazed with brown sugar or maple syrup.

I like to use cold-smoked fish for appetizers, rolling the thin slices into cornets to present atop a small piece of flatbread with a little herbed cream cheese or sour cream. It's also perfect draped over a salad or rolled into a flour tortilla. Hot-smoked fish, which is usually considerably cheaper, is perfect flaked in dips and cooked dishes, from soups and quiche to pasta dishes. Indian candy is great to sprinkle over a salad or take on the trail for snacking.

HOME SMOKING

It's easy to smoke fish at home. Here are a few tips:
• Add green willow or alder to the fire for a traditional smoke flavour.
• Avoid pine, poplar, and cedar, which produce a black, acrid smoke.
• Add juniper berries from your ornamental shrubs to fish marinade, or crush a few spruce or young pine needles into the mixture for a truly wild flavour. Try other fresh herbs and flavourings in the marinade, such as dill and thyme, or even lemon or orange zest.

1 tablespoon (15 mL) canola oil
1 teaspoon (5 mL) butter
6 sprigs of fresh thyme

1. Combine diced vegetables in a heavy roasting pan and toss with garlic, thyme, and canola or olive oil. Place pan in a preheated 450°F (230°C) oven and roast vegetables, stirring occasionally, for 15–20 minutes, until vegetables begin to brown and caramelize.
2. Meanwhile, season trout with salt and pepper. Place some cornstarch in a shallow dish and coat one side of each fish fillet, shaking off any excess cornstarch.
3. In a heavy, nonstick pan, heat canola oil and butter over medium-high heat and sear fish, dusted side down, for 2–3 minutes, or until golden.
4. Nestle browned fish in roasted vegetables, seared side up. Return roasting pan to oven and roast just until fish is cooked through, about 6–8 minutes.
5. To serve, pile some garlic mashed potatoes in centre of each of six wide dinner plates. Lean a fish fillet over top and surround with roasted vegetables. Garnish with a sprig of fresh thyme. Serves 6.

Pasta Salad with Smoked Trout

Make this pasta salad in the summer with young onions and fresh peas from the garden. Wasabi is a powdered green horseradish served with sushi. It has a fiery flavour, so add wasabi powder to taste. If you use wasabi, eliminate the mustard in this recipe.

1/2 pound (250 g) short pasta like farfalle, rotini, or orechiette
2 tablespoons (25 mL) cold-pressed canola or extra-virgin olive oil
1/2 cup (125 mL) mayonnaise
1/2 cup (125 mL) low-fat sour cream
3 tablespoons (45 mL) prepared horseradish, drained,
    or 1 tablespoon (15 mL) wasabi powder
1 tablespoon (15 mL) Dijon mustard (optional)
1 tablespoon (15 mL) fresh lemon juice
2 tablespoons (25 mL) chopped fresh dill
1/2 cup (125 mL) roasted red peppers, chopped (see tip, page 10)
1/2 cup (125 mL) chopped red onion
3 green onions, chopped
1/2 cup (125 mL) fresh peas (optional)
6 ounces (180 g) skinned and boned hot-smoked trout, shredded
salt and freshly ground black pepper

• Native cooks traditionally smoked fish whole, suspended on sticks over hot coals. Try this combination of barbecuing and smoking on your next camping trip. Butterfly a whole fish, remove the backbone from the inside, and impale it on a green willow branch. Weave smaller sticks through the fish at right angles to keep it flat, then smoke it slowly over a campfire. You can cheat by flattening the fish in a wire fish-grilling basket for easy smoking.

1. Cook pasta in plenty of boiling, salted water until al dente, about 8 minutes. Drain and rinse in cold water to chill. Toss with oil and set aside.
2. In a large bowl, mix mayonnaise, sour cream, horseradish or wasabi, mustard (if using), lemon juice, and dill. Stir until well combined.
3. Add pasta, red pepper, red onion, green onion, peas, and trout. Season with salt and pepper to taste. Toss until pasta has been coated with dressing and other ingredients are well distributed. Chill. Serves 6.

Home-Smoked Trout

Using this recipe, you can easily smoke your catch of trout, walleye, salmon, or whitefish in a home smoker or on the barbecue.

1/2 cup (125 mL) coarse kosher salt
1/4 cup (50 mL) brown or maple sugar
1 tablespoon (15 mL) crushed black peppercorns
1/4 teaspoon (1 mL) paprika
1 teaspoon (5 mL) crushed fresh juniper berries or
    spruce needles (optional)
4 lake trout fillets, skin on (scaling is not necessary for
    trout but should be done for larger-scaled fish)
4 tablespoons (50 mL) olive oil
rye bread, flatbread crackers, sour cream, and minced
    chives or red onion for serving

1. For cure, combine salt, sugar, peppercorns, paprika, and juniper berries.

2. Lay two fillets skin side down in a shallow ceramic dish and spread with cure. Top with remaining two fillets, skin side up.

3. Cover fish with plastic wrap. Place a plate or a cutting board over top, add some weight to the top (cans of food work well) and refrigerate fish overnight or up to 24 hours.

4. Rinse fish and pat dry. Let fish air dry uncovered in the refrigerator for 1 hour longer. Brush flesh side lightly with olive oil and smoke in top rack of a smoker for 2–3 hours, over wood of your choice. To smoke on your gas barbecue, heat only one burner. Soak wood chips and wrap in a foil packet. Punch holes in packet to release smoke and place it over lowest flame. Cook fish indirectly, on unlit side of grill, skin side down. Smoke over low heat until just cooked through, about 30–40 minutes.

5. Serve smoked fish on small pieces of heavy rye bread or thin flatbread crackers, with a dollop of sour cream and a garnish of chive sprigs or minced red onion. Smoked fish freezes well.

WHOLE GRILLED TROUT WITH LEMON MUSTARD BUTTER

You can make the lemon mustard butter in advance, roll it in plastic wrap to form a log, and refrigerate or freeze. The butter can then be cut into coins to set atop hot grilled fish or steamed green vegetables.

1/4 cup (50 mL) cold-pressed canola oil or extra-virgin olive oil
2 tablespoons (25 mL) fresh lemon juice
zest of 1 lemon
1 green onion, minced
1 clove garlic, minced
4 whole small trout (about 10–12 ounces/300–360 g each), cleaned but with heads and tails left on

Lemon Mustard Butter
1/2 cup (125 mL) soft butter
1 tablespoon (15 mL) chopped fresh lemon thyme or regular thyme
1/4 cup (50 mL) Dijon mustard
salt and white pepper

2 tablespoons (25 mL) fresh lemon juice
1 teaspoon (5 mL) finely grated lemon zest

1. Combine canola oil, lemon juice, lemon zest, green onion, and garlic in a blender or food processor and whirl to make a smooth marinade.

2. Slash skin in three places along both sides of trout. Brush trout liberally with marinade inside and out and refrigerate for 30 minutes.

3. Meanwhile, make lemon mustard butter. Process butter, lemon thyme, mustard, salt, white pepper, lemon juice, and lemon zest together in a food processor to combine well. Place butter alongside one edge of a piece of plastic wrap, roll into a log and twist the ends to enclose. Chill.

4. Place whole trout side by side in an oiled grilling basket. Grill over medium-high heat for 10–15 minutes, basting frequently with marinade. Serve one whole fish per person, topped with a round of lemon mustard butter. Serves 4.

CRISPY FRIED TROUT FILLETS WITH RED PEPPER MAYONNAISE

Roasted peppers and chiles give this mayonnaise a lovely rosy colour and a nice bite. Alternatively, for a cool summer supper, serve this crispy fried fish atop Cowboy Caesar Salad with Spicy Cilantro Mayonnaise (page 21). Try this cooking method with haddock or cod fillets, too.

1/4 cup (50 mL) milk
1/4 cup (50 mL) plain yogurt
1 egg, beaten
1 teaspoon (5 mL) mustard
1/2 teaspoon (2 mL) paprika
salt and freshly ground black pepper
1/2 cup (125 mL) all-purpose flour
1/4 cup (50 mL) cornmeal
1/4 teaspoon (1 mL) cayenne pepper
4 portions skinless and boneless trout fillet, about 1 1/2 pounds (750 g) in total
canola oil for frying
fresh lemon wedges

Red Pepper Mayonnaise

1/2 cup (125 mL) good-quality commercial mayonnaise

2 tablespoons (25 mL) plain yogurt or sour cream

1 roasted red pepper, peeled and seeded (see tip, page 10)

1 tablespoon (15 mL) fresh lime juice

1/4 teaspoon (1 mL) ground cumin

1 green onion, chopped

1/2 teaspoon (2 mL) hot chili sauce like Tabasco, or
    1/2 of a canned chipotle chile in adobo

1. To make red pepper mayonnaise, combine all ingredients in a blender or food processor and whirl until smooth. Chill.

2. Whisk together milk, yogurt, egg, mustard, paprika, salt, and pepper. Combine flour, cornmeal, and cayenne pepper in a shallow dish.

3. Dip fish fillets in milk mixture, then roll in cornmeal coating. Set aside in a single layer in refrigerator for 10 minutes.

4. Heat 1/4 inch (5 mm) of oil in a wide, nonstick pan over fairly high heat. Oil should be hot but not smoking. Fry fish for 2–3 minutes per side, until golden. Serve hot with red pepper mayonnaise. Serves 4.

GRILLED SALMON WITH MUSTARD GLAZE AND WILTED GREENS

Here's a simple way to dress up fresh salmon on the grill for an impromptu party. If you cut large salmon fillets into individual portions, they are easier to handle on the barbecue. Brush the glaze over vegetables like red onion wedges, red and yellow bell peppers, and zucchini to grill alongside the fish.

8 5-ounce (150 g) boneless salmon fillet pieces, skin on
    (2 large fillets, cut into portions)

canola oil

1/2 teaspoon (2 mL) salt

1/2 teaspoon (2 mL) white pepper

1/3 cup (75 mL) butter

1/4 cup (50 mL) honey

3 tablespoons (45 mL) Dijon mustard

1 tablespoon (15 mL) mustard seed

1 tablespoon (15 mL) fresh lime juice

assorted vegetables cut into large pieces for grilling
    (onion wedges, bell peppers, zucchini, or eggplant)

boiled or roasted tiny new potatoes

Wilted Greens

2 shallots

2 cloves garlic

3 tablespoons (45 mL) Highwood Crossing cold-pressed
    canola oil, or olive oil

12 cups (3 L) beet, turnip, and/or kohlrabi greens or
    chard, trimmed of tough stems

1 cup (250 mL) chicken stock

2 tablespoons (25 mL) balsamic vinegar

1 tablespoon (15 mL) tamari sauce

1. Rub the skin side of salmon pieces with a little canola oil to prevent sticking on the grill. Sprinkle flesh side with salt and white pepper. Set aside.

2. In a small saucepan, combine butter and honey and cook over low heat until melted and smooth. Stir in mustard, mustard seed, and lime juice. Set aside to cool.

3. Brush flesh side of the salmon pieces liberally with the sauce. Toss vegetables with some of the sauce.

4. Preheat barbecue to medium-high heat and lay vegetables on one side of grill (or use a barbecue wok or grill basket). Place fish, skin side down, on other side of preheated barbecue grill. Cook both for 10–15 minutes, until fish is barely cooked and vegetables are slightly charred. Brush fish with more sauce as it cooks. Turn vegetables as they brown.

5. To make wilted greens, mince shallot and garlic and sauté in canola oil in a large sauté pan. Wash greens well and remove stems. Roll leaves and slice. Add them to sauté pan in batches, stirring until greens begin to wilt and turn bright green. Add chicken stock, balsamic vinegar, and tamari sauce. Simmer over medium-high heat until almost all liquid has evaporated and greens are tender.

6. Present salmon on individual serving plates, each portion atop a mound of wilted greens and surrounded by grilled vegetables and steamed new potatoes. Serves 8.

RAINBOW TROUT CAKES WITH FRIZZLED LEEKS

This is a popular appetizer from The Ranche Restaurant, an historic ranch house with a contemporary cowboy menu. Serve the fish cakes with fresh salsa and a drizzle of cold-pressed canola oil or a homemade mayonnaise enhanced with fresh lemon.

2 rainbow trout fillets (about 8 oz/250 g), skinned, bones
  removed, and finely diced
2 tablespoons (25 mL) lemon juice
1/4 cup (50 mL) minced red bell pepper
2 tablespoons (25 mL) minced red onion
1 teaspoon (5 mL) capers, rinsed and chopped
1 teaspoon (5 mL) minced green onion
1/2 teaspoon (2 mL) finely chopped dill weed
1/2 teaspoon (2 mL) salt
2 cloves garlic, minced
1 egg
1/2 jalapeño pepper, seeded and minced
pinch of white or black pepper
5 oz (150 g) skinless salmon fillet
1 cup (250 mL) breadcrumbs
canola oil for frying

Garnish
1 leek, base only, sliced in julienne
oil for deep frying

1. In a bowl, combine the diced trout, lemon juice, red pepper, red onion, capers, green onion, dill, salt, garlic, egg, jalapeño, and white pepper.
2. Place salmon in a food processor and purée. Add the salmon purée to the bowl and mix to combine well.
3. Spread the breadcrumbs on a plate. Form mixture into 8 patties and roll each patty in crumbs to coat well. Set aside.
4. Meanwhile, make the frizzled leeks. Cut the green tops from the leek and discard. Cut the base in quarters, lengthwise, and rinse under running water to remove any sand or grit. Trim the room end and cut the quarters into thin julienne strips. Pat the strips dry on paper towels. Heat about 3 inches (8 cm) of oil in a wok until almost smoking. Toss the leeks into the hot oil, a few at a time, until they sizzle and curl. Remove with a slotted spoon and drain on paper towels . Set aside.
5. Heat 4 tablespoons (50 mL) of oil in a heavy sauté pan and, when the oil is very hot, fry the trout cakes until golden brown, about 5 minutes on each side. Arrange 2 trout cakes on each serving plate, garnish with leeks, and drizzle with canola oil. Serves 4.

ROASTED SALMON WITH RHUBARB CHIPOTLE GLAZE

Serve this elegant salmon dish with new potatoes and tiny green beans for a fresh, summer menu. The smoky chipotle chiles in the spicy sweet glaze add western flair. Rhubarb syrup, produced by home cooks and some Alberta fruit farmers, is a prairie pantry specialty.

1 tablespoon (15 mL) olive oil
8 5-ounce (150 g) portions of skinned salmon fillet
juice of half a grapefruit

Glaze
1/4 cup (50 mL) fresh grapefruit juice
1 tablespoon (15 mL) Dijon mustard
1 tablespoon (15 mL) chopped fresh dill
1 teaspoon (5 mL) coarsely ground black pepper
1/4 teaspoon (1 mL) salt
3 tablespoons (45 mL) rhubarb, maple, or other fruit syrup
1/4 teaspoon (1 mL) chipotle chile in adobo or Asian chili paste

1. For glaze, whisk together grapefruit juice, mustard, dill, black pepper, salt, syrup, and chipotle chile.

2. Heat olive oil in a heavy, nonstick, ovenproof pan over medium-high heat and sear salmon pieces for 4 minutes, until browned on the bottom. Turn over and spoon a small amount of glaze over each piece of fish.

3. Place pan in a preheated 400°F (200°C) oven and bake for 4 minutes longer, until just barely cooked through, brushing with glaze once or twice while cooking.

4. Heat remaining glaze. To serve, squeeze fresh grapefruit juice over hot salmon and drizzle with a little warm glaze. Serves 8.

> **TIP**
> When serving a whole fish, ask the fishmonger to sell you fish "pan-dressed" (the head, backbone, and other bones removed from the inside of the fish) or simply remove the bones as you eat the cooked fish. Make a cut lengthwise along the backbone, cutting through the skin, and carefully slide one fillet off the bones onto your plate. Pick up the tail, pull away the exposed skeleton from the second fillet, and you're done.

Sea Bass with Ancho and Pumpkin Seed Crust

Pumpkin seeds are common in Mexican and southwestern cooking. Look for them in health food stores. They give this very tender fish a tasty and crunchy coating. Serve it with a refreshing fresh tomato salsa, seasoned with lime juice and cilantro.

4 5-ounce (150 g) pieces sea bass, 1 inch (2.5 cm) thick
salt and white pepper
1/4 cup (50 mL) each: all-purpose flour and cornmeal
2 cups (500 mL) raw pumpkin seeds, ground in blender
   or food processor
1 tablespoon (15 mL) ancho chili powder
1 teaspoon (5 mL) garlic powder
2 tablespoons (25 mL) cold-pressed canola oil or olive oil
2 tablespoons (25 mL) regular canola oil

Salsa
4 Roma tomatoes, seeded and chopped
1/4 cup (50 mL) diced white or red onion
1 jalapeño pepper, seeded and minced
1/4 cup (50 mL) chopped fresh cilantro
1/2 teaspoon (2 mL) salt
1 tablespoon (15 mL) fresh lime juice
1 tablespoon (15 mL) olive oil
pinch of granulated sugar to taste

1. Season sea bass with salt and pepper. Preheat oven to 400°F (200°C). To make salsa, combine all ingredients gently and allow to stand at room temperature for up to 1 hour for flavours to meld.
2. Combine flour, cornmeal, ground pumpkin seeds, chili powder, garlic powder, and 2 tablespoons (25 mL) cold-pressed canola or olive oil. Mix well and press heavily over top of each piece of fish.
3. Heat regular canola oil in an ovenproof, nonstick skillet over high heat. When oil is almost smoking, add fish to pan, crusted side up, and sear for 2–3 minutes, until brown. Place pan in a preheated 400°F (200°C) oven and cook about 7–8 minutes longer, until fish is firm and crust is golden. Serve fish garnished with fresh tomato salsa and cilantro. Serves 4.

Candied Peppered Salmon

P.G. Cooper, the executive chef at Calgary's downtown Ramada Hotel, gets rave reviews for this oven-baked salmon fillet. The salmon is partially "cooked" in a gravlax process with salt and sugar, then baked with a sweet peppery glaze just before serving.

2 large fillets (about 4 pounds/2 kg) fresh Atlantic salmon, bones
   removed and skin on
garlic powder, dark brown sugar, and freshly ground or cracked
   black peppercorns

Marinade
1 teaspoon (5 mL) coarse salt
1/4 cup (50 mL) brown sugar
1/4 cup (50 mL) granulated sugar
4 cups (1 L) water
1/2 cup (125 mL) malt vinegar
1/2 cup (125 mL) white vinegar
1 bay leaf
1 cinnamon stick
1 tablespoon (15 mL) each: black peppercorns and
   crushed red chilies
1 tablespoon (15 mL) thyme leaves
1 teaspoon (5 mL) ground sage
1/4 cup (50 mL) minced garlic
1/2 teaspoon (2 mL) liquid smoke
6 whole allspice berries, coarsely crushed

1. Combine marinade ingredients. Place salmon in a shallow, non-reactive pan in a single layer. Pour marinade over top, cover, and refrigerate 24 hours or overnight.
2. Remove salmon from marinade and place skin side down on baking sheet lined with parchment paper. Allow salmon to dry at room temperature for 30 minutes. If desired, cut each fillet into four or five portions.
3. Lightly dust salmon flesh, non-skin side only, with garlic powder, then coat heavily with dark brown sugar, patting in a thick layer over fish. Sprinkle with cracked black peppercorns.

4. Bake salmon in a preheated 400°F (200°C) oven for 20 minutes, until just cooked through. The time will vary according to thickness of fish. While salmon is cooking, brush or spoon melting sugar mixture over it to glaze. Present whole fillets on buffet or serve portions on individual plates. Serves 8 to 10.

SALMON POT PIE

Pot pie is a homey dish that can be stylish when filled with fresh seafood. I like the traditional mashed potato topping, but for a more elegant presentation, top these pot pies with rounds of puff pastry.

1/4 cup (50 mL) butter, divided
1 cup (250 mL) minced brown mushrooms
2 cloves garlic, minced
1 medium onion, minced, or 1 cup (250 mL)
   tiny pearl onions, peeled
1 tablespoon (15 mL) all-purpose flour
1/2 cup (125 mL) white wine
1 cup (250 mL) fish stock (see page 64) or water
1/2 cup (125 mL) whipping cream or milk
1/4 cup (50 mL) chopped fresh parsley
1 tablespoon (15 mL) chopped fresh thyme or dill
1 tablespoon (15 mL) fresh lemon juice
salt and freshly ground black pepper
2 pounds (1 kg) salmon fillet, skin and bones removed,
   cut into large cubes

Topping
3 pounds (1.5 kg) Yukon Gold or other yellow-fleshed potatoes,
   boiled and mashed
3 tablespoons (45 mL) butter
1/4 cup (50 mL) milk or whipping cream
freshly ground black pepper

1. Heat 2 tablespoons (25 mL) of butter in pan and sauté minced mushrooms and garlic for 10 minutes, until mushrooms are tender and almost dry. Cool. Spread mushroom mixture over bottom of four individual 2-cup (500 mL) ovenproof ramekins or one 6–8-cup (1.5–2 L) soufflé dish.

2. Sauté onion in remaining butter on medium heat until tender and golden. If using pearl onions, blanch them in boiling water for 1 minute, peel, and brown lightly in butter. Stir in flour and cook for 1 minute. Slowly whisk in wine, stock or water, and cream or milk. Simmer, stirring, until you have a thick, smooth sauce. Mix in parsley, thyme or dill, and lemon juice. Season with salt and pepper to taste.

3. Meanwhile, boil potatoes in lots of salted water until very tender, then drain and mash with butter, milk or cream, and some black pepper. If you wish to pipe the potatoes over the pot pies, they should be very smooth. Otherwise, leave them a little chunky for texture.

4. Arrange salmon chunks over mushroom mixture in baking dishes. Pour sauce over top. Cover each pie decoratively with mashed potatoes. Bake in a preheated 350°F (180°C) oven for 40 minutes or until pies are bubbly and tops are golden. Makes 4 individual or 1 large pot pie.

TIP
For a fancier seafood pot pie, instead of salmon use 3/4 pound (375 g) of white fish like cod, cubed, 1 pound (500 g) of medium shrimp, shelled and deveined, and 1/2 pound (250 g) of sea scallops. Top with puff pastry.

PICKEREL IN BROWN BUTTER SAUCE

Freshly caught fish is best enjoyed with very little embellishment. Pickerel (also known as walleye) is a white and delicate prairie lake fish that is gaining popularity with Alberta chefs. Here's how it was cooked at Cuisine Canada's Northern Bounty conference by Jasper Park Lodge chef David Garcelon.

1/2 cup (125 mL) all-purpose flour
1/2 teaspoon (2 mL) salt
1/4 teaspoon (1 mL) freshly ground black pepper
1/4 teaspoon (1 mL) paprika
1 1/2 pounds (750 g) pickerel fillets, cut into serving pieces,
   skin and pin bones removed
3 tablespoons (45 mL) canola oil
1/4 cup (50 mL) butter, divided
1 lemon, halved, seeds removed
2 tablespoons (25 mL) chopped fresh parsley

1. Combine flour, salt, pepper, and paprika in a shallow dish. Dredge pickerel fillets in seasoned flour, coating both sides well and shaking off any excess flour.

2. Heat canola oil and 2 table-spoons (25 mL) butter in a nonstick frying pan over medium-high heat. When fat is sizzling, add floured fish and panfry until golden on both sides, about 2–3 minutes per side.

3. Remove fish from pan and place on a warm platter. Add remaining butter to pan and cook until it begins to brown. Squeeze juice of half a lemon into browned butter and sprinkle in chopped parsley.

4. Immediately pour butter sauce over fish and serve. Serves 4.

SMOKED FISH BREAKFAST HASH

Hash is a prairie staple—a way to use up leftover cold potatoes and corned beef for breakfast. This delicious version uses smoked trout or hot-smoked salmon. Cook it slowly for perfect crispy, crusty hash, then top it with a poached egg for the best brunch in the West.

2 tablespoons (25 mL) vegetable oil
1 tablespoon (15 mL) butter
1 medium onion, minced
3 cups (750 mL) cold boiled or baked potatoes, in small dice
1/2 cup (125 mL) each: diced carrot and rutabaga
1 clove garlic, minced
1/2 pound (250 g) hot-smoked trout or salmon (about 3
   cups/750 mL), skin and bones removed
freshly ground black pepper
1 tablespoon (15 mL) chopped fresh dill or sage
4 poached eggs (see tip, page 74)

1. Heat oil and butter in a large, nonstick frying pan over medium-high heat. Add onion and sauté until soft.

2. Add potatoes to pan and cook for 5 minutes, or until beginning to brown on the bottom. Add carrot, rutabaga, and garlic and continue to sauté over medium heat until all vegetables begin to brown, about 10 minutes longer.

3. Flake trout and remove any skin and bones. Stir smoked trout and black pepper into pan, turning potatoes in a mass with a wide spatula to brown on other side. Continue to cook until entire mass is brown and crispy. Stir in fresh dill or sage.

4. To serve, place some hash on each plate and top with a softly poached egg. Serves 4.

Vegetables and Side Dishes

MARKET TRENDS: HEIRLOOM TOMATOES, PURPLE POTATOES, AND OTHER FARMED FLAVOURS

It's the middle of December and Paul Hotchkiss is still picking tomatoes. The prairie wind is picking up skiffs of snow outside, but inside his big greenhouses the air is warm and heavy with the pungent aroma of freshly pruned tomato plants and steaming soil. Lanky stems spiral skyward up an elaborate system of wires, and multicoloured fruits peek out from under the leafy canopy, thinned to make the most of the waning winter Alberta sunlight.

Where other hothouse growers strive to produce evenly sized tomatoes, uniformly rosy and tough enough to transport long distances, Hotchkiss strives for something less tangible. What he's after is taste—that seductive blend of sweet meatiness and acidity that once gave this "apple of love"

a bad name, to the point of dismissal as a poisonous plant unfit for human consumption. How ironic that almost every famous Old World cuisine, from French and Spanish to Italian and Middle Eastern, was revolutionized by the discovery of the tomato and now relies on this New World fruit as a staple.

Hotchkiss makes no apologies for his addiction to this special vegetable, indigenous to Central and South America. In fact, it was his unsuccessful search for a perfectly ripe and flavourful tomato for a proper bacon and tomato sandwich (perhaps the sweet fruit's ultimate use) that first sent this one-time gas company executive back to the land. "I love a good bacon and tomato sandwich and that's what precipitated this

WILD MUSHROOMS

While it is far safer to leave a mushroom in the woods if you can't identify it positively, many Albertans make annual pilgrimages to their secret spots for spongy morels, golden chanterelles, spiky shaggy manes, and creamy puffballs.

Al Russow, an active retiree of Italian descent, can dig up a patch of morel mushrooms almost any spring day along the Bow River, or find you a nice selection of trumpet-shaped golden chanterelles in the fall. There are one thousand different mushrooms in Alberta and Russow is a walking field guide, fast to discard most of the fungus you'll find on the forest floor, and able to distinguish the one hundred edible varieties from the rest. Puffballs, shaggy manes, pine mushrooms, and oysters are all perfectly delicious, he says, if you know what you're doing. Morels look like little conical sponges, dark brown with lots of honeycomb holes. They appear in the spring along southern Alberta rivers and are as good as gold, so don't divulge your source. To make sure your wild mushrooms are free of any bugs and grit, soak them briefly in salted water then blot dry on paper towels before stuffing.

But don't eat wild mushrooms until you learn the ropes from a real expert. There are many mimics that look like your favourites but can make you very, very sick. It's wise to remember that even one poisonous mushroom in the pan can kill you, so don't take chances and learn the skill of identifying and picking wild mushrooms with someone who knows the ropes.

whole thing," he says of the quest that started as a backyard obsession and ended in his current commercial greenhouse operation. "I went to the supermarket in August and I couldn't find a decent tomato."

What Hotchkiss discovered was the sad truth that breeding tomatoes for uniformity, portability, and hydroponic production had virtually eliminated the wonderful taste he remembered from his youth. Nothing can compare to the juicy flavour of a fresh tomato, warm from the vine, but even in the height of the summer growing season, it's close to impossible to buy anything but that old-fashioned tomato's modern, engineered offspring.

It was in heirloom varieties that Hotchkiss finally found the holy tomato grail that he was seeking. Forget the perfectly shaped bags of red water that pass for tomatoes in today's produce departments. Hotchkiss had discovered the weird and wonderful branch of the tomato family tree—fat purple tomatoes, sweet green-fleshed tomatoes, and yellow teardrops with wacky names like 'Black Russian' from Tula, 'Green Zebra', and 'Dad's Sunset'.

It wasn't long before Alberta chefs began to discover the fruits of Hotchkiss's labours. Some, like David Garcelon, executive chef at the Jasper Park Lodge, began to serve plain, sliced heirloom tomato salads in the hotel's upscale restaurants. Now the name "Hotchkiss" appears on all of the best menus, and he is expanding his greenhouses to increase tomato production and move into other crops, from gourmet greens and edible flowers to sorrel, golden beets, red chard, and other organic edibles.

As he did for the tomatoes, Hotchkiss puts taste first when selecting new varieties. Everything is farmed organically, and there is a newly installed system of radiant hot water heating, keeping the temperature warm underground and overhead. He's recently converted from pricy natural gas to coal- and sawdust-fired boilers to generate the heat he needs to run his greenhouses efficiently year-round in this cold prairie climate.

Hotchkiss is a rare breed—the only organically certified heirloom tomato grower he knows of. He eliminates the need for chemical fertilizers by growing his crops in his own soil and organic compost. Biological controls like ladybugs and parasitic wasps deal with pests, and tiny frogs and tiger salamanders coexist among the rows of plants. Compared with the neat, compact plants of the average hydroponic tomato grower, which produce crops that ripen together and are easy to pick, his varieties are mutants. He's experimented with nearly one hundred varieties, and has eliminated many, but still grows about thirty-five different kinds of tomatoes. When up to full production, he will be picking as much as 2,300 pounds of unusual heirloom tomatoes every week.

These days Hotchkiss is partial to the big pink 'Brandywine' (which looks like an underripe red tomato when ready to eat) for sweetness, and the striped 'Green Zebra' (for its tangy, citrusy flavour). But there are always new varieties to taste, like next season's 'Orange Banana' (looks like a banana), 'Kellogg's Breakfast' (with black vertical stripes), and 'Old Ivory Egg' (an egg-like tomato), sprouting in nearby flats. Ironically, now that he is growing the tasty tomatoes of his dreams, Hotchkiss is not getting many BLTs. Chefs and consumers are happy to pay top dollar for as many tomatoes as he can deliver. "I can't afford to eat them myself," he says. "Certain clients have them on the menu and I have to make sure those folks are looked after."

Tomatoes aren't the only vegetable you'll find growing here in Alberta. In the rich soil of the central-Alberta farm belt and the warmer, irrigated areas east of Calgary, market gardeners produce peas and beans, gourmet potatoes, lettuce, sweet 'Thumbelina' carrots, golden yellow beets, and much more. From spring to late fall, prairie cooks can do their grocery shopping at the farmer's markets, where the bounty is spread out in an addictive array. Long winters are but a memory when there are piles of inexpensive and colourful peppers, crunchy pods of peas, pencil-thin asparagus and beans, tiny new potatoes, and fresh garden tomatoes to tempt.

In Calgary a crowd gathers at an outdoor neighbourhood farmer's market almost every afternoon during the dog days of summer, with more markets sprouting up in town and out every weekend. There are organic herbs, Hutterites with fresh geese and gigantic onions, sausages, fresh pies and breads, and lots and lots of vegetables. While early settlers made do with the vegetables from their home gardens and the fruit they collected in the wild, today's Albertans have the pick of the crop from local market gardeners and orchards, as well as produce trucked in overnight from growers in the warm Okanagan Valley of central British Columbia. Some chefs insist that it's all part of regional Alberta cuisine. When the peaches are perfect and the plums, peppers, and cherries just picked, they turn up on the most regional of menus.

But some things are local specialties, like the amazing assortment of potatoes Rosemary Wotske and Boshman grow at the Poplar Bluff Farm near Strathmore—'Purple Viking', 'All Blue', and fingerlings like Rose Fin Apple and La Ratte. Angela Vandershaaf and Tina Ray are also doing a roaring business in spuds. Their Little Potato Company has more than 300 hectares in production, digging up the latest in gourmet chic, tiny tubers like 'Russian Blue', 'Baby Bintje', 'Purple Peruvian', and miniature 'Rode Eerstling'. Their little potatoes are turning up on grocery store shelves and menus from Vancouver to Thunder Bay, and the pair of creative female farmers say their potatoes are a fast alternative to other starches like pasta and rice. You don't even have to peel a baby potato before you boil it, and if you follow the latest chefs' style, they're perfect to "smash," skin and all.

In addition to the markets, there are more than 120 farms across the province where you can pick your own vegetables and strawberries, or pick up produce at the market garden gate. The Alberta Market Gardeners Association publishes a guide to these farms that you can obtain by telephoning 1-800-661-AMGA.

Foraging is another way to obtain truly indigenous Alberta vegetables. Whether it's wild morels or chanterelles, or prairie sage, chefs rely on experts like Al Russow to bring them the flavours of the wild. An avid hunter and naturalist, Russow would never go hungry if he found himself alone in the woods. There are wild herbs like cress and mint, lamb's quarters and dandelion greens, edible cattails (winter roots or spring baby cattails) and berries, and even wild onions to eat. He throws in some edible flowers—dandelion blooms for sweet fritters, peppery nasturtiums, or pretty pansies from his own garden—and has the basis for an Alberta meal that's wildly delicious.

Squash and White Bean Sauté with Cold-Pressed Canola Oil

Beans and squash complement each other in both flavour and colour, and make a lovely dish to serve alongside roasted meats like lamb and beef. The cold-pressed canola oil, from Alberta's Highwood Crossing Farm, adds a nutty and rich note to this hearty side dish.

3 cups (750 mL) winter squash (acorn, butternut, delicata, or 'Golden Nugget'), seeded, peeled, and cut into 1/2-inch (1.5 cm) cubes
1 tablespoon (15 mL) butter
3 tablespoons (45 mL) cold-pressed canola oil or extra-virgin olive oil, divided
1/2 cup (125 mL) minced shallot or onion
1 clove garlic, pressed
2 tablespoons (25 mL) vegetable or chicken stock, or water
3/4 cup (175 mL) cooked white beans, rinsed and drained
salt and freshly ground black pepper
1 tablespoon (15 mL) chopped fresh sage or thyme

1. In a large nonstick sauté pan, heat butter and 1 tablespoon (15 mL) oil over medium-high heat. Add squash to pan and sauté for 10–15 minutes, until starting to brown.
2. Add shallot and garlic to pan and cook until tender, about 5 minutes more. Stir in water or stock if mixture begins to stick. Stir in cooked beans and season with salt and pepper. Cover and cook for 2–3 minutes longer, until beans are heated through.
3. Place mixture in a serving bowl and toss with sage and 1 tablespoon (15 mL) of oil. Serve immediately, drizzled with remaining oil. Makes 4 to 6 servings.

White Beans with Rosemary

Use tiny French flageolet beans or any small white beans for this elegant side dish for roast lamb or poultry. Flageolets are tender, pale green dried beans and are quite delicate. They cook faster than white beans, which will require at least 40 minutes of cooking time.

1 1/2 cups (375 mL) flageolets, navy, or other small white beans
1 onion, peeled and halved
5 whole cloves
1 carrot, peeled and quartered
1 stalk celery with leaves, quartered
4 sprigs fresh parsley
2 sprigs fresh thyme
2 sprigs fresh rosemary
1 bay leaf
2 tablespoons (25 mL) butter
2 large cloves garlic, minced
1/4 cup (50 mL) finely chopped shallots or onions
1/3 cup (75 mL) whipping cream
1 large Roma tomato, seeded and finely diced
2 tablespoons (25 mL) minced fresh rosemary
grating of fresh nutmeg
salt and freshly ground black pepper

1. Combine beans with 4 cups (1 L) of water in a large saucepan. Bring to a boil, remove pan from heat, and let beans stand, covered, for 1 hour.
2. Drain beans and add 8 cups (2 L) of fresh water. Stick cloves into onion and add to pot along with carrot, celery, parsley, thyme, rosemary, and bay leaf.
3. Bring flageolet beans to a boil and simmer, partially covered, for 20 minutes, or until beans are tender. If you are using white navy beans, you will have to cook beans a little longer. They should be tender through to the core, with no white spots in the middle. Drain beans and discard onion, carrot, celery, parsley, and bay leaf.

4. Meanwhile, melt butter in pan and sauté garlic and shallots or onions for 5 minutes, until tender. Add beans, along with cream, tomato, and rosemary.
5. Bring beans to a boil, then reduce heat and simmer until hot and creamy, about 10 minutes. Season with nutmeg, salt, and pepper. Serves 6.

POTATO, PARSNIP, AND GREEN CABBAGE PURÉE

Mashes of potatoes and other root vegetables, along with cabbage, are common in Ireland and Scotland, the homeland of many early immigrants to the Canadian prairies. A little cream added at the end makes the flavourful combination even richer.

6 medium potatoes, peeled and quartered
2 medium onions, finely chopped
2 parsnips, peeled and chopped
1/2 small green cabbage, shredded
1 teaspoon (5 mL) salt
1 cup (250 mL) water
freshly ground black pepper
1 tablespoon (15 mL) butter
1/4 cup (50 mL) whipping cream (optional)

1. Layer vegetables in a heavy pot—half of potatoes, onions, parsnips, and cabbage, and repeat. Add salt to water and pour over top.
2. Bring to a boil, then reduce heat to low. Cover tightly and simmer 1 hour. Drain.
3. Mash with a potato masher until mixture is almost puréed. Season with pepper and stir in butter and cream, if using. Serves 6.

Tomatoes Three Ways

Here are three ways to use the delicious heirloom varieties of tomatoes grown year-round by Tracey and Paul Hotchkiss in their Alberta greenhouses. The recipes were created by chef Michael Allemeier.

Oven-dried Tomatoes

1/2 cup (125 mL) extra-virgin olive oil or Highwood Crossing cold-pressed canola oil
2 tablespoons (25 mL) balsamic vinegar
1 teaspoon (5 mL) fresh thyme leaves
1/2 teaspoon (2 mL) salt
12 tomatoes, preferably fleshy heirloom or Roma

1. In a large bowl, mix oil, balsamic vinegar, and thyme. Cut tomatoes in half and add to bowl, tossing to coat with mixture.
2. Lay tomatoes on a clean sheet pan, sprinkle with salt, and bake for 2–3 hours in a preheated 250°F (120°C) oven until tomatoes have shrunk but are still soft.
3. Let cool. Serve at room temperature. The tomatoes will last for 4–5 days in the refrigerator. Serves 6.

Asiago-baked Tomatoes

1/2 cup (125 mL) extra-virgin olive oil or Highwood Crossing cold-pressed canola oil
1 shallot, finely minced
1 clove of garlic, minced
1/2 cup (125 mL) finely ground soft breadcrumbs
1/2 cup (125 mL) grated Asiago
salt and freshly ground black pepper
3 large tomatoes, preferably a beefsteak variety

1. Heat oil in a large frying pan over medium heat. Add shallots and garlic, and cook until tender and fragrant, about 5 minutes. Add breadcrumbs and cook for 1 minute, stirring constantly. Place crumbs in a bowl and let cool. Stir in Asiago, and season with salt and pepper.
2. Cut tomatoes in half and core. Season tomatoes with salt and pepper, set on a baking sheet and cover with crumbs. Bake in a preheated 400°F (200°C) oven until crumbs are golden, about 5–10 minutes. Serve at once. Serves 6.

Shallot and Tomato Butter

3 tablespoons (45 mL) extra-virgin olive oil or Highwood Crossing cold-pressed canola oil
4 large, ripe, fleshy tomatoes, cored and diced
1/2 pound (250 g) butter at room temperature
5 shallots, minced

1. Heat oil in a pan over low heat. Add tomatoes and cook for about 40 minutes over low heat, until moisture is cooked out. Stir often to prevent tomatoes from burning. Cool.
2. Combine tomatoes and butter in a food processor and purée. Transfer to a bowl. Fold in minced shallots.
3. Using a piping bag, pipe butter out onto a sheet pan. Refrigerate until needed. Alternatively, spread the butter along one side of a sheet of plastic wrap and roll into a log, twisting ends to seal. Refrigerate butter or freeze. Cut into slices to serve on grilled meats, poultry, or vegetables.

Heirloom Tomato Salsa

There's nothing better than fresh tomato salsa made with flavourful organic heirloom tomatoes. Serve salsa spooned over a piece of perfectly grilled fish or with taco chips for scooping.

1 cup (250 mL) diced fresh heirloom tomatoes
1/2 cup (125 mL) diced onion
1 jalapeño or serrano chile, stemmed and minced (serrano is hotter)
1/4 cup (50 mL) chopped fresh cilantro
1 tablespoon (15 mL) fresh lemon or lime juice
salt

Combine all ingredients in a bowl and add salt to taste. Mix well and refrigerate for 15 minutes to allow flavours to meld. Makes 1 1/4 cups (300 mL).

VEGETARIAN STUFFED PEPPERS

Using wholegrain bulgar wheat instead of meat makes a stuffed pepper that's low in fat and high in fibre. You can also use this savoury stuffing to fill hollowed-out baby eggplants, zucchini, or artichoke hearts. Eliminate the egg, cheese, and breadcrumbs to serve the filling as a bulgar pilaf.

2 tablespoons (25 mL) olive oil
1 tablespoon (15 mL) butter
1 large onion, chopped
3 cloves garlic, minced
1 hot serrano or jalapeño pepper, seeded and minced
4 large mushrooms, minced
4 cups (1 L) rich vegetable or chicken stock
1 tablespoon (15 mL) soy sauce
1/4 teaspoon (1 mL) freshly ground black pepper
2 cups (500 mL) coarse bulgar
1 cup (250 mL) walnuts, toasted and chopped
1 tablespoon (15 mL) honey
1 tablespoon (15 mL) chopped fresh basil
   (or substitute basil pesto)
1/2 cup (125 mL) grated Parmesan cheese
1/2 cup (125 mL) grated Sylvan Star Gouda or mozzarella cheese
2 large eggs, beaten
6 large red bell peppers, halved lengthwise, seeds and ribs removed
salt
1 tablespoon (15 mL) extra-virgin olive oil or
   cold-pressed canola oil
extra grated Parmesan cheese for topping

1. Heat oil with butter in a covered saucepan and sauté onion and garlic for 10–15 minutes, until onion is nicely browned. Add serrano or jalapeño pepper and mushrooms and cook 2 minutes longer.

2. Stir in stock, soy sauce, and pepper, and bring to a boil. Simmer, covered, for 5 minutes. Add bulgar, walnuts, and honey and stir to combine. Cover pot, reduce heat to low, and simmer until bulgar is tender, about 20 minutes. Remove from heat and set aside for 10 minutes longer to steam.

3. Fluff bulgar and cool slightly. Stir in fresh basil, grated cheeses, and beaten eggs.

4. Set red pepper halves snugly in an oiled baking dish and sprinkle with salt. Press some of the stuffing into each pepper half, mounding it slightly. Drizzle peppers with extra-virgin olive oil or cold-pressed canola oil and grate a little more Parmesan over top.

5. Bake in a preheated 375°F (190°C) oven for 40 minutes, until nicely browned on top. Serves 6.

FETTUCCINE WITH CREAMY BLUE GOAT CHEESE AND MASCARPONE SAUCE

Served alone or with grilled chicken or salmon steaks, this is a decadent and delicious way to sauce pasta. Mascarpone is a double cream cheese available at Italian markets. If you can't find arugula, substitute other greens like spinach, chard, or beet greens.

1 tablespoon (15 mL) olive oil
6 ounces (180 g) Canadian back bacon, slivered
1 clove garlic, minced
4 green onions, chopped
1/2 cup (125 mL) mascarpone cream cheese
1 pound (500 g) fresh fettuccine noodles
4 ounces (100 g) blue goat cheese
   (or other blue cheese), cut into small cubes
2 cups (500 mL) arugula leaves, cut into slivers
freshly ground black pepper

1. Heat olive oil in a large nonstick pan and sauté bacon until starting to brown. Add garlic and onions and cook another minute.

2. Stir in mascarpone and heat gently until creamy and smooth.

3. Meanwhile, cook pasta in a large pot of boiling, salted water until just al dente, about 3–5 minutes. Taste pasta after 3 minutes to ensure it's not overcooked. Drain well and add to cream sauce, tossing pasta to coat with sauce.

4. Add goat cheese and arugula to pan, continuing to toss until cheese just begins to melt and arugula is lightly wilted. Serve pasta in bowls with a good grinding of black pepper. Serves 4.

BAKED POTATO TORTE

This dish of crisp potatoes, bacon, and bright green Savoy cabbage is St. Patrick's Day in a pie. I think of my old friend John Fricker when I make this hearty side dish. Born on St. Paddy's Day, he's the kind of guy who knows how to enjoy a dram. Chef Brian Plunkett, a member of Canada's gold medal-winning culinary team and owner of Plunkett's restaurant in Calgary, helped devise this dish, based on his Irish heritage.

4–6 leaves Savoy cabbage
8 strips of smoky bacon, chopped
1 tablespoon (15 mL) butter
6 medium potatoes, peeled and thinly sliced
1 teaspoon (5 mL) fresh thyme leaves, or 1/2 teaspoon (2 mL) dried thyme
salt and freshly ground black pepper
2 cups (500 mL) old Cheddar cheese, shredded

1. Cook sliced cabbage in boiling, salted water for 2 minutes to blanch, then drain under cold running water to refresh and cool. Let cabbage stand in colander to drain for at least 5 minutes. Squeeze out excess moisture before slicing finely.
2. Chop bacon and sauté in butter until it starts to brown. Remove bacon from fat with a slotted spoon and reserve fat.

3. Rinse sliced potatoes and pat dry, then toss in a bowl with 3–4 tablespoons (45–60 mL) of reserved bacon fat, thyme, salt, and pepper.
4. Brush a nonstick pie plate or springform pan with reserved bacon fat and arrange a layer of sliced potatoes in pan. Top with some of the cheese, then a layer of cabbage and bacon, and another sprinkling of cheese. Continue layering in this fashion, ending with a layer of potatoes and cheese. It's important that each layer have some cheese to hold pie together.
5. Press layers down firmly and bake pie in a preheated 375°F (190°C) oven for 1 hour, until brown and crispy. Cut into wedges to serve. Serves 8.

ROASTED CARROTS WITH BASIL AND MINT

Simple but sublime. You can add other root vegetables to this roast— try tossing in some parsnips, rutabaga, onions, and potatoes.

1 pound (500 g) carrots, peeled and cut into chunks
2 tablespoons (25 mL) olive oil
salt and freshly ground black pepper
2 tablespoons (25 mL) each: chopped fresh basil and mint, or 1 teaspoon (5 mL) each: dried basil and mint

1. In a large bowl, toss carrots with olive oil, salt, and pepper. Spread in a single layer in a large baking pan and bake in a preheated 400°F (200°C) oven for 30–45 minutes, stirring occasionally, until carrots are cooked through and starting to brown.
2. Remove from oven, toss with herbs, and serve. Serves 4.

FRESH CORN AND ROASTED PEPPER SUCCOTASH

*Succotash is a true North American classic, a combination of beans and corn
that early American settlers learned to concoct from their Native neighbours.
Here's an updated version using dried beans and smoky, roasted hot peppers,
mixed with sweet summer corn. Serve it with barbecued beef brisket or
pulled pork, or over rice, for a healthy vegetarian meal.*

1 pound (500 g) dried navy beans or 2 cups (500 mL)
   black-eyed peas
2 tablespoons (25 mL) olive oil
2 medium onions, minced
4 cloves garlic
1 tablespoon (15 mL) ground cumin
1 tablespoon (15 mL) ground coriander
1 cup (250 mL) canned Roma tomatoes, chopped or puréed
4 Anaheim or Shepherd peppers
2 poblano or other medium-hot peppers
2 jalapeño peppers
1 each: red and yellow bell pepper, roasted (see tip, page 10)
2 cups (500 mL) fresh corn kernels (from 3 cobs of corn)

juice of 1 lime
1 teaspoon (5 mL) salt
freshly ground black pepper
1/2 cup (125 mL) chopped fresh cilantro

1. Cover beans with cold water and set aside to soak overnight, or use
   quick-soak method (page 29).
2. In a large pot, heat olive oil and sauté onions and garlic until tender. Add
   cumin and coriander and cook 1 minute. Add presoaked beans with 8
   cups of water, bring to a boil, and simmer for 1 1/2 hours, or until soft.
3. When beans are almost tender, add tomatoes, peppers, and fresh
   corn kernels. Simmer 30 minutes longer, uncovered, to thicken.
   Add lime juice, salt, pepper, and cilantro and stir to combine
   well. Serves 6 to 8.

CORNMEAL POLENTA TORTE WITH CARAMELIZED VEGETABLES AND GOAT CHEESE

Polenta, mamaliga, or cornmeal mush—whatever you call it, this porridge of flavoured cornmeal is as common on the prairies as cowboy cornbread. If fennel is not available, a mixture of wild or cultivated mushrooms like porcini, portobello, and oyster mushrooms makes a delicious addition.

Polenta Layer
4 cups (1 L) vegetable or chicken broth
2 cups (500 mL) water
1 1/2 cups (375 mL) cornmeal
1 tablespoon (15 mL) minced garlic
3/4 teaspoon (4 mL) salt
1/4 teaspoon (1 mL) pepper
2 tablespoons (25 mL) butter
1 tablespoon (15 mL) chopped fresh basil or rosemary
1 pound (500 g) goat cheese, crumbled or thinly sliced

Vegetable Layer
2 tablespoons (25 mL) good-quality olive oil
2 white onions, cut into slivers
1 tablespoon (15 mL) granulated sugar
1 large fennel bulb, trimmed and thinly sliced
2 red and/or yellow bell peppers, sliced
2 tablespoons (25 mL) balsamic vinegar

1. In a large saucepan, combine broth and water and bring to a boil. Slowly add cornmeal to boiling broth, whisking constantly to prevent lumps. Reduce heat to medium-low, add garlic, salt, and pepper and cook over low heat for 30 minutes, stirring regularly, until mixture comes away from the sides of the pan. Stir in butter and basil or rosemary, and keep warm.
2. Meanwhile, for vegetable layer, heat olive oil over medium heat and cook onions with sugar for 15 minutes or until golden. Add sliced fennel and peppers and cook until very tender, about 15 minutes longer. Remove from heat and stir in balsamic vinegar. Set aside.
3. Butter a 10-inch (25 cm) springform pan and add one-third of hot polenta. Press to form a smooth layer. Top with half of vegetables and one-third of goat cheese. Create a second similar layer of polenta and vegetables, then finish with remaining polenta. Smooth top and arrange remaining goat cheese over torte.
4. Bake for 30 minutes in a preheated 350°F (180°C) oven until brown and bubbly. Cool slightly before removing sides from pan. Serve warm or at room temperature, cut into wedges. Serves 6 to 8.

POLENTA WITH WILD SAGE, GOAT CHEESE, AND MUSHROOM RAGOUT

This is a flavourful vegetarian entrée or first course. You can use any kind of mushrooms at hand, but wild morels or chanterelles will give a richer taste to this comforting combination. Make sure to use coarse or stone-ground cornmeal—fine cornmeal makes a polenta that's too pasty.

Polenta
5 cups (1.25 L) water
1 teaspoon (5 mL) salt
1 tablespoon (15 mL) butter
1 cup (250 mL) coarsely ground cornmeal
1 cup (250 mL) soft goat cheese
1 tablespoon (15 mL) chopped fresh wild sage or garden sage

Mushroom Ragout
2 tablespoons (25 mL) butter
1 cup (250 mL) minced white onion
2 cloves garlic, minced
8 cups (2 L) assorted fresh wild mushrooms (oyster, shiitake, morel, or chanterelle), or cultivated mushrooms, thickly sliced
1/2 teaspoon (2 mL) salt
1/4 teaspoon (1 mL) freshly ground black pepper
1/2 cup (125 mL) vegetable or chicken stock, or white wine
1/4 cup (50 mL) whipping cream
sprigs of fresh wild or garden sage

1. Bring water to a rolling boil in a large pot and add salt and butter. Slowly add cornmeal to pot in a steady stream, whisking as you go to prevent lumps from forming. Stir for 5 minutes, then reduce heat to low and continue to cook for 15 minutes, stirring to make sure polenta does not stick to pot. Remove from heat and stir in goat cheese and sage. Keep warm.

2. To make ragout, melt butter in a wide pan and sauté onion and garlic until soft, about 5 minutes. Add sliced mushrooms to pan with salt and pepper and cook until mushrooms give up their liquid and begin to soften.

3. Add stock or wine, increase heat, and simmer until liquid in the pan is reduced by half. Stir in cream and bring to a boil. Cook 1 minute, until ragout is thick.

4. Serve polenta in deep bowls, topped with mushroom ragout. Garnish each bowl with a sprig of fresh sage. Serves 8 as a first course or 4 as a vegetarian main course with salad.

Black Bean, Taber Corn, and Smoked Tomato Cassoulet

Chef Michael Allemeier, who created this hearty bean dish, smokes the tomatoes in a wood oven using apple wood. Smoked tomatoes have a concentrated sweet and smoky flavour—if you don't have a home smoker, roast the tomatoes in a hot oven until softened and beginning to brown, and add a few drops of liquid smoke or a chipotle chile when you add the tomatoes to the dish.

1 cup (250 mL) black turtle beans
2 tablespoons (25 mL) canola oil
1 small onion, diced
2 cloves garlic, minced
3 tablespoons (45 mL) tomato paste
8 cups (2 L) water or chicken stock
5 Roma tomatoes, cut in quarters
1 cup (250 mL) corn kernels, from 1 or 2 cobs fresh Taber corn
1/4 cup (50 mL) chopped fresh cilantro
salt and freshly ground black pepper

1. Cover black beans with enough cold water to cover them by 3 inches (8 cm) and set aside to soak overnight. Drain beans well.

2. If you have a home smoker, smoke tomatoes over cold smoke. Tomatoes are infused with the flavour of wood smoke after only about 30 minutes in a home smoker. To smoke them on the barbecue, place soaked woodchips in a tinfoil package, poke some holes in the package to allow smoke to escape, and place it over the gas flame.

When the wood begins to smoke, place tomatoes on grill and reduce heat—they will begin to char and take on a smoky flavour in about 10 minutes. Peel away any blackened skin before chopping tomatoes.

3. In a large pot, heat canola oil over medium heat. Add onion and garlic and sauté until tender and starting to brown, about 10 minutes. Add tomato paste and cook for 30 seconds, stirring well.

4. Add water or stock and drained black beans. Bring to a boil, then reduce heat and simmer, covered, for 1 hour.

5. Chop smoked tomatoes and add to beans. Simmer 30 minutes longer or until beans are tender and sauce is nicely thickened.

6. Stir in corn kernels and cilantro and cook for 5 minutes longer. Season to taste with salt and pepper. Serves 6.

Easy Cookhouse Beans

Need to put together a pot of beans in a hurry? This combination, with smoky bacon and chipotle chiles, tastes like it's been on the campfire all day and works well with grilled burgers and coleslaw for a cowboy-style cookout.

4 slices double-smoked bacon, chopped
1 large onion, chopped
2 cloves garlic, minced
1/2 each: red and green bell pepper, chopped
2 14-ounce (398 mL) cans vegetarian baked beans
1 19-ounce (540 mL) can pinto beans, drained and rinsed
6 tablespoons (75 mL) maple sipping whisky, or equal parts maple syrup and rye whisky
1/4 cup (50 mL) ketchup
1 tablespoon (15 mL) mustard
1 teaspoon (5 mL) canned chipotle chile in adobo, chopped

1. Sauté bacon in a heavy Dutch oven until crisp. Remove and set aside.

2. In bacon drippings, sauté onion, garlic, and red and green pepper until tender and starting to brown. Stir in baked beans, pinto beans, maple whisky, ketchup, mustard, chipotle chile, and reserved bacon.

3. Pour into a heavy casserole dish or bean pot and bake in a preheated 250°F (120°C) oven for 1 hour. Serves 6 to 8.

Quinoa and Carrot Pilaf

Quinoa is a South American grain that is now grown in Alberta. The tiny grains cook in about 10–15 minutes and are perfect for pilafs, or make an interesting base for a cold grain salad. The seeds are commercially polished to remove the bitter natural coating, but should be rinsed in a colander for a minute or two to remove any residual dust.

2/3 cup (150 mL) quinoa
2 teaspoons (10 mL) olive oil
1 small onion, minced
1 clove garlic, minced
1 large carrot, peeled and finely grated, about 2/3 cup (150 mL)
1/4 teaspoon (1 mL) ground coriander
1 1/2 cups (375 mL) chicken stock, divided
1 tablespoon (15 mL) minced fresh cilantro
salt and freshly ground black pepper

1. Rinse quinoa under running water and drain.
2. Heat olive oil in a saucepan and sauté onion and garlic for 5 minutes. Add carrot and coriander and sauté for 1 minute. Stir in 1/2 cup (125 mL) of stock, bring to a boil, cover, then reduce heat to low and simmer for 5 minutes.
3. Add remaining broth to cooked vegetables and bring to a boil. Stir in quinoa, cover, then reduce heat to low and simmer for 15 minutes. Remove from heat and let stand 5 minutes to steam. Fluff quinoa with a fork, stir in cilantro, and season to taste with salt and pepper. Serves 4.

WILD RICE FRITTERS

These wild rice pancakes make a wonderful side dish to many meat and game meals, or can be served topped with smoked duck breast or trout as a first course.

2 tablespoons (25 mL) olive oil
2 tablespoons (25 mL) butter
1 cup (250 mL) minced onion
2 cloves garlic, minced
1/2 cup (125 mL) all-purpose flour
1/2 cup (125 mL) ground pecans
1 teaspoon (5 mL) baking powder
salt and freshly ground black pepper
1 egg
1/4 cup (50 mL) sour cream
1/4 cup (50 mL) milk
1 cup (250 mL) cooked wild rice
canola or olive oil for frying

1. Sauté onion and garlic in olive oil and butter until tender and starting to brown.
2. Combine flour, pecans, baking powder, salt, and pepper in a mixing bowl. Whisk together egg, sour cream, and milk, and add to batter. Stir in cooked onion, garlic, and wild rice.
3. Heat a little canola or olive oil in a nonstick pan and cook pancakes, using about 1–2 tablespoons (15–25 mL) of batter for each pancake. Pancakes should be bite-sized— about 2 inches (5 cm) in diameter. Make them a little larger if serving them as a side dish. Cook pancakes about 2 minutes on each side, or until golden. Set aside in a warm oven until all pancakes are cooked.
4. Serve as a side dish or as canapés topped with smoked duck and cranberry chutney, or smoked trout and dill mayonnaise. Serves 6 to 8 as a side dish.

MIXED POTATO MASH WITH GARLIC AND SAGE

This is a colourful and flavourful mashed potato mixture that goes beyond the usual garlic mashed potatoes. Sweet potatoes bring healthy beta-carotene to the mix, too.

4 medium to large yellow-fleshed potatoes
1 medium sweet potato or yam
1 clove garlic, minced
1 tablespoon (15 mL) minced fresh sage (don't substitute dry)
2 green onions, minced
1 tablespoon (15 mL) butter
1/4 cup (50 mL) fat-free sour cream
1/4 cup (50 mL) skim milk
salt and freshly ground black pepper

1. Peel yellow potatoes and sweet potato and cut into large cubes. Place in a saucepan. Cover with salted water, bring to a boil, then reduce heat and simmer for 20 minutes or until potatoes are tender.
2. Drain well and mash. Stir butter into hot potatoes along with garlic, sage, and green onion. Beat in sour cream and enough milk to make a smooth, orange purée. Season with salt and pepper to taste. Serves 4.

POTATO SCALLOP

The combination of buttery Yukon Gold potatoes and brilliant orange yams takes the classic potato and onion scallop to new heights. You can also add sliced rutabaga to this comforting side dish. Or for perfect presentation, make the layered dish in advance, chill, and cut into shapes (a cookie cutter makes nice rounds), then reheat on a baking sheet in a hot oven.

2 pounds (1 kg) Yukon Gold potatoes, peeled
2 medium orange-fleshed sweet potatoes or yams, peeled
2 cups (500 mL) thinly sliced onions or leeks
4 tablespoons (50 mL) all-purpose flour
salt and freshly ground black pepper
1/2 cup (125 mL) whipping cream, or 1/2 cup (125 mL) evaporated skim milk
1 1/2 cups (375 mL) chicken broth

1. Slice potatoes and sweet potatoes very thinly using the slicing blade of a food processor, a mandolin, or a sharp chef's knife. In a wide, shallow casserole dish, make alternating layers of potatoes, sweet potatoes, and onions or leeks, sprinkling a little flour and salt and pepper over each layer as you go.
2. Combine cream (or evaporated milk for a low-fat version) and broth and pour over vegetables. Liquid should come almost up to top layer of vegetables. Add more broth or cream if necessary.
3. Cover casserole with foil and bake in a preheated 350°F (180° C) oven for 1 hour. Remove foil and bake an additional 15 minutes, or until dish is nicely browned. Serves 6.

MUSTARD ROASTED NEW POTATOES

For an easy side dish, roast these new potatoes alongside anything else you might have in the oven.

2 pounds (1 kg) new nugget potatoes, red-skinned
1 tablespoon (15 mL) olive oil
salt and freshly ground black pepper
2 tablespoons (25 mL) grainy Dijon mustard
1 teaspoon (5 mL) honey
1 tablespoon (15 mL) chopped fresh rosemary and thyme
pinch of cayenne pepper

1. Leave small potatoes whole and cut larger potatoes in halves or quarters. Toss with olive oil, salt, and pepper. Spread on a baking sheet or in a shallow baking pan in a single layer. Roast potatoes, stirring occasionally, in a preheated 400°F (200°C) oven for 50–60 minutes, until nicely browned.
2. In a large metal bowl, whisk together mustard, honey, fresh herbs, and cayenne pepper. Toss hot roasted potatoes with mustard mixture to coat well. Serve immediately. Serves 6 to 8.

BAKED STUFFED POTATOES WITH ROOTS AND GINGER

*Alternatively, boil potatoes with root vegetables
for a tasty and colourful potato mash.*

2 large baking potatoes
2 carrots, cut into chunks
1 parsnip, cut into chunks
1/4 cup (50 mL) butter
3 green onions, minced
1 tablespoon (15 mL) minced fresh ginger root
1/4 cup (50 mL) milk or whipping cream
salt and freshly ground black pepper

1. Scrub potatoes, prick skins with a fork, and bake in a preheated 400°F (200°C) oven for 45 minutes or until soft. Meanwhile, put carrots and parsnips in a microwaveable dish with 1 tablespoon (15 mL) water, cover, and microwave on high for 4 minutes. Drain.
2. Cut each potato in half lengthwise, scoop out flesh, leaving 1/4-inch (5 mm) shell. Mash potato roughly with cooked vegetables.
3. Melt butter in a frying pan and sauté green onions and ginger for 5 minutes. Stir into mashed vegetables with milk or cream and season with salt and pepper to taste. Pile mash back into shells and bake for 10 minutes or microwave until heated through. Serves 4.

CHILI ROASTED SPUDS

This is a healthy, low-fat way to obtain crisp, spicy potatoes that are reminiscent of French fries. Feel free to eliminate the chili paste and cayenne pepper and replace them with herbs like basil or mint, and lemon pepper, for a more Mediterranean-inspired oven fry to match your main course.

2 tablespoons (25 mL) fresh lemon juice
2 tablespoons (25 mL) water
1 teaspoon (5 mL) Worcestershire sauce
1 teaspoon (5 mL) garlic chili paste
1/4 teaspoon (1 mL) each: ground cumin and cayenne pepper
1/2 teaspoon (2 mL) dried oregano

4 medium red-skinned potatoes, unpeeled, cut into 6 wedges
8 whole cloves garlic, peeled
2 red onions, cut into wedges
1 tablespoon (15 mL) olive oil

1. In a large bowl, combine lemon juice, water, Worcestershire sauce, garlic chili paste, cumin, cayenne pepper, and oregano. Add potatoes, garlic cloves, and onion wedges to bowl, and toss to coat well with spice mixture.
2. Pour into a large roasting pan and drizzle with olive oil. Roast in a preheated oven at 400°F (200°C) for 35–40 minutes, turning once or twice during cooking period so that vegetables brown evenly without burning. Vegetables will absorb sauce as they roast. Serves 4.

GRILLED MARINATED MUSHROOMS

Serve these mushrooms with steak or chilled with grilled eggplant, zucchini, leeks, and peppers as an antipasto or side dish. Brush this marinade on any vegetable before grilling.

1/2 cup (125 mL) cider vinegar
1 cup (250 mL) olive oil
3 cloves garlic, minced
2 tablespoons (25 mL) minced fresh parsley
2 tablespoons (25 mL) minced fresh herbs, such as oregano or sage, or 1 teaspoon (5 mL) dried herbs
1/2 teaspoon (2 mL) salt
1 dried hot chili pepper, crumbled
2 green onions, minced
2 pounds (1 kg) large mushrooms, such as portobellos or shiitake, cleaned, stems removed

1. Combine vinegar, oil, garlic, parsley, herbs, salt, chili pepper, and green onions in a food processor and purée. Put the mushrooms in a large bowl and add marinade, tossing to coat.
2. Cover and refrigerate overnight, stirring occasionally. Drain.
3. Brush barbecue grill with oil and heat barbecue to high heat. Grill mushrooms for about 3–5 minutes, turning until tender and starting to brown. Slice larger mushrooms before serving. Serves 8.

STUFFED MOREL OR PORTOBELLO MUSHROOMS

Serve stuffed mushrooms as a first course or artfully arranged alongside a grilled steak. If you use big portobello mushrooms for this recipe, use a spoon to scrape out the dark gills on the undersides of the mushrooms before stuffing.

1 pound (500 g) fresh morel mushrooms, stems removed and
   reserved, or 2 portobello mushrooms
2 shallots or 1 small onion, minced
1 tablespoon (15 mL) butter
1/2 cup (125 mL) whipping cream or milk
salt and freshly ground black pepper
1 teaspoon (5 mL) chopped fresh sage, or 1/4 teaspoon
   (1 mL) dried sage
1 cup (125 mL) cold mashed potatoes or soft breadcrumbs
3 tablespoons (45 mL) grated strong-flavoured cheese,
   such as aged Cheddar or Parmesan
melted butter

1. Clean mushroom tops and finely mince stems. (Don't use the tough stems of portobellos—discard and mince up an extra mushroom cap).
2. Sauté mushrooms with shallot or onion in butter until tender, about 5 minutes, then mix in cream or milk, salt, pepper, sage, mashed potatoes or breadcrumbs, and grated cheese.
3. Stuff this mixture into mushroom caps and lay them in a buttered baking dish. Brush with melted butter. Bake in a preheated 425°F (220°C) oven for 10 minutes. If using portobello mushrooms, bake until golden and cut into wedges to serve. Serves 4.

WILD MUSHROOM CUSTARDS

Serve these elegant individual souffléd custards with a handful of baby greens and a drizzle of Wild Mushroom Oil (page 115) as a starter or light luncheon dish, or to complement any roasted beef or game dish. Cooked in a single baking dish, the golden soufflé is always impressive.

2 cups (500 mL) chopped wild and/or cultivated mushrooms
   (brown, shiitake, portobello, morel, oyster, etc.)
1/4 cup (50 mL) minced onion
1 tablespoon (15 mL) butter
2 cloves garlic, minced
3 tablespoons (45 mL) soft breadcrumbs
3 large eggs, separated
1/4 cup (50 mL) hot chicken stock
1/2 cup (125 mL) whipping cream
salt and freshly ground black pepper
1/2 teaspoon (2 mL) sweet paprika

1. Use a food processor to finely chop mushrooms and onion. Melt butter in a frying pan and sauté mushrooms with onion and garlic in butter over medium heat until very tender and most of liquid has evaporated. Stir in breadcrumbs and cool.
2. Beat egg yolks with chicken stock and cream. Put mixture in a double boiler over hot water and whisk until custard thickens slightly. Combine with mushroom mixture and season with salt and pepper. Set aside.
3. Beat egg whites until very stiff. Carefully fold egg whites into mushroom mixture to lighten it. Spoon custard mixture into buttered muffin tins, individual custard cups, or small soufflé dishes, filling them two-thirds full.
4. Set custards in a larger pan that has been filled with 1 inch (2.5 cm) of hot water. Bake in a preheated 350°F (180°C) oven for 30 minutes, until custards are puffed and golden. Serve in dishes or run a knife around the edge and unmould onto plates. Sprinkle with paprika to serve. Makes 4 to 6 individual souffléd custards.

WILD MUSHROOM OIL

Anyone who has ever bought a big bag of dried mushrooms knows that the powder at the bottom of the bag adds flavour to soups, stews, breads, and even pizza dough. But you can also use home-made mushroom powder to infuse a neutral olive oil with intense mushroom flavour. Drizzle this wonderful oil over a salad, grilled steak, a pile of polenta or mushroom risotto, a pizza or omelette, or mash it into potatoes.

2 cups (500 mL) dried mushrooms (a single variety or a
    combination of several mushrooms)
3 cups (750 mL) olive oil or flavourless vegetable oil

1. Put mushrooms into a blender or clean coffee grinder and pulverize. The mushrooms must be very dry and crisp. If they are moist at all, dry them overnight in a 150°F (65°C) oven, or in a home dehydrator. If not using mushroom powder immediately, store in a cool, dry place.
2. In a heavy saucepan, combine mushroom powder and oil and warm very gently on low heat, stirring, for 30 minutes. The oil should not sizzle—you should be able to put your finger into it for a few seconds. If the oil is too hot, the flavour will be diminished.
3. Strain mushroom oil into a bottle through a very fine metal strainer lined with several layers of cheesecloth. Refrigerate. Makes 3 cups.

> ### TIP
> You can make herb-infused oil by macerating fresh herbs (like basil, scallions, rosemary, or thyme) in a food processor, then infusing with oil at room temperature for 8–24 hours before straining and bottling. The flavour of fresh herbs can easily be destroyed if you heat the oil.

CABBAGE WITH GRAINY MUSTARD AND CURRANTS

Colourful red cabbage stars in this dish. The acidity of the mustard is balanced by the sweetness of the dried fruit.

2 tablespoons (25 mL) olive oil
1 small head of red cabbage, thinly sliced
1 clove garlic, minced
1/4 cup (50 mL) dried currants, soaked in warm water to soften
2 tablespoons (25 mL) grainy mustard
1 tablespoon (15 mL) water
salt and freshly ground black pepper

1. Heat olive oil in a sauté pan and add cabbage and garlic. Sauté on high heat for about 3 minutes, until cabbage is starting to wilt.
2. When currants are soft, drain, discarding soaking liquid. Stir together mustard and water and add to cabbage in pan, along with drained currants.
3. Cover pan and simmer on low for 5 minutes, or until cabbage is tender but still a little crisp. Season with salt and pepper to taste. Serves 4.

CREAMED RUTABAGAS

Rutabagas are the big, orange-fleshed vegetables that are sometimes mislabelled as turnips. This comforting dish is perfect to serve with a roast turkey or chicken dinner.

2 medium rutabagas, about 3 pounds (1.5 kg), cut into chunks
1 large potato, peeled and cubed
2 tablespoons (25 mL) butter
4 tablespoons (60 mL) fat-free sour cream
salt and white pepper
2 green onions, chopped

1. Cook rutabagas and potatoes together in boiling water for 15–20 minutes, or until tender.
2. Drain and mash with butter and sour cream until smooth. Season with salt and pepper to taste and stir in green onions.
3. Transfer vegetables to an ovenproof dish and cook in a preheated 350°F (180°C) oven for 20 minutes, or until brown on top. Serves 6.

CREAMED KOHLRABI

Kohlrabi is a wonderful cruciferous vegetable that my father always grew in his prairie garden. The pale green globes grow above ground, like tennis balls with leafy appendages. They should be no bigger than a small orange (large ones can get woody inside). Serve creamed kohlrabi alongside roasted meats and poultry.

4 medium kohlrabi
2 cups (500 mL) water
1 small onion, halved
2 cloves
1/2 teaspoon (2 mL) salt
4 tablespoons (50 mL) butter
2 tablespoons (25 mL) all-purpose flour
1/2 cup (125 mL) whipping cream
salt and white pepper

1. Peel kohlrabi, removing leaves and tough outer skin, but leaving tender green layer just beneath skin intact. Cut into small cubes.
2. In a saucepan, heat water to boiling with onion, cloves, and salt. Add kohlrabi and blanch for 1–2 minutes. Drain kohlrabi, discarding onion and cloves, but reserving blanching liquid.
3. In another pan, melt butter and whisk in flour. Cook for 1–2 minutes, but don't let roux brown. Slowly whisk in about 1 1/4 cups (300 mL) of reserved blanching liquid, enough to make a smooth, thick sauce. Whisk in cream and bring sauce to a simmer. Add blanched kohlrabi and cook together for 3 minutes. Season to taste with salt and white pepper. Serve immediately. Serves 4 to 6.

GRILLED CORN ON THE COB WITH SPICY RED PEPPER BUTTER

Grilling fresh corn in the husk adds the most delicious smoky flavour—try it over a campfire on the trail, or on the gas barbecue at home. Freeze extra red pepper butter in a log for later use atop grilled fish, for a spicy garlic toast, or for sautéeing jumbo shrimp as an appetizer.

1 red bell pepper, chopped
1 canned chipotle chile in adobo
1 teaspoon (15 mL) chopped garlic
2 tablespoons (25 mL) canola oil
1 teaspoon (5 mL) granulated sugar
1/4 teaspoon (1 mL) salt
1/4 teaspoon (1 mL) ground cumin
1 cup (250 mL) butter, softened
2 green onions, minced
3 tablespoons (45 mL) chopped fresh cilantro
8 large cobs sweet Taber corn

1. Place red pepper, chipotle, garlic, and canola oil in a food processor or blender and process until smooth. Heat pepper paste in a sauté pan with sugar, salt, and cumin, and cook until most of the liquid has evaporated. Cool. Blend with softened butter, green onions, and cilantro and refrigerate.
2. To prepare corn for grilling, remove heavier outer leaves and peel back husk, keeping leaves intact at base of cob. Pull off all silk. Rub corn with softened red pepper butter and pull husk back up around the cob, tying strips of discarded husk or strings around each cob at intervals to hold leaves together. Submerge ears of corn in a sink full of cold water and soak for 25 minutes. You want the water to soak in between leaves, so corn will steam as it cooks on the barbecue.
3. Grill corn over medium-high heat for 15–20 minutes, until leaves are slightly blackened and kernels are steamy and tender. Serve with husk on, letting diners peel away charred leaves.
4. Alternatively, boil husked corn in a 4 to 1 solution of water to milk, with a little salt, for 3–4 minutes. The milk will help keep the corn's colour and sweetness. Drain corn and grill on barbecue for 4–5 minutes, until outside is marked but not charred.
5. Serve corn with additional red pepper butter for melting over cobs. Serves 8.

SECRET CREAMED TABER CORN

Although there's nothing like fresh corn on the cob, sometimes it's easier for your guests if you remove it from the cob first. In this combination of fresh corn cut from the cobs and simmered in rich cream, the secret ingredient is a splash of rye whisky.

4 or 5 cobs fresh Taber corn
2 tablespoons (25 mL) butter
1/4 cup (50 mL) minced onion
2 tablespoons (25 mL) maple syrup
3 tablespoons (45 mL) rye whisky
1/2 cup (125 mL) whipping cream
salt and white pepper

1. Cut kernels from cobs using a sharp knife. Stand cobs upright in a large bowl and cut from top to bottom. Use back of knife to scrape cobs, to make sure you get all kernels and milky juice. You should have about 4 cups (1 L) of corn kernels. It takes about 2 cobs of corn to make 1 cup (250 mL) of kernels.
2. Heat butter in a sauté pan and cook onion until tender. Add corn and sauté for a couple of minutes.
3. Stir in maple syrup, whisky, and cream. Bring to a boil and simmer until corn is creamy and thickened. Season with salt and white pepper to taste. Serves 4.

BARLEY RISOTTO WITH BUTTERNUT SQUASH AND ALBERTA GRANA

This is a real prairie version of a popular dish that's traditionally made with short-grained arborio rice. Barley is a wonderful wholegrain stand-in—fluffy, toothsome, and good for you.

2 cups (500 mL) pot barley
5 cups (1.25 L) good chicken stock or brown stock
2 tablespoons (25 mL) butter
1 tablespoon (15 mL) olive oil
1 onion, chopped
2 cloves garlic, minced
2 carrots, cut into small cubes
2 parsnips, cut into small cubes

1 cup (250 mL) butternut squash, seeded, peeled, and cubed
1/4 cup (50 mL) white wine
1/2 cup (125 mL) whipping cream
2 cups (500 mL) shredded Parmesan or Asiago cheese
salt and freshly ground black pepper
2 tablespoons (25 mL) chopped fresh parsley

1. Combine barley and stock in a large saucepan. Bring to a boil, cover, then reduce heat and simmer for 45–50 minutes, until grains are tender. Add more water if necessary.
2. In a sauté pan, heat butter with olive oil over medium-high heat and sauté onion and garlic until softened and beginning to brown, about 5 minutes. Add carrots, parsnips, and squash, and continue to cook until vegetables are caramelized. Deglaze with white wine, stirring up any browned bits from the bottom of the pan, and cook until half of liquid has evaporated.
3. Stir cooked barley into pan, add cream, and heat through. Sprinkle cheese over risotto, stirring until mixture is creamy. Add a little water if risotto seems too dry—it should be creamy, but not soupy. Season risotto with salt and pepper to taste, and garnish with parsley. Serve immediately with grilled meat, poultry, or game. Serves 8.

WILD RICE AND BARLEY PILAF

When you combine two prairie grains like wild rice and barley, the result is a nutty, chewy pilaf that melds well with hearty local mains like wild game and Alberta beef. If you have any leftover pilaf, add some sautéed carrots, leftover meat, and beef broth, and the soup's on!

2 large shallots, minced
2 cloves garlic, minced
2 tablespoons (25 mL) olive oil
2 cups (500 mL) sliced mushrooms
1/2 cup (125 mL) wild rice
1/2 cup (125 mL) pot barley
1/4 cup (50 mL) dry sherry
1 1/2 cups (375 mL) beef stock
1/2 teaspoon (2 mL) salt
1 1/2 cups (375 mL) water
2 tablespoons (25 mL) butter

1. Combine shallots, garlic, and olive oil in a saucepan and sauté over medium-high heat until golden. Stir in mushrooms and cook until they begin to give up their liquid.
2. Add rice and barley and stir well. Cook grains for 2 minutes, then add sherry and cook until it's absorbed. Stir in beef stock, salt, and water and bring to a boil.
3. Reduce heat and simmer, covered, for 45 minutes or until wild rice is split and barley is tender. Remove from heat and stir in butter. Serves 4.

PRAIRIE FRIED RYE

Rye is another prairie grain to serve in pilafs tossed with butter and herbs, or to add to soups and stews. This dish, using precooked rye berries, is reminiscent of fried rice.

1 cup (250 mL) rye berries
2 cups (500 mL) water
2 tablespoons (25 mL) butter
1 tablespoon (15 mL) canola oil
1 small onion, minced
2 stalks celery, chopped
1/2 cup (125 mL) sliced mushrooms
2 teaspoons (10 mL) soy sauce
3 tablespoons (45 mL) chopped fresh cilantro or Thai basil

1. Wash rye in a colander under running water to remove chaff and dust. Place grain in a saucepan, cover with plenty of cold water, and bring to a boil. Reduce heat, cover pan, and simmer for 40–50 minutes, or until grains begin to burst open. Drain in a colander and cool.
2. Meanwhile, melt butter with canola oil in a large nonstick sauté pan and sauté onion, celery, and mushrooms until tender, about 10 minutes in total.
3. Add cooked rye berries and soy sauce to pan, and toss to combine. Cook, stirring, over medium-high heat until grain is just beginning to brown. Stir in fresh herbs and serve immediately. Serves 4.

WILD RICE WITH CRANBERRIES AND CARAMELIZED ONIONS

Serve this combination of wild rice, tart dried cranberries, and sweet onions alongside grilled or roasted meats. You can also try it as a stuffing for duck, game birds, and chicken, or, without the fruit, inside a whole baked fish.

3 cups (750 mL) chicken stock
1 cup (250 mL) wild rice
3 tablespoons (45 mL) cold-pressed canola oil or extra-virgin olive oil
1 large white or purple onion, sliced thinly
2 teaspoons (10 mL) granulated sugar
1 teaspoon (5 mL) chopped fresh thyme leaves
1/2 cup (125 mL) dried cranberries
freshly ground black pepper

1. Bring chicken stock to a boil. Add wild rice. Cover pan, reduce heat to low, and simmer for 45–60 minutes, until rice is chewy but tender and all stock has been absorbed.
2. Meanwhile, heat oil and sauté onion over medium heat until tender. Sprinkle with sugar and thyme and reduce heat to low. Continue to cook until onion is brown and caramelized, about 45 minutes longer.
3. Stir cranberries into onion and cook for 5 minutes to soften. Stir into rice and heat through. Season with black pepper to taste. Serves 4.

Breads and Baking

BREAD BASKET OF THE WORLD

It's 5 AM and a handful of young bakers are halfway through their daily shift. They have already milled the grain, proofed the yeast, and mixed the dough for several different breads. Now they are up to their ball caps in sugar and cinnamon, rolling a gigantic whole-wheat cinnamon roll across a big baking table. The dough is patted and stretched, drizzled with a gallon of melted butter, and sprinkled with cinnamon sugar before two of them can begin the tandem task of rolling the sugary snake. It will be sliced, baked, and on the shelf in their bakery before anyone else in this town is even thinking about breakfast.

This is the way it's done early every morning at Prairie Mill bakery in Calgary, where co-owner John Juurlink works alongside his staff, turning out hearty, whole-grained breads the old-fash-

John Juurlink

ioned way. There is a big Hobart mixer and a commercial bread oven in this small city bakery, but the goal here is to keep the bread as natural as possible, as Juurlink says, "Made the way it used to be, fresh from the field to the table."

Prairie Mill Bread Co. is unique in that it mills its own grains on site—mainly organic hard spring wheat—into stone-ground flour for a variety of breads and pastries. The best Canadian wheat, with 14 to 16 percent protein level, makes the best bread, and at Prairie Mill Bread Co. they take time to make their bread from scratch, never relying on the mixes or frozen bread doughs that are so common in today's baking business. Starting with a sponge, they use a slow-rise process to create heavy, dense loaves of natural sourdough, honey whole-wheat, and nine-grain bread, and huge, hearty

cinnamon buns. Their Mediterranean bread is shot with chunky black olives; the rye is heavy and rustic; the banana bread an inky loaf that's often on the bread board in the front of the bakery so customers can hack off a slice to eat while they shop. The bakers at Prairie Mill are offering Albertans the kind of bread that their grandparents grew up eating. It's wholegrain bread that you can really get your teeth into, something entirely different from today's ubiquitous loaves of white, commercial bread.

Dwayne and Doreen Smith are at the other end of that new bakery food chain. On a small family farm in southern Alberta, the Smiths have created Grainworks, an organic grain company devoted to growing and distributing organic grains, flours, seeds, and beans. From their own certified organic wheat, rye, triticale, and barley, to low-gluten grains like spelt, buckwheat, quinoa, amaranth, and teff, Grainworks ships 110 different grains under their own label to health food stores, gourmet groceries, and chefs around the province.

There is Grainworks garbanzo bean flour, quinoa flour, light and dark buckwheat, and stone-ground blue cornmeal, piled in brown paper bags in a steel storage building next to their farm-based organic mill. Set in an old seed-cleaning plant, in a miniature wooden grain elevator, their specially-designed Grainworks Mighty Fine Mill grinds whole grains into fine, wholegrain flour that makes wholegrain breads lighter than traditional stone-ground flours. Unlike commercial whole-wheat flour, white flour with the bran mixed back in, this flour is 100 percent wholegrain, with even the delicate germ intact.

Wheat makes up nearly 90 percent of all grain consumed in Canada. Most of that grain turns up in white flour, used to make bread, pasta, and breakfast cereal. There are two main types of wheat grown on the prairies, hard red spring wheat and soft winter wheat. Spring wheat, planted in the spring and harvested in the fall, has high levels of gluten, a gluey protein that helps bread hold its structure as it rises. This is why Canadian wheat is known all over the world as the best for bread and quality pasta. Soft winter wheat, planted in winter for late summer harvest, is lower in gluten and is favoured for pastry and cake flours.

Although grain, mainly wheat, remains Alberta's primary crop and a leading export, organic grain is still a very small part of the Alberta grain industry. Of the 58,000 grain farmers in Alberta, only about 250 are growing organically. Over the last fourteen years, the Smiths have made Grainworks the largest organic grain wholesaler in western Canada, shipping 100,000 pounds of dried products every month to customers from Calgary to California. Smith says there is growing interest in organic products, and sales of organic foods continue to grow across the country at a rate of about 30 percent per year.

While you won't likely detect a flavour difference in organic grains, pulses, and seeds, consumers choose them for other reasons. Dwayne Smith, an organic activist and the first president of the Canadian Organic Advisory Board, says people are concerned about reducing pesticides in the environment and keeping genetically modified organisms (GMO) off their plates. Most of the country's canola crop is being grown from GMO seed and by 2002, he expects farmers to begin harvesting the first GM wheat. It's risky to farm grain organically in Alberta, as the Smiths learned through trials and some costly errors that made survival difficult in the early years. Finally, experiments with crop rotation, and underseeding with clover to smother weeds and fix nitrogen in the soil, have helped the Smiths become competitive with their non-organic neighbours. Smith expects the price for conventional grains to fall as more consumers demand organic and GMO-free foods, making his products easier to market.

Back in Calgary, chefs like Myra Matson are looking for the best local products for their brand of high-end, regional Alberta cuisine. Matson, the former pastry chef at Calgary's River Café, says any foods and flavours are fair game in her creative breads. Like a soup cook, she uses yesterday's cooked wheat berries, wild rice, and roasted vegetables to augment her hearty breads. "I don't like to follow recipes," she says, kneading a new combination together. "This is mixed with onion, wild rice, and lentil hummus. Whatever we have—beets and apples or chutney—I'll throw anything into my bread."

Matson is especially fond of sourdoughs, creating bread with the wild yeasts found on fresh organic fruits and vegetables. On this day, she checks her apple-based starter, made by fermenting organic apples and apple juice and combining the resulting liquid with equal parts of organic white flour and rye flour. She says the starter will sit for a couple of days at room temperature to develop, then will be refrigerated and used instead of conventional yeast in breads—about 1 cup (250 mL) of starter for 4 cups (1 L) of water in a recipe.

With organic wheats and designer flours to play with, there's no telling where these creative bakers and chefs will take the idea of regional Alberta baking. What's already certain, it's taken your morning toast choices way beyond "Will that be white or whole-wheat?"

PRAIRIE FLAX BREAD

This recipe comes from Highwood Crossing Farm and is designed for bread machines. Use their nutty cold-pressed canola oil and whole flax seed for a healthy wholegrain bread.

1 egg
1 1/4 cups (300 mL) water
2 tablespoons (25 mL) honey
2 tablespoons (25 mL) organic cold-pressed canola oil
2 cups (500 mL) all-purpose bread flour
1/2 cup (125 mL) dark rye flour
1/2 cup (125 mL) whole-wheat flour
1 1/2 teaspoons (7 mL) salt
1/3 cup (75 mL) organic whole flax seed
2 tablespoons (25 mL) sunflower seeds
1 tablespoon (15 mL) poppy seeds
1 tablespoon (15 mL) sesame seeds

2 teaspoons (10 mL) fast-rising instant yeast

1. Measure ingredients and place in bread machine in order recommended by manufacturer.
2. Use 'Whole Wheat Rapid Cycle' or 'Large Light Cycle' depending on machine type. Makes 1 loaf.

ICELANDIC BROWN BREAD

Icelandic immigrants settled in central Alberta around Markerville, home of the famed Icelandic poet Stephan Stephannson. John Juurlink of Prairie Mill Bread Co. shared this recipe for hearty Icelandic-style bread. If you like a sweeter brown bread, add 1/2 cup (125 mL) of brown sugar with the molasses.

2 tablespoons (25 mL) fresh yeast, or 1 package
   (1 tablespoon/ 15 mL) dry yeast
1/2 cup (125 mL) molasses
1/2 cup (125 mL) warm (95°F/35°C) water
3 cups (750 mL) hot (110°F/45°C) water
4 cups (1 L) stone-ground whole-wheat flour
1 1/2 tablespoons (20 mL) salt
3–4 cups (750 mL–1 L) unbleached all-purpose flour

1. In a large bowl, combine fresh or dry yeast with molasses and warm water. Set aside for 10 minutes to activate the yeast.
2. Stir in the hot water and whole-wheat flour. Let stand in a warm place for 30 minutes. This allows the gluten to develop and enhances the whole-wheat flavour of the bread.
3. Add salt and gradually mix in all-purpose flour. The dough should be soft but not too wet. Cover and let bread proof for 1 hour at room temperature. This is considered a dry proof.
4. Divide dough into two or three pieces and form into large, round peasant loaves or smaller oval loaves for loaf pans. Place on oiled pans, cover, and leave in a warm place to rise again, for about 45 minutes. Bake loaves in a preheated oven at 350°F (180°C) for 40–45 minutes, until nicely browned. Makes 2 or 3 loaves.

THE BARLEY SANDWICH

Another classic use of prairie grains is booze, especially Canadian rye whisky and beer.

Alberta two-row barley is the basis of the malting barley that goes into excellent local beers like those made at Big Rock Brewery. Big Rock and other smaller breweries, such as Alley Kat in Edmonton and Wild Rose in Calgary, have been at the forefront of the microbrewing business in western Canada. Big Rock's Traditional Ale has been a benchmark brew for Bernd Pieper, the company's longtime brewmaster. Malts from a malting plant in Alix, Alberta, give the beer its distinctive flavour. No adjuncts are used in these kinds of microbrewed, unpasteurized beers, which are brewed with 100 percent barley, water, hops, yeast, and nothing else. Larger breweries may use other grains, from rice to corn, in the brewing process, as well as sugars, additives, colourings, and chemical preservatives.

A 12-ounce serving (355 mL) of Big Rock Ale contains 145 calories, 2.24 g of protein, 12.7 g of carbohydrate, and no cholesterol or fat. Dark unpasteurized beer is high in B vitamins, antioxidants, and flavinoids that make blood platelets less sticky. So a barley sandwich a day may be just what the doctor ordered!

HARVEST BREAD

Here's Myra Matson's recipe for the grainy harvest bread flavoured with golden acorn squash and seeds that she created for Calgary's River Café.

3 packages dry yeast
4 cups (1 L) warm water
1/4 cup (50 mL) canola oil
1/2 cup (125 mL) buckwheat honey
2 cups (500 mL) roasted acorn squash, puréed
3 tablespoons (45 mL) salt
2 teaspoons (10 mL) ground cinnamon
1/2 teaspoon (2 mL) ground nutmeg
2 teaspoons (10 mL) freshly grated ginger root
1 cup (250 mL) pumpkin seeds
1/4 cup (50 mL) sunflower seeds
2 tablespoons (25 mL) sesame seeds
1/2 cup (125 mL) dried cranberries
1/2 cup (125 mL) cooked wild rice
1/2 cup (125 mL) chopped fresh sage
8 1/4 cups (2 L) unbleached all-purpose flour
5 cups (1.25 L) whole-wheat flour
1 egg beaten with 2 tablespoons (25 mL) water

1. In a large bread bowl, dissolve yeast in warm water. Stir in canola oil, honey, and squash purée. Add salt, cinnamon, nutmeg, and ginger.
2. Mix in pumpkin, sunflower, and sesame seeds, dried cranberries, and cooked wild rice. Stir in sage.
3. Add all-purpose and whole-wheat flour gradually, mixing with a wooden spoon and then with your hands as dough stiffens. Knead dough for at least 10 minutes, until smooth, elastic, and satiny.
4. Place dough in a big oiled bowl and cover. Set in a warm place and let rise until doubled in bulk. Punch dough down and shape into five long or round loaves.
5. Set loaves on a baking sheet sprinkled with cornmeal, cover, and let them rise again until doubled.
6. Brush tops of loaves with a wash of egg and water, and score lightly with a very sharp knife. Sprinkle tops of loaves with extra pumpkin seeds to decorate.
7. Bake in a preheated 350°F (180°C) oven for approximately 35–40 minutes, until loaves are golden brown and sound hollow when tapped. Makes 5 dinner-size loaves.

Myra Matson

BRAIDED EASTER BREAD (UKRAINIAN PASKA)

This is a traditional bread served at Easter dinner in Ukrainian homes. The beautiful braided loaves are impressive for a brunch at any time of the year.

6 eggs, beaten
1/2 cup (125 mL) granulated sugar
1 teaspoon (5 mL) salt
3 cups (750 mL) lukewarm water
1/2 cup (125 mL) butter, melted
1/2 cup (125 mL) canola oil
13–14 cups (3–3.5 L) unbleached all-purpose flour

Proofing Mix
1 1/2 cups (375 mL) warm water
1 teaspoon (5 mL) granulated sugar
1 1/2 tablespoons (20 mL) yeast

1. Combine 1 1/2 cups (375 mL) warm water, 1 teaspoon (5 mL) sugar, and yeast and set aside in a warm place to proof for 10 minutes.
2. In a large bowl, combine eggs, sugar, salt, 3 cups (750 mL) water, butter, and canola oil with softened yeast. Stir in flour and knead until smooth and elastic—a bit stiffer than regular bread dough.
3. Cover and let rise in a warm place until doubled. Punch down and let rise again. Punch down and divide dough into thirds or quarters, to make three or four loaves.
4. Divide each piece in half and press one half into the bottom of a 9-inch (2.0 L) greased round cake pan. Take remaining half of dough and divide in half again. From one of the pieces, roll two long ropes, each about 36 inches (90 cm) long. Entwine pieces to make a rope, and encircle it around the outside edges of the pan, joining ends.
5. Divide remaining piece of dough into quarters and roll into 8-inch (20 cm) ropes. Entwine to make two twisted ropes. Cross ropes over in middle of pan, then unravel ends slightly and curl each end into centre. Repeat with remaining loaves.
6. Let loaves rise until doubled in bulk. Glaze carefully with a mixture of beaten egg and water. Bake loaves in preheated 350°F (180°C) oven for 15 minutes, then reduce heat to 325°F (160°C) and bake for 40 minutes longer. Makes 4 loaves.

MULTI-GRAIN CEREAL BREAD

Sunny Boy or Red River cereals are Canadian classics—mixed-grain hot cereals that have long been part of any hearty prairie breakfast. These mixtures are also the basis for hearty wholegrain breads like this one.

2 1/2 cups (625 mL) milk
1 cup (250 mL) wheat germ
1 cup (250 mL) Sunny Boy or Red River cereal
2 tablespoons (25 mL) instant yeast
3 cups (750 mL) whole-wheat flour, divided
1/2 cup (125 mL) molasses
1/2 cup (125 mL) canola oil
1/2 cup (125 mL) unsalted sunflower or sesame seeds
1 1/2 cups (375 mL) warm water
2 teaspoons (10 mL) salt
2 tablespoons (25 mL) brown sugar
5 cups (1.25 L) all-purpose flour

1. Heat milk in a saucepan over medium heat until bubbles begin to appear around edges. Remove from heat. Pour scalded milk over wheat germ and cereal in large mixing bowl to soften. Set aside to cool until just warm.
2. In another large bowl, mix yeast with 2 cups (500 mL) of whole-wheat flour. Stir in cooled cereal mixture, molasses, canola oil, sunflower or sesame seeds, warm water, salt, and brown sugar. Beat in remaining whole-wheat flour, then add all-purpose flour until it forms a soft but sticky dough.
3. Turn out onto a floured surface, let rest for 5 minutes, then begin kneading. Add more flour until dough is smooth and silky, but be cautious and add flour slowly. The bran in the mixture can suddenly absorb liquid and you may be left with dough that is too dry.
4. Form into three large loaves and let rise in greased bread pans, covered, until doubled, about 45 minutes. Bake in a preheated 375°F (190°C) oven for 20 minutes. Reduce heat to 350°F (180°C) and bake 20–25 minutes longer. Makes 3 loaves.

CHEDDAR CHEESE BISCUITS

Serve these cheese biscuits with soup, stews, chili, or brunches. For variety, use other cheeses, like Gouda, Havarti, or even blue cheese.

4 cups (1 L) all-purpose flour
2 tablespoons (25 mL) baking powder
1 tablespoon (15 mL) granulated sugar
1/2 teaspoon (2 mL) salt
1 teaspoon (5 mL) dry mustard
pinch of cayenne pepper
3/4 cup (175 mL) cold butter
2 cups (500 mL) grated Cheddar cheese
4 egg yolks
1 whole egg
2/3 cup (150 mL) milk
1 egg beaten with 2 tablespoons (25 mL) water

1. Combine dry ingredients in a large bowl. Cut in butter using a pastry blender or a fork to form coarse crumbs. Stir in cheese. Beat egg yolks, egg, and milk together and quickly add to dry ingredients. Do not overmix. The secret to fluffy biscuits is not overworking dough or heating it with your hands.
2. Roll or pat dough about 1-inch (2.5 cm) thick on a floured surface. For wedges, form dough into two 10-inch (25 cm) circles and cut each into eight wedges. You can also cut these biscuits into tiny squares or traditional rounds using a 3-inch (8 cm) cookie cutter or a floured water glass.
3. Place biscuits slightly apart on a baking sheet. Brush tops with a wash of beaten egg, mixed with a little water.
4. Bake biscuits in a preheated 400°F (200°C) oven for about 15–20 minutes, until golden brown. Makes 16 large biscuits.

CORN STICKS

I have a great cast-iron baking pan that makes this simple cornbread into cob-shaped sticks. You can use a heavy cast-iron muffin pan instead, or bake it in an 8-inch (1.5 L) square pan. If you bake in cast-iron, preheating the pan gives your cornbread a lovely golden crust.

1 cup (250 mL) cornmeal
1/2 cup (125 mL) all-purpose flour
1 teaspoon (5 mL) granulated sugar
2 teaspoons (10 mL) baking powder
1/4 teaspoon (1 mL) baking soda
1/2 teaspoon (2 mL) salt
1/4 cup (50 mL) butter, melted
1 egg, beaten
3/4 cup (175 mL) buttermilk
1/2 cup (125 mL) whipping cream

1. Preheat oven to 450°F (230°C) and brush heavy cornstick pan or muffin pan with oil. If using a cast-iron pan, preheat it in the oven for 10 minutes.
2. To make batter, combine cornmeal, flour, sugar, baking powder, baking soda, and salt. Whisk together butter, egg, buttermilk, and cream. Stir quickly into batter. Don't overmix.
3. Remove hot baking pan from oven and spoon batter in, filling three-quarters full. Bake for 15 minutes, until golden and firm. Turn out of pans immediately and serve warm. Makes 12 cornsticks or small muffins.

> **TIP**
> For more savoury and substantial cornsticks to serve with chili, add 1/4 cup (50 mL) cooked corn kernels and 1 or 2 minced jalapeño peppers to batter. Alternatively, flavour the cornsticks with 1/2 cup (125 mL) grated Jalapeño Jack cheese.

BUTTERMILK HERB AND SEED BREAD

This is a variation of a recipe that my sister Deanna passed on to me many years ago. You can make it without herbs or use your favourites fresh from the garden.

3 cups (750 mL) whole-wheat flour
1 cup (250 mL) unbleached all-purpose flour
2 teaspoons (10 mL) baking soda
1/2 teaspoon (2 mL) salt
1/2 cup (125 mL) mixed seeds and nuts (raw sunflower seeds, sesame seeds, poppy seeds, flax, ground walnuts, or others)
3–4 tablespoons (45–50 mL) chopped fresh herbs (thyme, rosemary, oregano, dill, or others)
1 tablespoon (15 mL) honey or corn syrup
2 cups (500 mL) buttermilk or low-fat plain yogurt
extra seeds, oat bran, or wheat germ for topping

1. In a large bowl, combine whole-wheat and all-purpose flours with baking soda, salt, seeds, and herbs.
2. Whisk together honey or syrup with buttermilk or yogurt. Add to dry ingredients and mix until just moistened.
3. Pour batter into a greased loaf pan and sprinkle top with additional seeds or wheat germ.
4. Bake in preheated 350°F (180°C) oven for 45–55 minutes, until a toothpick inserted in the centre comes out clean. Turn bread out on a rack to cool. Serve warm. Makes 1 large loaf.

ALBERTA GRAINS

There are many different grains that can be used in hearty breads, soups, stews, and pilafs. Here is a look at some whole grains and their uses:

AMARANTH: Tiny amaranth seeds, from the red-root pigweed family, have little or no gluten but the highest level of protein of all grains, and are also high in calcium and lysine. Grown by the Aztecs of Central America more than five hundred years ago, amaranth has been rediscovered and dubbed "new" in the food world. Also, the leaves can be eaten like spinach.

BARLEY: Alberta farmers grow about 6 million tonnes of barley every year (as much as is grown in the entire United States). Barley is the whole grain that traditionally is used for hearty beef soups, but today's chefs like to use barley for pilafs and risottos, too. Cooking barley in stock adds flavour; use three parts liquid to one part barley. You can buy pearl barley, pot barley, and hulled, wholegrain barley. Pearl barley is the most highly processed and hulled barley the least processed product. Pearl barley cooks a little faster than pot barley, which takes about 40 minutes. Hulled barley is the kind of wholegrain barley used to feed cattle. It can take twice as long to cook as pot barley and should always be soaked overnight before cooking. If you presoak pearl or pot barley, it's extra fluffy and cooks in 15 minutes. Like oats, barley contains soluble and insoluble fibres that can reduce cholesterol. Barley flour, like that milled by the Hamilton family near Olds, is low in gluten and high in fibre, and can be substituted for wheat flours in muffins, cookies, pancakes, and quick breads. For yeast breads, you can substitute up to one-quarter of the wheat flour with barley flour with good results.

BUCKWHEAT: Originating in Siberia, buckwheat is not a true grain, but its triangular seeds have been used in Eastern European cuisine for centuries. Buckwheat flour makes great pancakes and breads, and whole buckwheat groats can be purchased raw or toasted. To toast raw buckwheat, toss the raw groats with beaten egg (to keep the grains separate once cooked) and toast in a dry, hot pan. Buckwheat flour is also used in Japanese soba noodles.

RUSTIC WHITE BREAD

This is a rustic, French-style peasant bread—a round, golden brown loaf of heavy white bread. The sponge starter, which works overnight before you make your bread, gives the loaf a wonderful complex flavour that you don't get with faster methods.

Sponge Starter
1 teaspoon (5 mL) active dry yeast
1 teaspoon (5 mL) honey or granulated sugar
1/2 cup (125 mL) warm water
1/2 cup (125 mL) milk, room temperature
1 cup (250 mL) unbleached all-purpose flour

Dough
1 cup (250 mL) room temperature water, divided
1 teaspoon (5 mL) yeast
3–4 cups (1.5–2 L) unbleached all-purpose flour
1 tablespoon (15 mL) salt

1. For sponge starter, stir yeast and honey or sugar into warm water and let stand about 10 minutes to proof. When yeast begins to foam, stir in milk and flour and beat until smooth. Cover with plastic wrap and let stand at room temperature until bubbly—at least 5–6 hours. When the mixture has risen up in the bowl, then fallen, it is ready.

2. Proof remaining yeast in 1/4 cup (50 mL) room temperature water. Add this to sponge starter with remaining water and mix well in a large bowl.

3. Combine flour and salt and add, 1 cup (250 mL) at a time, to the starter mixture, beating with a wooden spoon very well between each addition. When it's too stiff to mix by hand, turn out onto a well-floured surface and let rest 5 minutes. Knead in more flour until dough is smooth and satiny. This will take about 5–10 minutes of kneading.

4. Place dough in a well-oiled bowl, turning to coat ball of dough with oil. Cover with plastic wrap and let rise for 2 hours or until doubled in bulk. Punch it down.

5. Cut dough in half and shape each piece into a large round or oblong loaf. Place loaves on a heavy baking sheet, lined with parchment. Lightly sprinkle flour over loaves and let them rise, covered, for 1 hour, until doubled again.

6. Using a sharp knife or razor blade, slash loaves three times across top. Bake in preheated oven at 400°F (200°C) for 45 minutes, until they are golden and sound hollow when tapped on bottom. Cool loaves on wire racks. Makes 2 large loaves.

WALNUT ROLL

My grandma used to make two kinds of rolled sweet breads—one filled with poppy seeds, the other with a sweet ground walnut filling. She rolled the dough into rectangles and filled them like jelly rolls, creating long loaves swirled with sweet fillings. I make them into long, narrower rolls coiled into big round breads, or layered in a big bread pan.

Dough
1 package (1 tablespoon/15 mL) dry yeast
1/4 cup (50 mL) warm water mixed with 1 teaspoon
 (5 mL) granulated sugar
1 cup (250 mL) milk
1/4 cup (50 mL) granulated sugar
1/3 cup (75 mL) butter
1 egg plus 1 egg yolk, beaten
1/4 teaspoon (1 mL) salt
3 1/2–4 cups (875 mL–1 L) unbleached all-purpose flour
1 egg beaten with 2 tablespoons (25 mL) water

Filling
4 cups (1 L) walnut halves or pieces
1 cup (250 mL) brown sugar
1/2 cup (125 mL) whipping cream
2 eggs
2 teaspoons (10 mL) vanilla extract
1/4 cup (50 mL) butter, softened

1. Sprinkle yeast over warm sugar water and let stand 10 minutes to proof. In a small saucepan, scald milk—bring it just to a simmer and remove from heat—then stir in sugar and butter. Stir until butter is melted. When cool, add beaten egg and egg yolk, salt, and dissolved yeast.
2. Put 3 1/2 cups (875 mL) of flour into a food processor (or large bowl) and add milk mixture, processing or mixing until dough forms a ball. If dough is too wet, add a little more flour. The dough should be soft, not sticky.
3. Set dough in a greased bowl in a warm spot, cover with a clean towel and let rise for an hour, until doubled. Punch dough down and roll (or wrap well and refrigerate overnight and roll the next day).
4. To make filling, grind walnuts in a food processor, then add remaining ingredients. Process to combine well.

BULGAR: Bulgar is a processed wheat product. The whole grains are cracked, steamed, and then dried and broken up. The result is a product that cooks almost instantly; fine-grind bulgar only needs to be soaked to be rehydrated. Although cracked wheat looks like bulgar, it is simply ground raw wheat, with the germ removed, and must be cooked.

Rehydrated bulgar is the perfect base for grain salads and can be added to hamburgers and meat loaves. I prefer a coarse-grained product for salads and pilafs.

CORN: When dried and ground, corn makes a prairie staple, cornmeal. While polenta (made from cornmeal) has just recently become trendy, cornbread, mush, and mamaliga have been on the menu in Alberta for a long time. Use cornmeal in yeast breads, soda breads, pancakes, and to thicken stews. Cooked with 6 cups (1.5 L) of water, salt, and butter, 1 cup (250 mL) of cornmeal is a soft, creamy side dish; with 4 cups (1 L) of water, it makes a thick mass that solidifies when cool, and can be shaped, cut, fried, or grilled.

FLAX: Flax seed contains lignans and high levels of Omega-3 fatty acids, the essential fatty acids found in fish oils that reduce the risk of heart disease and some cancers. Whole flax seed is not digestible, so some prairie companies sell milled flax, breaking the hard little seeds open, and coldpressed flax oil. You can also "mill"  your own flax seed by grinding it in a coffee grinder or blender. Once broken, the seed is highly perishable as the oils quickly oxidize and become rancid. Purchase milled flax seed in light-proof vacuum packages that have been refrigerated for storage. Once open, store oils and milled flax seed in the refrigerator or freeze. Milled flax has a nutty, fishy flavour and can be used as a topping for cereal or in salads, breads, meat loaves, muffins, and pancakes. Milled or ground flax seed is also high in soluble fibre or mucilage, which reduces the absorption of cholesterol from foods and stabilizes blood sugars.

MILLET: Millet originated in central Asia and came to Europe during the Middle Ages. Once only sold for bird seed, millet is a popular whole grain for use in grainy breads and pilafs. Cook it with twice as much water or broth for about 20 minutes.

Oats: Oats are the latest in the functional foods category, the first to be approved for labelling health claims. Studies show that the soluble fibre found in wholegrain oats, rolled oats, oatmeal, and oat bran can lower cholesterol levels and reduce heart disease. Rolled oats are the basis for hot oatmeal cereal and muesli and can be incorporated into breads, meat loaves, and muffins, and even used for coating fish or chicken before frying.

Quinoa: Quinoa (pronounced *keen*-wah) is an ancient grain, first grown by the Incas. Primarily a South American crop, quinoa is being grown by the Smillie family at their Artesian Acres farm in central Alberta. It is considered one of the world's most perfect foods, high in protein and amino acids. Quinoa seeds have a natural bitter coating and should be rinsed well under running water before cooking. Try combining quinoa and rice in pilaf recipes.

Rye: Rye berries add contrasting colour and chewiness to grain pilafs and combine well with brown rice. Rye can take 1 1/2–2 hours to cook; pressure cooking reduces the cooking time to about 30 minutes.

Spelt: Spelt is similar to wheat, but longer, softer, and containing a different type of fibre that is easier to digest. While spelt contains some gluten, and is therefore not recognized as an option by those who suffer from celiac disease, it is used as an alternative to wheat. Kamut is a trademark for a type of Polish wheat with elongated grains about twice the length of regular wheat or spelt grains. Kamut is grown and marketed here under the Artesian Acres brand. These and other wheats can be soaked overnight before cooking with about four times as much liquid. To partially cook before adding to soups and stews, simmer for 15 minutes. To fully cook for salads, boil for 1 hour or pressure cook for 30–40 minutes.

Teff: An African grain, teff is most often seen in the injera flat bread that is the basis of Ethiopian cuisine.

Triticale: A cross between Durham wheat and rye, triticale was developed in Scotland in the late 1800s. Higher in protein than either wheat or rye, it's available whole, flaked, and as flour. Cook whole

5. Divide dough in half and roll out each piece on a floured surface. Dough should be quite thin—each piece should make a rectangle of about 12 x 24 inches (30 x 60 cm). Divide walnut filling evenly and spread over two pieces of dough. From long side, start rolling a tight jelly roll. You'll have two rolled "snakes," each about 24 inches (60 cm) long. Pull and stretch them until they are longer and thinner, about 40 inches (102 cm) long.

6. Form rolls into coils on a baking sheet or cut them into 8-inch (20-cm) lengths and arrange in 8 x 4-inch (1.5 L) greased bread pans, two rolls on the bottom and three on top. Press down. Cover and allow loaves to rise again, about 45 minutes longer.

7. Brush loaves with a little beaten egg and water to glaze the tops. Bake in preheated oven at 375°F (190°C) for 35–40 minutes, until nicely browned. Remove loaves from pans and cool well before slicing. Makes 2 loaves.

TIP

To make more traditional walnut rolls, roll dough into two 8 x 15-inch (20 x 38 cm) rectangles, spread with filling, and roll into large oval loaves, pinching ends to seal. Place loaves on an oiled baking sheet, glaze with egg and water mixture, and bake in a preheated oven at 350°F (180°C) for 30–40 minutes, until golden.

This dough can also be used to make cinnamon rolls. Roll dough into two large rectangles, each about 10 x 18 inches (25 x 46 cm). Drizzle each with 1/4 cup (50 mL) melted butter, and sprinkle heavily with a mixture of brown sugar and cinnamon. Roll up, jelly roll style, slice into twelve 1 1/2-inch (4 cm) disks, and set on a baking pan, covered, to rise for 45 minutes. Bake rolls in preheated 375°F (190°C) oven for 20–25 minutes.

Orange Molasses Spice Bread

Low in fat with a crunchy texture from the cornmeal, this unusually spiced quick bread is not very sweet, but makes a great tea treat or breakfast toast.

1 1/4 cups (300 mL) each: all-purpose and whole-wheat flour
1/2 cup (125 mL) cornmeal
2 teaspoons (10 mL) baking powder
1 small orange, zest grated and flesh chopped
1/4 cup (50 mL) brown sugar
1 teaspoon (5 mL) aniseed, crushed
1/4 teaspoon (1 mL) each: ground cardamom and nutmeg
3/4 teaspoon (4 mL) ground coriander
3/4 teaspoon (4 mL) salt
1/2 teaspoon (2 mL) baking soda
1 1/3 cups (325 mL) buttermilk

1/4 cup (50 mL) molasses
3 tablespoons (45 mL) canola oil
1 egg

1. Combine flours, cornmeal, baking powder, orange zest, brown sugar, spices, salt, and baking soda in a large bowl.
2. In another bowl, whisk together the buttermilk, molasses, and canola oil, and egg. Stir in the chopped orange. Add wet ingredients to dry ingredients and stir until just blended. Don't overmix.
3. Spoon batter into a greased 9 x 5-inch (2 L) loaf pan and smooth top. Bake in a preheated oven at 350° (180°C) for 50–60 minutes, until springy to the touch and golden brown. Cool in pan for 10 minutes, then turn bread out onto a rack to finish cooling. Makes 1 loaf.

BLACKFOOT FRY BREAD

Bannock, or fry bread, is classic Native fare. It's just the thing to serve alongside a bison stew or other braised game dishes.

1 cup (250 mL) each: all-purpose and whole-wheat flour
1 tablespoon (15 mL) baking powder
2 pinches of salt
3/4–1 cup (175–250 mL) warm water, enough to make a soft dough
vegetable shortening or oil

1. Mix all dry ingredients and water together with your hands to make a soft dough.
2. Form dough into egg-sized balls, then stretch and flatten with your hands into thin, 6-inch (15 cm) rounds.
3. Fry in about 1 inch (2.5 cm) hot vegetable shortening or oil in a cast-iron frying pan, until golden on both sides. Serve with stew, or sprinkle with icing sugar and spread with jam for a snack. Serves 4.

berries with three to four times as much water for 1 hour, and serve it in soups, salads, or pilafs.

WHEAT: Wholegrain wheat is also known as wheat berries and is the perfect grain to serve in a salad or pilaf. To cook wheat berries, cover the grain in three to four times as much boiling water or stock and simmer, covered, for 60 minutes. To speed up the cooking process to about 35 minutes, use a pressure cooker.

WILD RICE: Wild rice is not a grain, but the seed of an aquatic grass that grows in northern lakes. Natives long harvested the rice from the wilds of northern Alberta, Saskatchewan, and Manitoba by pulling the ripening seed heads into their canoes and shaking the long, black seeds free. Today, wild rice is grown commercially, planted in shallow water, and harvested with special air boats that skim the water and thrash the seeds from the plants into big scoops with rotating paddles. Wild rice should be simmered in three to four times its volume of water or broth for 45 minutes to 1 hour, until the grains soften and burst.

MOUNTAIN MUESLI WITH CPR STRAWBERRIES

When real strawberries were few and far between on the prairies, the only fruit that came west on the train were portable prunes, what cowboys called "CPR strawberries." They're a welcome addition to this healthy dish that you can make on Sundays and keep in the refrigerator for breakfasts all week.

1 1/2 cups (375 mL) large flake rolled oats (not instant)
1 1/2 cups (375 mL) water
2 cups (500 mL) shredded unpeeled apple, about 2 apples
1 1/2 cups (375 mL) pitted prunes, chopped
2 tablespoons (25 mL) each: honey and fresh lemon juice
1/2 teaspoon (2 mL) ground cinnamon
chopped fresh fruit (bananas, melons, pineapple, grapes, or others)
fat-free plain yogurt
chopped nuts

1. Combine oats, water, apples, prunes, honey, lemon juice, and cinnamon. Stir well and refrigerate overnight, covered.
2. In the morning, spoon some muesli in a bowl, stir in some yogurt and fresh fruit, and serve sprinkled with nuts. Makes about 8 servings.

BANANA BREAD

Here is another recipe using healthy flax seed and organic canola oil from Highwood Crossing Farm. Use bananas if you have them, or substitute pumpkin purée or applesauce in this substantial and healthy fruit bread. The secret to a really dark banana bread is super-ripe bananas—freeze them to save for this classic.

1/2 cup (125 mL) brown sugar
1/2 cup (125 mL) buttermilk
1 large egg
3 tablespoons (45 mL) organic cold-pressed canola oil,
   or regular canola oil
3/4 cup (175 mL) all-purpose flour
1/2 cup (125 mL) whole-wheat or rye flour
3/4 cup (175 mL) ground flax seed
1 teaspoon (5 mL) baking powder
1 teaspoon (5 mL) baking soda
1 cup (250 mL) mashed banana, pumpkin purée, or applesauce

1. In a large bowl, combine brown sugar, buttermilk, egg, and canola oil and whisk until smooth.
2. In another bowl, combine all-purpose flour, whole-wheat or rye flour, ground flax seed, baking powder, and baking soda. Add to wet ingredients and stir just to mix. Add bananas and blend together quickly. Do not overmix.
3. Oil and flour an 8-inch (1.5 L) loaf pan. Pour in batter and bake in a preheated oven at 350°F (180°C) for 40–50 minutes, until a toothpick inserted in centre of loaf comes out clean. Turn loaf out of pan onto a rack to cool. Makes 1 loaf.

SAVOURY POTATO AND CHEESE BISCUITS

You can cut the fat in these tender baking-powder biscuits by using plain mashed potatoes in the mix.

1 1/2 cups (375 mL) all-purpose flour
2 teaspoons (10 mL) baking powder
1/2 teaspoon (2 mL) salt
2 tablespoons (25 mL) unsalted cold butter, chopped
2/3 cup (150 mL) mashed potatoes
2 green onions, minced
1/4 cup (50 mL) sharp Cheddar cheese, grated
1/4 cup (50 mL) skim milk

1. Combine flour, baking powder, and salt. Add butter and cut in with a pastry blender to form coarse crumbs. Mix in mashed potatoes, green onions, cheese, and enough skim milk to form a soft dough.
2. Turn out onto a floured surface and knead lightly. Roll or pat out to a 1/2-inch (1.5 cm) thickness. Place biscuits on a baking sheet sprayed with nonstick cooking spray or lined with parchment.
3. Bake in a preheated oven at 425°F (220°C) for 10–15 minutes, until golden and well risen. Serve warm. Makes 12 biscuits.

Lemon Scones with Crabapple and Rose Geranium Jelly

*For an elegant breakfast on the terrace or afternoon tea, you
have to have scones. These are particularly yummy.*

2 cups (500 mL) all-purpose flour
2 tablespoons (25 mL) granulated sugar
2 teaspoons (10 mL) baking powder
1/2 teaspoon (2 mL) baking soda
pinch of salt
1/2 cup (125 mL) cold butter or vegetable shortening
1 tablespoon (15 mL) finely grated lemon zest
1 cup (250 mL) buttermilk

Crabapple and Rose Geranium Jelly
16 cups (4 L) crabapples, washed and quartered
4 cups (1 L) water
granulated sugar
rose geranium leaves, washed and dried

1. Combine flour, sugar, baking powder, baking soda, and salt. Cut in butter or shortening with a pastry blender to form a coarse, crumbly mixture. Stir in lemon zest.
2. Add buttermilk and stir quickly with a fork, just until dough clings together in a soft, sticky mass. Knead lightly on a floured board for 1 minute, then pat into 1-inch (2.5 cm) thick rounds.
3. Set on an ungreased baking sheet and cut into eight pie-shaped wedges with a large-bladed knife. Bake in a preheated 425°F (220°C) oven for 15 minutes, until golden. Break apart into scones, split, and serve warm with rose geranium jelly and clotted cream.
4. Place crabapples in a large kettle and add water. Bring to a boil and simmer for 30 minutes, crushing crabapples well as they cook.
5. Pour crushed apples into a jelly bag, suspended over a large bowl to catch juice. Let drip overnight. Do not squeeze bag or jelly will become cloudy.
6. The next day, measure crabapple juice into a saucepan, adding 1/2 cup (125 mL) sugar for every 1 cup (250 mL) juice. Bring to a boil and keep boiling for 15 minutes. Continue to boil and test jelly until a few drops on a plate chilled in freezer become stiff. Remove from heat.
7. Place 1 rose geranium leaf in the bottom of each sterilized jelly jar. Pour hot jelly over leaves, leaving 1/4-inch (5 mm) headspace, then seal jars and store in a cool place. Makes 4–5 cups.

Carrot Health Muffins

*These are substantial muffins—healthy enough for breakfast on
the go and tough enough to pack for a hike or a bike trip.
Just like carrot cake, but without all the fat.*

1 cup (250 mL) each: all-purpose and whole-wheat flour
1 cup (250 mL) chopped dates, cut into small pieces
3/4 cup (175 mL) brown sugar
1 tablespoon (15 mL) ground cinnamon
1 teaspoon (5 mL) ground nutmeg
2 teaspoons (10 mL) baking soda
1/2 teaspoon (2 mL) salt
1/2 cup (125 mL) chopped nuts
2 eggs
1 egg white
2/3 cup (150 mL) low-fat plain yogurt
2 teaspoons (10 mL) vanilla extract
3 cups (750 mL) grated carrots
1 cup (250 mL) grated apple

1. Combine flours, dates, sugar, cinnamon, nutmeg, baking soda, salt, and nuts.
2. In another bowl, whisk together eggs, egg white, yogurt, and vanilla. Stir in grated carrots and apple. Pour over dry ingredients and stir until just mixed.
3. Spoon into greased or paper-lined muffin cups. Bake in a preheated 350°F (180°C) oven for 40 minutes, until tops are firm. Makes about 18 muffins.

RHUBARB STREUSEL MUFFINS

*The sweet, nutty streusel topping makes these muffins a little decadent—
serve them for Sunday brunch on the deck when spring arrives.*

1 1/4 cups (300 mL) each: all-purpose and whole-wheat flour
1 cup (250 mL) brown sugar
1 teaspoon (5 mL) baking powder
1 teaspoon (5 mL) baking soda
1/2 teaspoon (2 mL) ground cinnamon
1/4 teaspoon (1 mL) ground nutmeg
1/4 teaspoon (1 mL) salt
1/4 cup (50 mL) canola oil
1 teaspoon (5 mL) vanilla extract
1/4 cup (175 mL) buttermilk
1 large egg
1 1/2 cups (375 mL) finely chopped rhubarb

Streusel Topping
2 tablespoons (25 mL) butter, softened
1/3 cup (75 mL) brown sugar
1 teaspoon (5 mL) ground cinnamon
1/2 cup (125 mL) chopped pecans

1. Combine flours and sugar in large bowl. Add baking powder, baking soda, cinnamon, nutmeg, and salt.
2. Whisk together canola oil, vanilla, buttermilk, and egg, and slowly add to dry ingredients, mixing to form a stiff batter. Fold in chopped rhubarb.
3. Mix streusel topping ingredients together until crumbly. Set aside.
4. Spoon batter into greased or paper-lined muffin tins, filling them two-thirds full and sprinkling each with a little streusel topping. Bake in a preheated 350°F (180°C) oven for 20–25 minutes. Makes 12 large muffins.

BIG BATCH BARLEY BRAN MUFFINS

This recipe was supplied by the Alberta Barley Commission—it makes a big batch of three dozen muffins, or you can store the batter in the refrigerator for up to a week and make muffins whenever the mood strikes.

5 cups (1.25 L) wheat bran
5 cups (1.25 L) buttermilk
1 cup (250 mL) firmly packed brown sugar
1 cup (250 mL) canola oil
4 eggs
1 cup (250 mL) blackstrap molasses
1 1/2 cups (375 mL) water
5 cups (1.25 L) wholegrain barley flour
2 cups (500 mL) raisins or dried cranberries
1 cup (250 mL) wheat germ
1 tablespoon (15 mL) salt
4 teaspoons (20 mL) baking powder
4 teaspoons (20 mL) baking soda
1 teaspoon (5 mL) ground cinnamon

1. In a very large bowl, combine wheat bran and buttermilk. Whisk together brown sugar, canola oil, and eggs, and add to the bowl. Stir in molasses and water.
2. In a second bowl, combine barley flour, raisins or cranberries, wheat germ, salt, baking powder, baking soda, and cinnamon. Add to wet mixture and stir until dry ingredients are just moistened.
3. Set paper liners in muffin pan and fill to top edge. Bake in a preheated 375°F (190°C) oven for 20 minutes. Makes 36 muffins.

WHOLE-WHEAT ZUCCHINI BREAD

Every prairie cookbook needs to include a good way to get rid of zucchini. Even if you've never contemplated cultivating zucchini, this is one vegetable that every gardener wants to give away, and you may end up with a friendly contribution on your doorstep in August.

1 cup (250 mL) whole-wheat flour
3/4 cup (175 mL) all-purpose flour
1 teaspoon (5 mL) ground cinnamon
1/2 teaspoon (2 mL) baking soda
1/4 teaspoon (1 mL) baking powder
1/2 teaspoon (2 mL) salt
zest of 1 lemon, minced
3/4 cup (175 mL) packed brown sugar
1/2 cup (125 mL) milk
1/4 cup (50 mL) vegetable oil
1 large egg, lightly beaten
1/2 teaspoon (2 mL) vanilla extract
1/2 pound (250 g) zucchini, grated (about 1 cup/250 mL)
1/2 cup (125 mL) raisins, currants, or chopped nuts

1. Combine flours, cinnamon, baking soda, baking powder, salt, and lemon zest in a bowl.
2. In another bowl, beat together sugar, milk, oil, egg, and vanilla. Mix in zucchini and raisins, currants, or nuts. Add flour mixture and stir until just combined.
3. Spoon into a greased 9 x 5-inch (2 L) loaf pan. Bake in a preheated 350°F (180°C) oven for 50–60 minutes, until a toothpick inserted in centre of loaf comes out clean. Cool in pan for 10 minutes, then turn out onto a rack to finish cooling. Makes 1 loaf.

DRIED FRUIT AND NUT GRANOLA

This is truly the tastiest way to get your whole grains every day. There's nothing on the supermarket cereal shelf that compares with home-made granola. Try it once and you'll be hooked. Substitute any chopped nuts for the pecans in this recipe.

8 cups (2 L) rolled oats
2 cups (500 mL) wheat germ
2 cups (500 mL) unsweetened shredded coconut
1 cup (250 mL) chopped pecans
1 cup (250 mL) slivered almonds
2 cups (500 mL) shelled, raw sunflower seeds
1/2 cup (125 mL) sesame seeds
1/2 cup (125 mL) flax seeds
1 cup (250 mL) canola oil
1 cup (250 mL) honey
1 teaspoon (5 mL) salt
2 teaspoons (10 mL) ground cinnamon
1 teaspoon (5 mL) grated nutmeg
1 tablespoon (15 mL) vanilla extract
2 cups (500 mL) dried blueberries, cherries, and/or dried cranberries, or substitute raisins or currants
2 cups (500 mL) raisins
2 cups (500 mL) chopped dried apricots
zest of 4 oranges

1. Mix oats, wheat germ, coconut, pecans, almonds, sunflower seeds, sesame seeds, and flax.
2. Heat canola oil, honey, salt, cinnamon, nutmeg, and vanilla almost to boiling, then drizzle over dry ingredients, mixing well.
3. Spread granola in one or two shallow roasting pans and bake in a preheated 300°F (150°F) oven for 30–45 minutes, stirring often to prevent it from burning. Cool.
4. Stir in dried fruits and orange zest. Store in a large jar in a cool place. Serve with milk.

MULTI-GRAIN PANCAKES

When you're hosting breakfast, nothing beats a stack of home-made pancakes chock full of whole grains and nuts. Drizzle these pancakes with an Alberta fruit syrup made with local saskatoon berries or chokecherries, birch syrup, or top with fresh sliced strawberries.

1 1/2 cups (375 mL) barley flour
1 cup (250 mL) all-purpose flour
1 cup (250 mL) rolled oats
1/2 cup (125 mL) cornmeal
2 teaspoons (10 mL) baking powder
2 teaspoons (10 mL) baking soda
1/2 cup (125 mL) brown sugar
1 teaspoon (5 mL) salt
1/2 cup (125 mL) cold butter, cut into small pieces
4 eggs
4 cups (1 L) buttermilk
1 cup (250 mL) chopped almonds
melted butter

1. In a food processor, process barley flour, all-purpose flour, oats, cornmeal, baking powder, baking soda, brown sugar, and salt until well blended. Add butter and process until mealy.
2. Beat eggs with buttermilk in a large bowl. Stir flour mixture into bowl and fold in chopped nuts.
3. Brush a heavy pan or griddle with butter. Ladle batter on, making 6-inch (15 cm) pancakes. Cook until golden on both sides, turning when bubbles begin to break on the first side. Serve with butter and your choice of syrup. Serves 6 to 8.

LOGAN BREAD

This is a classic and substantial snack cake to take on mountain hikes and backpacking trips. If you want it to last even longer, slice it and dry in a low oven for an hour, and enjoy the crunchy sweet like biscotti or mandelbrot.

1 cup (250 mL) rolled oats
1 cup (250 mL) each: all-purpose flour and whole-wheat flour
1/3 cup (75 mL) brown sugar
1/2 teaspoon (2 mL) salt
2 teaspoons (10 mL) baking powder
3/4 cup (175 mL) chopped nuts
1 cup (250 mL) chopped dried fruit (apricots, raisins, dried cranberries, or others)
1/2 cup (125 mL) milk
1/4 cup (50 mL) oil
1/2 cup (125 mL) corn syrup
2 tablespoons (25 mL) molasses

1. Combine oats, flours, brown sugar, salt, baking powder, nuts, and dried fruit in a bowl.
2. In another bowl, whisk together milk, oil, corn syrup, and molasses. Stir wet ingredients into dry until just mixed.
3. Spread batter evenly in a greased 9-inch (2 L) square baking pan and bake in a preheated 325°F (160°C) oven for 1 hour, or until a toothpick inserted in middle of cake comes out clean. Cut into squares and wrap in plastic wrap for packing. Alternatively, cut into fingers and dry in a 250°F (120°C) oven for 2 hours.

Desserts

SASKATOONS, CHOKECHERRIES, AND PRAIRIE FRUIT

Heat, haze, the background buzz of bees and bugs—there's a definite drone that surrounds the saskatoon berry season. Paul Hamer is displaying all of the telltale signs of a saskatoon picker. He is purple up to the elbows, his jeans are stained and sticky from wiping the inky juices of this famous prairie berry from his hands. His face is deeply tanned by this time in late July, and there is a faint aroma of perspiration mingled with mosquito repellent in his van as we head out into the deep coulees where his 20 hectares of 'Smoky' and 'Northline' saskatoon bushes stand in thick, even rows.

Hamer's Saskatoon farm is only minutes from Calgary's southern extremities. There is little to announce it as you head across the flat, dry landscape past fancy country residences and grain farms. But when you arrive, you find a little irrigated oasis of fruit and fun in the steep river valley. Hamer's U-pick saskatoon farm is a destination for city dwellers still addicted to that unique prairie berry, the saskatoon, or serviceberry. They arrive by the carload in midsummer to comb the stocky, gnarled shrubs for the juicy berries, with their deep purple colour and musky, almond-like sweetness. "With saskatoons, it's almost a cult-like following," says Hamer, who has combined his U-pick orchard and tree farm with a café and store where you can buy saskatoon pies, jams, syrups, and pie fillings made on the premises.

While it looks a lot like a blueberry, there's nothing quite like the saskatoon, and anyone who has picked pails of them in the wilds of the West would never mistake the two. Saskatoons are a western berry, growing plentifully along river banks and in coulees across the Canadian prairies. Although saskatoons grow wild in every part of the country, and into the western United States, it's the fruit from the western species, *Amelanchier alnifolia*, that's the most delicious. Central-Canadian and west-coast serviceberries are described by some authors as "insipid"—hardly a word true prairie dwellers would apply to their beloved saskatoon berry.

The bushes are covered in white blooms in the spring, and if spared the common late-spring Alberta frost, they are hanging heavily with sweet, nearly black berries by mid-July. Like the wild bison, the saskatoon is a hardy prairie food source,

THE BRITISH CONNECTION

Dessert in this part of the world has a distinctly British heritage. Pies and puddings abound on our Alberta menus, whether traditional fruit concoctions or made with the prunes, raisins, and other dried fruits that were typically available to early pioneers and easy to store all winter.

Dense fruitcakes—like the ones still baked for Christmas—have also long been traditional for weddings in these parts, and steamed puddings, rice puddings, carrot puddings, and the like, all have familiar English or Scottish pedigrees. Many of these old-fashioned desserts, especially the baked, custardy bread pudding, are making a comeback in this age of cocooning and comfort foods.

the berry that supplied essential vitamins to early Native tribes. Saskatoons were dried and pounded with dried bison meat and fat to make pemmican, the portable, preserved staple that sustained these indigenous people over long prairie winters for generations. Early Canadian explorers, and the voyageurs who first came to the West for furs in the early 1800s, noted that the saskatoon berry was an integral part of the local diet, that the straight-grained wood was used by the Natives for their arrows, and that the fruit was so delicious that it should be cultivated in Britain and other parts of Canada.

While you'll still find berries like saskatoons, chokecherries, and tiny alpine strawberries in the wild, most of the berries consumed today are cultivated. Like grapes, saskatoons don't perform well with too much water and rich soil. When they suffer in rockier soil with less water, the bushes produce more concentrated, flavourful fruit, says Hamer.

The first commercial saskatoon orchards only came into existence in the 1970s, but there's been a renewed interest in the prairie berries in recent years as chefs and consumers search for unique, local products. According to Alberta Agriculture, there are more than 250 berry operations in the province. Second only to saskatoons, strawberries are now a multi-million-dollar industry, and raspberries are a third major berry crop. Demand for local berries continues to outstrip supply.

Like Hamer, John Schussler has planted saskatoons, along with other prairie fruits like chokecherries, red currants, black currants, and rhubarb. At his Bridge Berry Farm near Lethbridge, Schussler experimented with these indigenous ingredients to create juices, syrups, and other berry products. Using a Florida citrus press, Schussler created juices, like his rich, concentrated Black Rhubarb Juice, from local berries and fruits. Such combinations are incredibly high in vitamin C and electrolytes, making them perfect as sports drinks.

With the remaining fruit, he's experimenting with fruit leathers and dehydrated fruit powders or flours that he's adding to baked goods. There are also fruit jams and unique syrups—like his blush-coloured rhubarb syrup that's perfect to drizzle over a warm waffle or brush onto a pork tenderloin before grilling.

Like saskatoons, strawberries and raspberries are another sweet treat in the Alberta summer. While you'll come upon tiny, delicious alpine strawberries on mountain hikes, the majority of Alberta strawberries are the big, cultivated kind, available from U-pick farms around the province. At The Garden, just east of Calgary, ripe, juicy strawberries rest on their straw mulch, just waiting to be picked. Families arrive in droves to fill four-litre baskets that they haul away for making strawberry jams, summer puddings, and summer shortcakes.

There's nothing like a warm strawberry, plucked from the vine and popped into your mouth when no one's looking. It's part of the pick-your-own experience and it's expected that everyone will eat their fill as they stoop over the rows, lifting the round, saw-tooth leaves to reveal the luscious red fruit hiding in the shadows. While strawberry picking was once only a late-June pastime, new varieties of day-neutral strawberries bear fruit right into the fall.

Rhubarb is another longtime staple for prairie cooks. The almost indestructible perennial plant is dubbed the "pie plant" for its perfect role as a pie filling, either alone or mixed with strawberries or apples, or set in creamy custard. Rhubarb is the first thing to break through the frozen ground in the spring, and you can keep pulling the big, celery-like stalks until the weather turns hot and the plant sends up its big, spiky, green flower heads.

Rhubarb is actually a vegetable, but it's eaten as a fruit since the tartness needs to be tamed with a substantial amount of sugar to make it edible. Many a prairie kid remembers dunking fresh rhubarb into a bowl of sugar and biting it off like a piece of candy. Don't eat the big, shiny leaves, though—they're actually very poisonous. Choose rhubarb that's young and red for the best flavour; strawberry or crimson varieties are red right to the centre and make bright red desserts (green-centred stalks will taste good but give you a fairly dull-looking pie filling). Rhubarb is very juicy when cooked, so stew it first to cook it down, or add extra thickener to your pie filling or fruit crisp. The tangy, tart flavours of rhubarb also work well in savoury dishes and sauces for game, and make the perfect background for a spicy chutney. Native to the Himalayas, rhubarb appears in traditional dishes from Poland to the Middle East.

SEDUCED BY CHOCOLATE

Chocolate, an indigenous North American ingredient in the most historic sense, with its roots in ancient Mexico, has always been a popular ingredient in prairie sweets, from sheet cakes and brownies to cookies, fudge, and, of course, our own Bernard Callebaut chocolates.

Calgary-based chocolatier Bernard Callebaut, a transplant from the famous chocolate-making family in Belgium, hand-makes his chocolates for thirty-five Callebaut chocolate shops across Canada and the United States. And it's not only Albertans who will tell you that they are the best chocolates in the world. Bernard Callebaut won that honour in a recent world chocolate competition in France, where his bon bons beat out the best offered by European chocolatiers. Cooks can visit his main Calgary store for slabs of good-quality white, dark, and milk chocolate for baking, or order online.

SUGAR AND OTHER SWEET STUFF

Sugar is a major Alberta-made commodity, most of it refined from sugar beets grown in the southern irrigation belt. Every fall trucks haul and pile mountains of these grey roots outside the processing facilities. The sugar beets are then shovelled by front-end loaders into the industrial plants that will turn them into pure white crystals.

At the other end of the scale is Warren Bard, the Edmonton-area entrepreneur who produces a dark, heavy syrup from birch trees. Natives tapped the birch trees in a similar manner, then boiled the sap to make syrup. Top chefs like to drizzle Bard's Indian Head Birch Syrup over their desserts for regional flair, although it is an expensive and rare commodity—it takes almost 3,000 mL of sap to make 30 mL of his thick, molasses-like syrup, three times sweeter than maple sap. You may find Bard dispensing his sweet elixir at Edmonton farmer's markets.

SASKATOON PIE

*Saskatoon pie is the quintessential prairie fruit pie. Today you
can even purchase saskatoon pie filling, but it isn't the same
as a pie made with freshly picked whole berries.*

Pastry
5 cups (1.25 L) all-purpose flour
1 tablespoon (15 mL) salt
1 pound (500 g) lard or vegetable shortening
1 egg, lightly beaten
1 tablespoon (15 mL) white vinegar, added to 1/2 cup (125 mL)
   ice-cold water

Filling (per pie)
4 cups (1 L) saskatoon berries
2 tablespoons (25 mL) all-purpose flour, divided
1/4 cup (50 mL) butter
1/2 cup (125 mL) granulated sugar
pinch of salt
2 tablespoons (25 mL) fresh lemon juice

1. For pastry, mix together flour and salt in a food processor. Add lard
   or shortening, cut into cubes, and pulse until mixture is crumbly.
   Whisk egg with vinegar and ice water and add to processor. Pulse in
   short bursts, just until pastry comes together. Don't overprocess.
   Gather up into two balls, wrap in plastic, and let rest for 10 minutes.
   This will make enough pastry for two double-crust pies. Divide each
   ball in half and roll out on a floured surface, forming two rounds,
   each about 10 inches (25 cm) in diameter. Extra pastry can be
   wrapped well and frozen.
2. Lay one round of pastry in a large, well-greased pie plate. Sprinkle 1
   teaspoon (5 mL) flour onto the surface before adding clean,
   uncooked saskatoon berries. Fill pie plate heaping full. Dot with
   butter. Sprinkle with remaining flour, sugar, salt, and lemon juice.
3. Rub a little cold water over exposed edge of pastry. Cover berries
   with top crust and press edges together to seal, then flute between
   your fingers. Make some holes in top crust with tip of a sharp knife
   so steam can escape. Set pie on a baking sheet to catch any juice
   that overflows.
4. Bake in a preheated 350°F (180°C) oven for 45–50 minutes. Cool and
   serve warm with ice cream. Makes 1 pie. Serves 6.

RHUBARB MERINGUE TARTE

This is a pretty summer dessert that resembles a lemon meringue pie with a pale pink filling. For the best colour, use young strawberry rhubarb stalks that are red all the way through, or include some chopped fresh strawberries in the filling.

Base
3/4 cup (175 mL) butter
2 cups (500 mL) all-purpose flour
3 tablespoons (45 mL) granulated sugar

Filling
4 cups (1 L) rhubarb
1 cup (250 mL) granulated sugar
1/2 cup (125 mL) brown sugar
1/2 cup (125 mL) whipping cream or milk
1/4 teaspoon (1 mL) salt
4 egg yolks
1/3 cup (75 mL) all-purpose flour
juice and minced zest of 1 lemon

Meringue
4 egg whites
pinch of cream of tartar
1/2 cup (125 mL) granulated sugar

1. For base, combine ingredients in a food processor and pulse until crumbly, or cut butter into flour and sugar using a pastry blender. Press into bottom and up sides of a greased 10-inch (3 L) tart pan with removable base. Bake in a preheated 350°F (180°C) oven for 12 minutes. Cool.
2. Mix ingredients for filling and pour into baked tart base. Place tart on a cookie sheet to catch spills and bake for another 45 minutes at 350°F (180°C). Cool.
3. In a clean bowl, beat egg whites with cream of tartar until soft peaks form. Beat in sugar, 1 tablespoon (15 mL) at a time, until meringue is stiff and glossy. Spoon evenly over rhubarb, sealing to edges of crust to prevent shrinking. Using the back of a spoon, make decorative spikes and swirls in meringue.
4. Return tart to oven for 10 minutes, until meringue is golden brown. Let cool thoroughly before cutting, but do not refrigerate or meringue will weep. Serves 6 to 8.

SASKATOON BERRY AND LIME CHEESECAKE

This recipe comes from Rosemary Harbrecht, the talented pastry chef and owner of Brulée Bakery in Calgary. Rosemary devised this method of swirling tart lime- and berry-flavoured batter together when she discovered a wonderful new product, saskatoon berry jam. If you substitute blueberry jam and fresh blueberries it will be just as beautiful—it just won't have that real prairie punch!

Crust
1 1/2 cups (375 mL) all-purpose flour
1/3 cup (75 mL) icing sugar
1/2 cup (125 mL) plus 1 tablespoon (15 mL) unsalted butter

Filling:
1 pound (450 g) regular cream cheese
1 cup (250 mL) granulated sugar
1 cup (250 mL) sour cream
4 eggs
1 teaspoon (5 mL) vanilla extract
juice and zest of 2 limes
1/2 cup (125 mL) saskatoon berry or blueberry jam
1 cup (250 mL) fresh saskatoon berries or blueberries

1. To make crust, combine flour, sugar, and butter in a food processor and pulse until crumbly and just starting to come together. Press dough firmly over bottom and halfway up sides of a 10-inch (3 L) springform pan. Bake in a preheated 350°F (180°C) oven for 12 minutes. Remove from oven and cool.

2. Cream cheese and sugar together in an electric mixer until smooth. Add sour cream, then beat in eggs, one at a time. Add vanilla, lime juice, and lime zest, and mix well. Scrape down sides of mixing bowl to make sure everything is incorporated.

3. Remove 1/2 cup (125 mL) of filling and place it in a bowl. Stir in saskatoon berry or blueberry jam, mixing well.

4. Pour lime filling into prepared crust and spoon berry-flavoured filling in dollops on top. Use a knife blade to swirl the berry filling artfully into the lime base. Sprinkle fresh berries evenly over the cheesecake and bake in a preheated 300°F (150°C) oven for 1 hour. Turn oven off, and leave cheesecake in oven for 25 minutes longer.

5. Remove from oven, cool, and refrigerate. Serve slices of cheesecake with more fresh berries to garnish. Serves 12.

WHITE CHOCOLATE FLAN WITH SASKATOON BERRY SAUCE

*Cold white chocolate pudding with warm berry sauce—
it's a contrast of textures and flavours that can't be beat. Easy, too.*

Flan
1/2 cup (125 mL) granulated sugar
1 tablespoon (15 mL) water
1 cup (250 mL) milk
1 cup (250 mL) whipping cream
2 squares white chocolate, chopped
3 egg yolks
2 whole eggs
icing sugar
white chocolate curls

Saskatoon Berry Sauce
1 1/2 cups (375 mL) saskatoon berries, or substitute blueberries, strawberries, black currants, or other berries
1 cup (250 mL) red wine
1/3 cup (75 mL) brown sugar
1 tablespoon (15 mL) cornstarch
1 teaspoon (5 mL) vanilla extract

1. Heat sugar and water in saucepan over low heat, shaking pan to dissolve sugar. Turn heat to high and boil, without stirring, until sugar is caramelized and golden brown. Keep a pastry brush dipped in water to wash sugar down from side of pan. Watch carefully so that it doesn't burn. When sugar is nicely browned, remove from heat and carefully stir in milk and cream. Bring almost to a boil, add white chocolate, and stir until melted.

2. In a bowl, whisk egg yolks with whole eggs to combine. Stir a small amount of chocolate mixture into eggs, then slowly whisk in remaining custard to combine. Pour mixture into six lightly oiled custard cups. Place cups in a baking dish and add hot water to come halfway up sides of custards. Bake in a preheated 350°F (180°C) oven for 35 minutes. Cool, then chill.

3. To make sauce, cook berries with wine, sugar, and cornstarch over medium heat until thick and bubbly. Remove from heat, stir in vanilla, and keep warm. To serve, spoon saskatoon berry sauce over custards in dishes, or unmould custards on individual serving plates, dust with icing sugar, and top with warm sauce, fresh berries, and shavings of white chocolate. Serves 6.

APPLE BERRY CRISP

We grew up calling apple crisp "Apple Betty"—the kind of everyday dessert that even a kid could whip together for the family. This adult version includes a little brandy and some fresh berries to add colour and zing, but it's still a dead easy and delicious dessert.

3/4 cup (175 mL) granulated sugar
2 tablespoons (25 mL) honey
1/2 teaspoon (2 mL) ground cinnamon
1/4 teaspoon (1 mL) ground nutmeg
3 tablespoons (45 mL) brandy, Calvados, or Grand Marnier
2 cups (500 mL) saskatoon berries, or substitute cranberries or sliced rhubarb
5 large Granny Smith apples, peeled and sliced
2 tablespoons (25 mL) all-purpose flour

Topping
1/4 cup (50 mL) whole-wheat flour
3 tablespoons (45 mL) butter, softened
1/2 cup (125 mL) brown sugar
1/2 cup (125 mL) rolled barley or rolled oats
pinch of salt
1 teaspoon (5 mL) ground cinnamon

1. Combine sugar, honey, cinnamon, nutmeg, and brandy, Calvados, or Grand Marnier and mix well. Toss with saskatoon berries and apples and marinate for 1 hour, until fruit releases its juices. Add flour and combine well. Pour into a greased shallow baking dish.

2. Combine whole-wheat flour with butter and brown sugar, mixing to form coarse crumbs. Stir in rolled barley or oats and season with salt and cinnamon. Scatter over fruit in dish.

3. Set baking dish on a baking sheet or pizza pan to catch any juice that may run over. Place in a preheated 350°F (180°C) oven and bake for 45–55 minutes, until bubbling and golden brown. Serve warm with vanilla ice cream or lemon yogurt. Serves 6 to 8.

SNOW CANOES

This recipe is inspired by something I found in a crumbling old recipe book that I picked up at a flea market—the Farm Women's Union of Alberta cookbook. It's really just a variation on the classic "floating island" meringues in custard, or snow pudding, as it's sometimes called. But I love the name that this early Alberta farm wife devised. What could be more Canadian?

Meringues
4 large egg whites
1/2 cup (125 mL) granulated sugar
pinch of cream of tartar
saskatoon berry jam, grated bittersweet Callebaut
chocolate shavings, and/or icing sugar

Custard
1 cup (250 mL) milk
1 cup (250 mL) whipping cream
4 large egg yolks
1/2 cup (125 mL) granulated sugar
1 teaspoon (5 mL) vanilla extract

1. To make custard, rinse a small saucepan with water but don't dry. This will help to ensure that the custard doesn't burn onto the pan.

2. Pour in milk and cream and bring to a boil. Remove from heat. Meanwhile, whisk egg yolks, sugar, and vanilla until pale yellow in colour. Gradually add about 1/2 cup (125 mL) of hot milk mixture to yolks, whisking to combine, then gradually whisk egg mixture back into hot milk.

3. Cook custard over low heat, whisking constantly, until thickened, but do not boil or mixture will curdle. Pour custard into a large ovenproof glass or ceramic baking dish. Chill.

4. For snow canoes, beat egg whites with sugar and cream of tartar until very stiff and glossy, like marshmallow cream. Using two soup spoons, form canoe-shaped scoops of meringue. Use second spoon to slide meringues into the custard. Use the tip of a spoon to make a long indentation in each oval mound of meringue for filling later. You should have enough meringue for twelve to sixteen canoes. Set custard in a large pan of ice water.

5. Put pan in a preheated 350°F (180°C) oven and lay a sheet of parchment paper over top. Bake for 10 minutes, until meringues are just set. Remove from oven and cool to room temperature. If desired, chill before serving.

6. To serve, place two or three snow canoes on each individual dessert plate, in a pool of custard sauce. Carefully fill indentation in each meringue with a little saskatoon berry jam or a line of grated chocolate. If desired, decorate edges of plates with chocolate shavings and a dusting of icing sugar. Serves 4 to 6.

> **TIP**
> To dust desserts with sugar, put icing sugar into a fine mesh sieve or sugar shaker and lightly sprinkle over top of plates. To decorate a plain chocolate cake just before serving, set a paper doily on top of the cake, dust heavily with icing sugar, and carefully remove the doily. You will have an instant pretty pattern on your cake.

Strawberry Napoleons with Lemon Mascarpone Cream

As easy to assemble as strawberry shortcake, these pretty desserts make an impressive finale to any summer dinner. Mascarpone is a triple-cream soft cheese, available in Italian groceries. The components of this dessert can be made in advance, then layered just before serving.

1 package frozen puff pastry, thawed
2 tablespoons (25 mL) plus 1/4 cup (50 mL) granulated sugar
3 cups (750 mL) fresh strawberries
3 tablespoons (45 mL) Cointreau or other brandy
icing sugar

Lemon Mascarpone Cream
2 lemons
1 cup (250 mL) mascarpone cheese
1 cup (250 mL) whipping cream
1/2 cup (125 mL) icing sugar

1. Roll puff pastry out into two sheets, about 1/16 inch (1 mm) thick, and cut each into nine even rectangles. Wipe a baking sheet with a wet cloth, then place squares on sheet. Prick pastry squares with a fork, sprinkle with 2 tablespoons (25 mL) granulated sugar, and bake in a preheated 450°F (230°C) oven for 20 minutes. If pastries puff too high, place a second baking sheet on top to hold them down while they bake. Remove from oven and cool.

2. Wash lemons well. Using a zester or peeler, remove zest and chop finely. Press lemons under your palm to release juice, then cut in half and juice with a lemon reamer, discarding any seeds.

3. Whisk lemon juice and zest into mascarpone. Whip cream with icing sugar until stiff, then carefully fold into mascarpone. Cover and chill.

4. Quickly rinse, hull, and slice strawberries. Combine strawberries, Cointreau or brandy, and 1/4 cup (50 mL) granulated sugar and set aside for 10 minutes.

5. To assemble napoleons, place a little lemon mascarpone cream on each dessert plate and top with a piece of pastry. Spoon more lemon mascarpone cream on top, spreading it evenly, then top with strawberries. Repeat with pastry, cream, and strawberries, ending with a piece of pastry. Dust each dessert with icing sugar and serve immediately. Serves 6.

STICKY TOFFEE PUDDING WITH MOLASSES SAUCE

Chef Alan Groom is known for this homey and simple dessert rooted in British tradition. These steamy little date puddings are served in a pool of warm molasses sauce with a big dollop of Jersey cream, similar to British clotted cream. Groom prefers the cream from British Columbia's Jersey Farms.

Puddings
1/2 cup (125 mL) unsalted butter
1 cup (250 mL) brown sugar
1 large egg
1 teaspoon (5 mL) vanilla extract
1 cup (250 mL) all-purpose flour
1 teaspoon (5 mL) baking powder
1 teaspoon (5 mL) baking soda
2 cups (500 mL) pitted dates, finely minced
1 1/4 cups (300 mL) boiling water
1/4 cup (50 mL) blackstrap molasses
Jersey cream

Molasses Sauce
1 cup (250 mL) brown sugar
1/4 cup (50 mL) light unsulphured molasses or treacle
1/2 cup (125 mL) cold butter, cubed
2 cups (500 mL) whipping cream

1. To make puddings, cream butter with an electric mixer until fluffy. Slowly add brown sugar and continue to beat until well combined. In another bowl, whisk together egg and vanilla. Combine flour, baking powder, and baking soda. Alternately add flour mixture and egg mixture to the butter, beating well after each addition.

2. Combine dates, boiling water, and molasses and set aside to cool. Stir into batter.

3. Butter ten individual ovenproof ramekins or small soufflé dishes. Divide batter evenly between ramekins and place them on a baking sheet. Bake in a preheated 350°F (180°C) oven for 20 minutes. Reduce heat to 300°F (150°C) and continue baking for an additional 30 minutes.

4. Meanwhile, to make sauce, combine brown sugar and molasses or treacle in a saucepan and bring to a boil over medium-high heat, stirring constantly. Boil for 1 minute, then whisk in butter, a few cubes at a time. Add cream and boil until sauce is reduced and thickened. You should have about 2 cups (500 mL) of sauce.

5. Remove puddings from oven and cool slightly on a rack. Run a knife around edge of each ramekin to loosen pudding, and invert on individual serving dishes. Serve puddings warm, drizzled with molasses sauce and topped with Jersey cream. Serves 10.

GINGER CAKE WITH WARM APPLE COMPOTE

Nothing could be more comforting than warm gingerbread with chunky apple compote, topped with a generous spoonful of whipped cream or mascarpone.

1 1/2 cups (375 mL) cake flour
1 teaspoon (5 mL) baking soda
1/4 teaspoon (1 mL) salt
1 large egg
1/4 cup (50 mL) blackstrap molasses
1/4 cup (50 mL) maple syrup
1/2 cup (125 mL) buttermilk
1/2 cup (125 mL) butter
1/2 cup (125 mL) brown sugar
1 tablespoon (15 mL) lemon zest
1 tablespoon (15 mL) grated fresh ginger root
icing sugar

Compote
2 tablespoons (25 mL) butter
6 apples, peeled, cored, and cut into wedges
1/2 cup (125 mL) brown sugar
1/4 cup (50 mL) water
1/2 teaspoon (2 mL) ground cinnamon
1/4 teaspoon (1 mL) ground ginger
2 tablespoons (25 mL) Calvados or brandy

1. Butter and flour a 9-inch (2 L) round cake pan.
2. Combine flour, baking soda, and salt. In another bowl, beat egg lightly. Whisk together molasses, maple syrup, and buttermilk.
3. With an electric mixer, cream butter until soft. Add brown sugar and continue to cream until fluffy. With mixer running, slowly add egg.
4. Remove bowl from mixer and stir in lemon zest and ginger by hand. Then alternately add molasses mixture and flour mixture to batter, mixing until smooth after each addition.
5. Pour batter into prepared pan and bake in a preheated 350°F (180°C) oven for about 45 minutes, until a toothpick inserted in the centre comes out clean. Cool cake on a wire rack and remove from pan.

6. To make apple compote, melt butter in a large nonstick sauté pan and cook apples over medium-high heat until starting to become tender, about 5 minutes. Add brown sugar, water, cinnamon, and ground ginger and continue to cook until apples are beginning to caramelize. Remove from heat and stir in Calvados or brandy.
7. Cut cake into wedges, top with warm apple compote, and dust lightly with icing sugar. Serve with a dollop of whipped cream or mascarpone, if desired. Serves 6 to 8.

MARIANNE'S LEMON SOUFFLÉ TART

Desserts have never been my strong suit, but luckily I have friends who are brilliant in that department. One is former Calgary pastry chef Marianne Sanders, who generously shared some of her best recipes with me, including this one. For a more intense flavour, spread a thin layer of lemon curd on the crust before adding the filling with the soufflé mixture.

Crust
2 1/4 cups (550 mL) all-purpose flour
1/2 cup (125 mL) granulated sugar
1 cup less 2 tablespoons (225 mL) butter
1 egg
1 egg yolk
splash of fresh lemon juice
splash of vanilla extract

Filling
5 eggs, separated
1/2 cup (125 mL) plus 2 tablespoons (25 mL) granulated sugar
1/2 cup (125 mL) fresh lemon juice
grated zest of 2 lemons
1/4 cup (50 mL) all-purpose flour

1. For the crust, pulse flour, sugar, and butter in a food processor until finely blended. Add remaining ingredients and pulse just until a ball forms. Divide dough in half and press one portion into a tart pan with a removable bottom. (This makes enough for two 10-inch tarts—the extra dough can be frozen.) Chill crust, then bake in preheated 350°F (180°C) oven for 15 minutes. Cool.

2. For filling, whisk together egg yolks and 1/2 cup (125 mL) sugar by hand or in food processor. Add lemon juice and zest, and pulse to combine, then incorporate flour. Cook mixture until slightly thickened, either in a double boiler or in the microwave. If using the microwave, stop and whisk mixture every 30 seconds to prevent lumps. Cool.

3. Beat egg whites until soft, then add 2 tablespoons (25 mL) sugar and beat until stiff. Carefully fold cooled lemon custard into egg whites to make a light, fluffy filling.

4. Pour lemon soufflé mixture into prepared crust and bake in a preheated 350°F (180°C) oven for 18–20 minutes, just until custard is puffed, light brown, and firm. Cool to room temperature, dust with icing sugar, and serve. Serves 8.

THIERRY'S TARTE TATIN

Many old-time ranch cooks were famous for their fruit pies, which usually came with sturdy crusts—cowboys liked to pick up their slices of pie and eat them out of their hands. A little fancier than those everyday pies, this upside-down apple tart was on the menu at Chef Thierry Meret's former restaurant, La P'Tite Table in Okotoks. And although Chef Thierry Meret never would, you can make it even easier by using frozen puff pastry.

1/2 cup (125 mL) unsalted butter
2 tablespoons (25 mL) honey
1/2 cup (125 mL) granulated sugar
8–10 Golden Delicious apples, peeled, cored, and halved
1 package puff pastry dough (thawed if frozen)
1 egg beaten with 2 tablespoons (25 mL) milk

1. In a 10–12 inch (25–30 cm) ovenproof skillet, melt butter and honey. Spread sugar evenly over butter mixture and add a layer of apples, rounded side down, to completely cover the pan. Cut remaining apples in chunks and spread over top, filling in spaces between apple halves.

2. Place skillet over high heat and cook until butter and sugar start to lightly caramelize and bubble up around edges of pan, about 10 minutes. Then turn heat down to medium-low and continue to cook apples until softened or "confit," about 45 minutes longer. Cool apples in pan. Tarte may be made ahead to this point.

3. Roll out puff pastry and place over cooked apples in pan. Trim pastry and push edges down around apples using a spoon. Brush pastry with a mixture of beaten egg and milk, then place in a preheated 400°F (200°C) oven and bake for 30 minutes, until golden.

4. Cool the tarte for 1 hour before unmoulding. You can also make it ahead to this point and chill. If chilled, heat in pan for a few minutes over high heat, just to release caramel, then place a serving plate over pan and invert tarte onto plate. Cut into wedges and serve with vanilla ice cream. Serves 6.

MAPLE WALNUT APPLE KUCHEN

A kuchen is a kind of German crumb cake—a biscuit crust filled with fruit and topped with a sweet crumble. Other seasonal fruits, such as peaches, plums, and rhubarb and strawberries, make great kuchen, too. This coffee cake is perfect to serve warm on a brunch buffet.

3 Granny Smith apples
1/2 cup (125 mL) maple syrup
2 1/2 cups (625 mL) all-purpose flour
2 teaspoons (10 mL) baking powder
1/4 teaspoon (1 mL) salt
1/4 cup (50 mL) butter, softened
1/2 cup (125 mL) granulated sugar
1 large egg
2/3 cup (150 mL) buttermilk

Walnut Topping
1/2 cup (125 mL) granulated sugar
1/3 cup (75 mL) all-purpose flour
1 teaspoon (5 mL) ground ginger
grated zest of half a lemon, minced
1/4 cup (50 mL) butter
1/2 cup (125 mL) chopped walnuts

1. Peel apples, remove cores, and cut into 1/4-inch (5 mm) wedges. Combine apples and maple syrup in a skillet and bring to a boil over high heat. Simmer for 5 minutes then remove from heat and allow fruit to cool in syrup.

2. Combine flour, baking powder, and salt. Beat butter and sugar

together in a mixer until fluffy, then beat in egg. Add dry ingredients alternately with buttermilk, mixing well after each addition.

3. Combine topping ingredients, using your hands to incorporate butter and make a crumbly mixture.

4. Grease a 10-inch (3 L) springform pan or a 9 x 13-inch (3.5 L) cake pan. Spread two-thirds of batter evenly in pan and arrange apples in a pattern on top. Dot remaining batter over fruit, leaving spaces between spoonfuls of batter. Sprinkle walnut topping over kuchen.

5. Bake in a preheated 350°F (180°C) oven for 45–55 minutes, until a toothpick inserted in centre comes out clean. Serve warm with ice cream or frozen yogurt. Serves 8.

CALLEBAUT CHOCOLATE MOCHA PUDDING WITH COFFEE CREAM SAUCE

Many prairie cooks make steamed puddings at Christmas time, when a flaming fruit-filled or carrot pudding takes them back to their British roots. When there were no fancy moulds or pudding basins to be had, early puddings were boiled in flour sacks and steamed in old tomato juice cans. This decadent chocolate pudding is like a big steamy brownie in a puddle of coffee cream sauce.

3 squares Callebaut bittersweet chocolate, chopped
1/2 cup (125 mL) butter, room temperature
3/4 cup (175 mL) granulated sugar
2 large eggs, separated
1 teaspoon (5 mL) instant espresso powder
2 teaspoons (10 mL) coffee liqueur
1 cup (250 mL) all-purpose flour
1 teaspoon (5 mL) baking powder
pinch of salt
2/3 cup (150 mL) milk

Coffee Cream Sauce
1 cup (250 mL) whipping cream
3/4 cup (175 mL) brown sugar
2 tablespoons (25 mL) unsalted butter, melted
1/2 teaspoon (2 mL) vanilla extract
1 large egg yolk
2 tablespoons (25 mL) Kahlua or other coffee liqueur

1. Generously oil a pudding mould or heatproof glass bowl.

2. Melt chocolate in a double boiler or in a bowl in the microwave. Stir until cool. Beat butter and sugar together until fluffy. Beat in egg yolks, espresso, and coffee liqueur.

3. Combine flour, baking powder, and salt, and add alternately to batter with milk until smooth. Beat on low speed and mix in chocolate.

4. In a clean bowl, beat egg whites until stiff, then fold gently into batter. Pour batter into mould or bowl, cover with lid or foil, and place on a rack in a deep pot. Fill pot with enough boiling water to come halfway up side of the mould, cover pot, and simmer for 3 hours, adding more boiling water as necessary. To speed things up, you can also steam this pudding at low pressure in a new-generation pressure cooker, which cuts steaming time down to about 45 minutes.

5. To make coffee cream sauce, stir cream, sugar, butter, and vanilla together in a saucepan and heat over medium-high heat until sugar dissolves. Simmer, uncovered, for about 30 minutes, until thick. Remove from heat. Whisk egg yolk with Kahlua. Stir a little hot cream sauce into egg mixture, then add egg mixture to pot and whisk until smooth. Serve sauce warm or cold over steamed pudding.

6. When pudding has steamed, remove it from pot and set on a rack to cool for 30 minutes before unmoulding. To serve, slice pudding and top with sauce. Serves 8 to 10.

Callebaut chocolates

Coconut Oatmeal Chocolate Chip Cookies

There is a commercial version of this cookie made in the West, perfect to dip in a glass of cold milk after school. These crunchy cookies are classics.

1 cup (250 mL) butter
1 cup (250 mL) granulated sugar
1/2 cup (125 mL) brown sugar
2 eggs, well beaten
1 1/2 cups (375 mL) quick-cooking rolled oats
1/2 teaspoon (2 mL) salt
3/4 cup (175 mL) finely chopped coconut
1 teaspoon (5 mL) vanilla extract
1 1/2 cups (375 mL) whole-wheat flour
1 teaspoon (5 mL) baking powder
3/4 cup (175 mL) chocolate chips

1. Cream butter with white and brown sugars until fluffy.
2. Add eggs, oats, salt, coconut, and vanilla and beat well.
3. Combine flour and baking powder and add to mixture, stirring to combine well. Stir in chocolate chips.
4. Grease cookie sheets or line with parchment paper. Roll cookie dough into 1-inch (2.5 cm) balls and place 3 inches (8 cm) apart on cookie sheets. Use a fork or bottom of a drinking glass to flatten cookies lightly. Bake in a preheated 400°F (200°C) oven for 15 minutes, until cookies are golden brown. Makes 24 cookies.

Caramel Pumpkin Custard

This is a perfect Thanksgiving dessert—like pumpkin pie but without the crust and all of the extra work and calories.

3/4 cup (175 mL) granulated sugar
3 tablespoons (45 mL) water
1 cup (250 mL) half-and-half cream
1 cup (250 mL) evaporated skim milk
2 tablespoons (25 mL) dark rum
pinch of salt
3 large eggs
1 cup (250 mL) canned pumpkin purée
1/3 cup (75 mL) brown sugar
1 teaspoon (5 mL) cornstarch
1/2 teaspoon (2 mL) each: ground cinnamon,
   ground ginger, and mace
whipped cream

1. In a heavy skillet, melt granulated sugar and water over medium heat, stirring, until sugar dissolves. Increase heat and boil without stirring until mixture turns golden brown, swirling pan occasionally and using a wet pastry brush to rinse any sugar from sides of the pot. This should take about 10 minutes.
2. Working quickly, pour caramelized sugar into an 8-cup (2 L) round soufflé or baking dish, swirling to coat with sugar. Set aside to allow sugar to harden.
3. Bring cream, evaporated milk, and rum to a boil in a heavy saucepan. Remove from heat and stir in salt.
4. Whisk eggs, pumpkin, brown sugar, cornstarch, and spices together in a large bowl to blend well. Gradually whisk in hot milk mixture.
5. Pour custard into prepared baking dish. Place dish in a larger baking pan filled with 2 inches (5 cm) of hot water. Bake custard in a preheated 350°F (180°C) oven for about 1 hour, until set and puffed. Remove from water and cool. Cover with plastic wrap and chill overnight.
6. Before serving, run a knife around edge of dish and invert custard onto a rimmed plate. The caramel sauce should form a pool around custard. Cut into wedges, spoon a little sauce over each piece, and serve whipped cream on the side. Serves 6 to 8.

SPOTTED DOG (RAISIN RICE PUDDING)

It's the raisins that give this dog its spots. Rice pudding studded with raisins is an old-fashioned dessert that cowboys enjoyed on the range because all of the ingredients, even the canned milk, were portable. Many early Canadian cooks baked rice pudding for about 2 hours in a medium oven, until a light-brown crust formed on top. This is an update of that classic recipe, boiled on the stovetop for speed.

1 tablespoon (15 mL) butter
1/3 cup (75 mL) short-grain rice
1/3 cup (75 mL) granulated sugar
1/4 teaspoon (1 mL) salt
1/2 teaspoon (2 mL) ground cinnamon (optional)
1 teaspoon (5 mL) vanilla extract
3 1/2 cups (875 mL) milk, or 3 cups (750 mL) milk and
    1/2 cup (125 mL) whipping cream
1/2 cup (125 mL) raisins
1/4 cup (50 mL) Grand Marnier or cognac
1 teaspoon (5 mL) minced orange zest

1. In a saucepan, melt butter and stir in rice until coated. Add sugar, salt, cinnamon, vanilla, and milk, and bring to a boil.
2. Cover rice, reduce heat to low, and simmer for 40 minutes or until rice is tender and pudding is creamy but thick.
3. To plump raisins, place in a bowl with Grand Marnier or cognac and microwave on high power for 1–2 minutes. Cool.
4. When rice is tender and milk is absorbed, remove from heat. Stir in plumped raisins and minced orange zest. Serve warm or chilled. Serves 4.

TIP
For an elegant, make-ahead dessert, pour the warm rice pudding into ovenproof ramekins, cover, and chill. Just before serving, top each pudding with a layer of brown sugar. Place puddings under a preheated broiler for a minute to melt and caramelize the sugar before serving.

NUTTY APRICOT FRUIT CAKE SOAKED IN SCOTCH WHISKY

The fruit cake is a classic prairie tradition, lovingly constructed of the finest dried fruits and soaked in the best booze for special occasions like weddings and Christmas. Try this version that comes to Alberta via our Texas connection (where pecans are a major cash crop and cowboys go to escape winter).

2 cups (500 mL) sultana raisins
2 1/2 cups (625 mL) chopped dried apricots
1 cup (250 mL) mixed candied lemon and orange peel
2 cups (500 mL) scotch or rye whisky
1 pound (500 g) butter, room temperature
2 cups (500 mL) granulated sugar
2 cups (500 mL) brown sugar
8 large eggs, separated
3 cups (750 mL) chopped pecans
5 cups (1.25 L) all-purpose flour
1 teaspoon (5 mL) baking powder
1 teaspoon (5 mL) salt
2 teaspoons (10 mL) ground nutmeg
1/2 teaspoon (2 mL) ground cloves

1. Cover raisins, apricots, and peel with scotch and soak overnight. Drain and reserve scotch.
2. With an electric mixer, cream butter with white and brown sugars, then beat in egg yolks one at a time.
3. Toss pecans with 1/2 cup (125 mL) of flour and set aside. Combine remaining flour, baking powder, salt, nutmeg, and cloves. Add flour mixture and reserved scotch alternately to egg mixture to make a smooth batter. Carefully fold in marinated fruit and nuts. Beat egg whites until stiff and fold into batter.
4. Pour batter into two buttered and floured 8-inch (1.5 L) tube pans or springform pans. Pans should be no more than three-quarters full. If you're using a straight-sided pan, line it with waxed paper or buttered parchment to prevent over-browning. If desired, you can also divide batter between smaller pans, and adjust baking time accordingly. This recipe makes enough for about six miniature bread pans. Reduce the baking time to 1 1/2–2 hours if making smaller cakes.

5. Place a shallow pan of water in oven to keep cakes moist during baking. Bake fruit cakes in a preheated 300°F (150°C) oven for 2–2 1/2 hours, until cakes are set and browned and a skewer inserted in the centre of the cakes comes out clean. Brush tops of cakes with 2 tablespoons (25 mL) of scotch as soon as they're out of the oven.

6. Cool cakes and remove from pan. Wrap in several layers of cheesecloth soaked in scotch, then wrap well in foil. Let cakes ripen for 2–3 weeks, then soak cloth again in scotch and rewrap. Fruit cakes must age for at least a month to develop and meld flavours. Like all good fruit cake, this one will keep indefinitely if tightly wrapped. Makes 2 medium or several small cakes.

CHEWY CHOCOLATE BROWNIES

Every country cook can whip up a batch of brownies in a blink. These are especially addictive because they are both nutty and chewy. If you have a miniature muffin pan, try making tiny two-bite brownies, halving the cooking time. Remember, the better the chocolate, the better the brownie.

1 cup (250 mL) butter
4 ounces (125 g) unsweetened chocolate, chopped
2 cups (500 mL) granulated sugar
4 eggs
1 teaspoon (5 mL) vanilla extract
1 cup (250 mL) all-purpose flour
1/2 teaspoon (2 mL) salt
1 cup (250 mL) coarsely chopped walnuts or pecans

1. Lightly grease a 13 x 9 (3.5 L) baking pan. Heat butter over low heat until half melted. Add chocolate and stir until both are completely melted. Remove from heat and stir in sugar.

2. Beat in eggs, one at a time, until mixture is shiny. Stir in vanilla, then add flour and salt. Stir in chopped nuts.

3. Pour batter into prepared pan and bake in a preheated 350°F (180°C) oven for 30 minutes, or until firm. A cake tester or toothpick inserted in the middle of the pan should come out clean. Let cool completely in pan. Makes 24 to 36 bars.

COWBOY COFFEE CUSTARD

This is a flan recipe shared with me by Mexican-born cook Norma Schmill de French. For more intense coffee flavour, drizzle a little Kahlua on top just before serving and garnish with chocolate-covered coffee beans.

1 cup (250 mL) granulated sugar
3 tablespoons (45 mL) water
3 cups (750 mL) milk
1/3 cup (75 mL) icing sugar
1/2 cup (125 mL) espresso or very strong coffee
3 eggs
2 egg yolks
pinch of salt
1/4 cup (50 mL) Kahlua
chocolate-covered coffee beans to garnish

1. Place granulated sugar and water in a heavy saucepan over medium-high heat. Swirl pan constantly until sugar melts and caramelizes, turning golden brown. Use a pastry brush dipped in water to wash sugar crystals down from inside of pot as it caramelizes.

2. Pour caramelized sugar into eight ovenproof ramekins, tilting them so that caramel covers bottom. Set aside.

3. In another pan, combine milk, icing sugar, and coffee. Bring to a boil. Reduce heat and stir until sugar dissolves completely. Set aside.

4. Beat eggs and egg yolks in a large bowl with salt. Slowly pour in warm milk mixture, beating constantly. Add Kahlua, mix well, and pour into prepared ramekins.

5. Place ramekins in a large pan of hot water and bake in a preheated 350°F (180°C) oven for 35 minutes, or until custards are set but still a little jiggly. Remove from hot water bath, cool for 30 minutes, then refrigerate overnight. To serve, invert the custards on individual dessert plates. Drizzle with a little more Kahlua and garnish each with a couple of coffee beans. Serves 8.

RASPBERRY AND SASKATOON CRÈME FRAÎCHE TART

To make your own crème fraîche, mix 2 cups of whipping cream with 1/2 cup of sour cream and let stand, covered, at room temperature for 12 hours. When the mixture is nicely thickened, you can store it in the refrigerator for up to 2 weeks.

Pastry
2/3 cup (150 mL) all-purpose flour
2/3 cup (150 mL) cornmeal
pinch of salt
grated rind of 1 lemon
1/2 cup (125 mL) cold butter
1 egg

Filling
1 1/2 cups (375 mL) fresh raspberries
1 1/2 cups (375 mL) saskatoon berries
3/4 cup (175 mL) crème fraîche
3 eggs
1/4 cup (50 mL) ground almonds
2/3 cup (150 mL) granulated sugar
icing sugar

1. For pastry, pulse ingredients together in food processor just until dough forms a ball. Alternatively, combine flour, cornmeal, salt, and lemon rind, and cut butter into mixture with a pastry blender until crumbly.
2. Press dough into bottom and up sides of a 10-inch (3 L) tart pan with removable base. Bake in preheated 350ºF (180ºC) oven for 15 minutes.
3. Arrange berries in tart shell. Whisk together crème fraîche, eggs, almonds, and sugar. Pour over fruit and bake at 350ºF (180ºC) for 20 minutes until firm, puffed, and lightly golden. Dust with icing sugar before serving. Serves 6 to 8.

RUDY'S BREAD PUDDING

Bernard "Rudy" Vallee created this tasty bread pudding at the Memories Inn in Longview "cowboy-style for city slickers" by dousing it with a buttery whisky sauce he kept simmering in a crock pot on the sideboard.

Pudding
1 loaf day-old French bread, crumbled (about 6–8 cups/1.5–2 L)
4 cups (1 L) milk
2 cups (500 mL) granulated sugar
1/2 cup (125 mL) butter, melted
3 eggs, beaten
2 tablespoons (25 mL) vanilla extract
1 cup (250 mL) raisins

1 cup (250 mL) shredded coconut
1 cup (250 mL) chopped pecans
1 teaspoon (5 mL) ground cinnamon
1 teaspoon (5 mL) ground nutmeg

Whisky or Rum Sauce
1/2 cup (125 mL) butter
1 1/2 cups (375 mL) icing sugar
2 egg yolks
1/2 cup (125 mL) rye whisky or rum

1. Combine all pudding ingredients in a large bowl. Mixture should be very moist, but not soupy. Pour into a buttered 13 x 9-inch (3.5 L) baking dish.
2. Bake in a preheated 350°F (180°C) oven for 75 minutes, until top is golden.
3. To make sauce, melt butter in a saucepan and stir in sugar. Cook until sugar dissolves. Remove from heat and whisk in egg yolks. Gradually add rye or rum, stirring constantly. Sauce will thicken as it cools. Serve warm over bread pudding. Serves 8 to 10.

DOUBLE CHOCOLATE CHUNK COOKIES

For chocoholics everywhere, these are the ultimate way to end a meal (or start one). The recipe is from my old friend Marianne Sanders, who knows a good cookie when she sees one. Don't overbake these. They should be crispy on the outside and chewy on the inside.

1 cup (250 mL) butter
1 1/2 cups (375 mL) granulated sugar
7/8 cup (225 g) Dutch-process cocoa
2 eggs
2 teaspoons (10 mL) vanilla extract
1 teaspoon (5 mL) baking powder
1 1/4 cups (300 mL) all-purpose flour
1/4 pound (125 g) white chocolate chunks, preferably Callebaut
3/4 cup (175 mL) salted peanuts

1. Using a mixer, cream butter and sugar until light and fluffy. Add cocoa and mix to incorporate. Add eggs, one at a time, at medium speed, then vanilla.
2. Combine baking powder and flour and fold into batter to combine. Fold in white chocolate chunks and peanuts.
3. Drop about 2 tablespoons (25 mL) of batter per cookie onto a cookie sheet lined with parchment paper, leaving 2 inches (5 cm) between cookies to allow them to spread. Bake in a preheated 350°F (180°C) oven for 12 minutes. Makes 24 cookies.

SHORTBREAD COOKIES

This is my mother's simple Scottish-style shortbread recipe, which I'm sure is exactly what her Scottish mother made when she settled on the farm in Saskatchewan. Don't bother with fancy cookie presses or shortbread moulds. Make it the old-fashioned way in simple, rectangular fingers.

1 pound (500 g) unsalted butter, room temperature
1 cup (500 mL) granulated sugar
4–5 cups (1–1.25 L) all-purpose flour, sifted

1. Cream butter and sugar together until smooth and fluffy.
2. Gradually add flour until mixture just starts to crumble. Mix with a spoon, not your hands. The mixture should be very stiff, or short, and will barely hold together.
3. Turn mixture out onto a work surface and, using a wide knife, pat into a square, about 1/2–3/4 inches (1.5–2 cm) thick. Cut shortbread into squares, or fingers, each about 3/4 inch (2 cm) wide and 2 inches (5 cm) long.
4. Using a spatula, lift shortbread onto an ungreased cookie sheet, placing pieces about 1/2 inch (1.5 cm) apart. Make a pattern on the top of each piece with the tines of a fork.
5. Bake in a preheated 325°F (150°C) oven for 30–40 minutes, or until edges just barely start to colour. Cool on racks. Makes about 48 shortbread cookies.

GINGER CRACKLE COOKIES

These great little cookies from my friend Jane Fournier are the prairie cook's biscotti, just right with a good cup of coffee or cappuccino. Add the candied ginger if you're feeling adventurous.

3/4 cup (175 mL) shortening or butter
1 cup (250 mL) granulated sugar
1 egg
1/2 cup (125 mL) molasses
3 cups (750 mL) all-purpose flour
1/2 teaspoon (2 mL) salt
2 teaspoons (10 mL) ground ginger
1 teaspoon (5 mL) baking powder
1 teaspoon (5 mL) baking soda
2 teaspoons (10 mL) ground cinnamon
1/2 teaspoon (2 mL) ground cloves
2 tablespoons (25 mL) minced candied ginger (optional)
extra granulated sugar for dipping

1. With an electric mixer, cream shortening or butter with sugar until fluffy. Add egg and beat until smooth. Beat in molasses, leaving mixer running for several minutes to make a fluffy base.
2. Combine flour, salt, ground ginger, baking powder, baking soda, cinnamon, and cloves. Gradually add to batter and combine well. If using candied ginger, add it now. Cover batter and chill.
3. Roll batter into small balls and dip one side in sugar to coat. Set balls 1 1/2 inches (4 cm) apart on an ungreased cookie sheet and bake at 350°F (180°C) for 10 minutes. The cookies will crackle on top and should still be chewy. Don't overbake. Place cookies on a rack to cool. Makes 24 cookies.

SESAME DATE BARS

I always make these chewy little energy bars for cycling trips and hikes in the mountains because they offer a fast burst of energy in a healthy package. They can be a bit sticky, so wrap them individually in plastic wrap before you put them in your pack.

1/2 cup (125 mL) sesame seeds
1/4 cup (50 mL) butter
1 cup (250 mL) granulated sugar
2 eggs
1 cup (250 mL) chopped pecans
1 cup (250 mL) chopped dates
3/4 cup (175 mL) whole-wheat flour
1/3 cup (75 mL) quick-cooking rolled oats

1. Toast sesame seeds in a heavy pan over medium heat until golden. Set aside.
2. Beat butter with sugar until fluffy, then beat in eggs until blended. Stir in pecans, dates, toasted sesame seeds, flour, and oats. Blend well.
3. Spread batter in a greased 9-inch (2 L) square baking pan. Bake in a preheated 350°F (180°C) oven for 20–25 minutes. Cut into small bars while still warm and wrap individually in plastic wrap. Makes 16–24 bars.

CHOCOLATE MATRIMONIAL BARS

For whatever reason, the typical date squares you find in every Canadian kitchen are known as "matrimonial" cake or squares on the prairies. These sweet squares filled with a layer of chocolate fudge are a variation on that theme.

1 cup (250 mL) butter
2 cups (500 mL) brown sugar
2 eggs
2 teaspoons (10 mL) vanilla extract
2 1/2 cups (625 mL) all-purpose flour
1 teaspoon (5 mL) baking soda
1 teaspoon (5 mL) salt
3 cups (750 mL) rolled oats, quick or old-fashioned
1 cup (250 mL) chopped nuts (walnuts or pecans are best)
1 12-ounce (375 g) bag semi-sweet chocolate chips
1 14-ounce (398 mL) can sweetened condensed milk

1. Cream butter and sugar together until fluffy. Add eggs and vanilla and stir well.
2. Mix flour, baking soda, and salt, and gradually add to butter mixture until combined. Slowly stir in oats and nuts and blend well.
3. For fudge layer, combine chocolate chips and condensed milk in a saucepan and cook over low heat, stirring, until chocolate is melted.
4. To assemble, pack two-thirds of the oat mixture into a 13 x 9-inch (3.5 L) baking pan. Press mixture down well, compacting it with a fork. Spread chocolate mixture evenly over top.
5. With your fingers, crumble remaining oat mixture evenly over top of pan to cover chocolate. Press down lightly. Bake in a preheated 350°F (180°C) oven for 25 minutes, until golden. Cool and cut into bars, each about 1 x 2 inches (2.5 x 5 cm). Makes 36 bars.

BAKED STUFFED PEARS WITH CARAMEL SAUCE

Olive oil is the basis for this caramel sauce, created by Jean Faivre at Avignon's hotel school when I was a visitor there. The recipe transfers perfectly to the prairie home kitchen and makes a wonderful fall dessert. Baking the pears concentrates the fruit flavours.

1/2 cup (125 mL) each: dried chopped apricots,
    raisins, chopped almonds, or chopped hazelnuts
1/2 cup (125 mL) pear brandy
1 tablespoon (15 mL) brown sugar
1 teaspoon (5 mL) ground cinnamon
6 pears (Comice, Bosc, or Bartlett pears hold their shape best)
1 tablespoon (15 mL) olive oil

Caramel Sauce
1 cup (250 mL) granulated sugar
1/4 cup (50 mL) fruity olive oil
1 cup (250 mL) whipping cream

1. Finely dice dried fruit and nuts and marinate with pear brandy, brown sugar, and cinnamon for 1 hour. Set aside.
2. Peel and halve pears, using a melon baller to remove core, and stuff with marinated fruit. Arrange stuffed pears in a shallow baking dish and drizzle with olive oil. Bake in a preheated 350°F (180°C) oven for 30 minutes, until tender.
3. Meanwhile, combine sugar and olive oil in a saucepan and cook over medium heat until lightly browned. Add cream and cook gently for 20 minutes. Whip with a wire whisk while cooling. Serve warm pears drizzled with caramel cream sauce. Serves 6.

ALBERTA PRODUCTS

ALBERTA PRODUCER GROUPS

Alberta Barley Commission
200, 3601A - 21 Street NE
Calgary, AB T2E 6T5
Phone: 403-291-9111
Web Site: www.albertabarley.com

Alberta Canola Producers Commission
170, 14315 - 118 Avenue
Edmonton, AB T5L 4S6
Phone: 780-454-0844,
(toll free) 1-800-551-0844
Web Site: www.canola.ab.ca

Alberta Egg Producers Board
101, 90 Freeport Boulevard NE
Calgary, AB T3J 5J9
Phone: 403-250-1197,
(toll free) 1-877-302-2344
Web Site: www.eggs.ab.ca

Alberta Farm Fresh Producers Association
Phone: (toll free) 1-800-661-2642
Web Site: www.albertafarmfresh.com
Comments: free "Come to Our Farm" map
and guide

Alberta Farmer's Market Association
106, 7000 - 113 Street
Edmonton, AB T6H 5T6
Phone: 780-644-5377
Web Site: www.albertamarkets.com

Alberta Goat Breeders Association
Box 330
Hay Lakes, AB T0B 1W0
Phone: 780-878-3814
Web Site: www.albertagoatbreeders.ca

Alberta Milk
1303, 91 Street SW
Edmonton, AB T6X 1H1
Phone: 780-453-5942, (toll free) 1-877-361-
1231
Web Site: www.albertamilk.com

Alberta Pork
103, 14707 Bannister Road SE
Calgary, AB T2X 1Z2
Phone: 403-256-2764
Web Site: www.albertapork.com

Alberta Pulse Growers
4301, 50 Street
Leduc, AB T9E 7H3
Phone: 780-986-9398,
(toll free) 1-877-550-9398
Web Site: www.pulse.ab.ca

Alberta Sheep and Wool Commission
Agriculture Centre, 97 East Lake Ramp NE
Airdrie, AB T4A 0C3
Phone: 403-948-8533
Web Site: www.absheep.com

Alberta Turkey Producers
4828, 89 Street
Edmonton, AB T6E 5K1
Phone: 780-465-5755
Web Site: www.albertaturkey.com

Beef Information Centre
Calgary Office
310, 6715 - 8 Street NE
Calgary, AB T2E 7H7
Phone: 403-275-5890
Web Site: www.beefinfo.org

Bison Producers of Alberta
4603 - 61 Avenue
Leduc, AB T9E 7A4
Phone: 780-986-4100
Web Site: www.bisoncentre.com

Fruit Growers Society of Alberta
Web Site: www.albertafruit.com
Comments: represents fruit and berry
growers in Alberta (no permanent office);
links to u-pick farms

Growing Alberta
201, 8704 - 51 Avenue
Edmonton, AB T6E 5E8
Phone: 780-466-7928
Web Site: www.growingalberta.com

DAIRY FOODS AND CHEESE

Bles-Wold Dairy
RR5
Lacombe, AB T0C 1S0
Phone: 403-782-3322
Web Site: www.bles-wold.com
Comments: plain and flavoured farm-
made yogurt and sour cream

Fairwinds Farm
Fort Macleod, AB
Phone: 403-553-0127
Comments: goat milk, goat yogurt, and
unripened goat cheese (chevre) and feta

Fiasco Gelato
736 - 17 Avenue SW
Calgary, AB
Phone: 403-229-2503
Web Site: www.fiascogelato.com
Comments: Thirty-plus flavours of freshly
made gelato

Janice Beaton Fine Cheese
1708, 8 Street SW
Calgary, AB T2T 2Y9
Phone: 403-229-0900
Web Site: www.jbfinecheese.com
Comments: retail cheese shop with exten-
sive selection of regional and imported
cheeses, a second Calgary location in
Kensington

Mackay's Cochrane Ice Cream
Cochrane, AB
Phone: 403-932-2455
Web Site: www.mackaysicecream.com
Comments: ice cream, frozen yogurt, and
sorbet available by the scoop, litre, or
wholesale quantities

Paddy's International Cheese Market
10732, 82 Avenue NW
Edmonton, AB T6E 6P4
Phone: 780-413-0367

Pinocchio Ice Cream
12814, 163 Street
Edmonton, AB
Phone: 780-455-1905
Web Site: www.pinocchioicecreamcom
Comments: premium gourmet ice creams
and sorbets, custom flavours

Sylvan Star Cheese
RR1
Red Deer, AB T4N 5E1
Phone: 403-340-1560
Comments: plain, smoked, and flavoured
Gouda cheese (2000 Canadian champion),
aged cheddar

Tiras Dairies
3712 42 Avenue
Camrose, AB T4V 4W3
Phone: 780-608-2487
Comments: feta cheese

BISON AND WILD GAME

Canadian Rangeland Beef and Bison
Box 857
Rimbey, AB T0C 2J0
Phone: (toll free) 1-877-844-2231
Web Site: www.rangelandbison.ca
Comments: beef and bison raised with no
growth hormones, antibiotics, or stimulants

Canadian Rocky Mountain Ranch
Web Site: www.crmr.com/ranch
Comments: game, including elk, bison, and
caribou from the ranch that supplies the
CRM resorts and restaurants

Carmen Creek Gourmet Meats
1919B, 4 Street SW
Box 914
Calgary, AB T2S 1W4
Phone: 403-233-9393
Web Site: www.carmencreek.com
Comments: Carmen Creek brand bison
products

Dirt Willy Game Bird Farm
53116 Range Road 210
Ardrossan, AB T8G 2E4
Phone: 780-922-6080
Web Site: www.dirtwilly.com
Comments: farm-raised wild turkey, partridge, pheasant

Full Course Strategies
Phone: 780-413-9266
Comments: distributor of alternative meats including bison, elk, beef, pork, rabbit, lamb

Hog Wild Specialties
Box 1209
Mayerthorpe, AB T0E 1N0
Phone: 780-786-4627, (toll free) 1-888-668-9453
Web Site: www.hogwild.ab.ca
Comments: wild boar meat (fresh or frozen), wild boar smokies, paté, jerky

Horizon Meats
3610, 29 Street NE
Calgary, AB T1Y 5Z7
Phone: 403-291-0595
Web Site: www.horizonmeats.ca
Comments: specialty meats: from wild turkey and bison to alligator to ostrich, homemade sausages

North Country Bison Meats
10718, 180 Street
Edmonton, AB T5S 2J6
Phone: 780-454-8858
Web Site: www.ncbison.com
Comments: bison meat, burgers, sausage, jerky

Specialty Fine Foods & Meats
4820 Northland Drive NW
Calgary, AB T2L 4L3
Phone: 403-282-7412
Comments: retail source of bison, venison, wild boar, caribou, emu, organic chicken

Valbella Meats & Specialty Foods
104 Elk Run Industrial Park
Box 8121
Canmore, AB T1W 2T8
Phone: 403-678-4109
Web Site: www.valbellagourmetfoods.ca
Comments: wild game and sausages, smoked bison carpaccio, venison smokies, gourmet food

Valta Bison
Box 22
Valhalla Centre, AB T0H 3M0
Phone: 780-356-3627
Web Site: www.valtabison.com
Comments: bison products, available at Calgary Farmer's Market

Wapiti Ways
Year-round location, Calgary Farmer's Market
Phone: 403-238-3120,
(toll free) 1-888-927-4849
Web Site: www.wapitiways.com
Comments: ranched elk and venison

Windy Ridge Exotic Meat
339, 13 Street N
Lethbridge, AB T1H 2S1
Phone: 403-381-7508
Comments: bison, farm direct

MEAT AND POULTRY

Broek Pork Acres
Coalhurst, AB
Phone: 403-381-4753
Web Site: www.broekporkacres.com
Comments: pastured pork, sausages, smoked meats, heritage Berkshire pork, no growth hormones, antibiotics, or animal by-products

Diamond Willow Organics
Box 1718
Pincher Creek, AB T0K 1W0
Phone: 403-627-1800
Comments: certified organic beef from seven Alberta ranches

Driview Farms
Fort Macleod, AB
Phone: 403-553-2178
Web Site: www.driviewfarms.ca
Comments: specializing in lamb and beef raised without antibiotics or growth hormones

Ewe-Nique Farms
Box 794
Picture Butte, AB T0K 1V0
Phone: 403-824-3050
Web Site: www.eweniquefarms.com
Comments: free range natural Alberta lamb, processed and cut on the farm

First Nature Farms
Box 123
Goodfare, AB T0H 1T0
Phone: 780-356-2239
Web Site: www.firstnaturefarms.ab.ca
Comments: certified organic chicken, turkey, bison, eggs, wild turkey, and organic pet food

Hoven Farms
RR 3
Eckville, AB T0M 0X0
Phone: 403-746-3072, (toll free) 1-800-311-2333
Web Site: www.hovenfarms.com
Comments: certified organic Alberta beef from the farm or at Calgary Farmer's Market
(403-217-2343)

Old Country Sausage Shop
Box 775
Raymond, AB T0K 2S0
Phone: 403-752-3006
Comments: fresh, natural sausages with no additives, fillers or preservatives; available at Klaus Schurmann's booth at the Calgary Farmer's Market

Pine Terra Farm
Onoway, AB T0E 1V0
Phone: 780-967-3012
Comments: certified organic, grass-fed beef

Spolumbo's Fine Foods
1308, 9 Avenue SE
Calgary, AB T2G 0T3
Phone: 403-264-6452
Web Site: www.spolumbos.com
Comments: Italian, chicken and apple, chorizo, and other fresh gourmet sausages made with pork and poultry

Sunshine Organic Farm
Warburg, AB
Phone: 780-848-2288, (toll free) 1-866-648-2288
Web Site: www.sunshineorganicfarm.com
Comments: organic pasture-raised beef, chicken, pork, and eggs

Sunworks Farm
Box 55
Armena, AB T0B 0G0
Phone: 780-672-9799,
(toll free) 1-877-393-3133
Web Site: www.sunworksfarm.com
Comments: certified organic pastured poultry, raised in moveable pens, at Calgary Farmer's Market

TK Ranch Natural Meats
123 Wildflower Lane
PO Box 2050
Hanna, AB T0J 1P0
Phone: 403-578-2404,
(toll free) 1-888-857-2624
Web Site: www.natural-beef.net
Comments: natural, ethically raised meats including 100% grass-fed beef from Alberta ranches, pastured poultry, bison, natural, hormone-free pork and lamb

Wagyu Canada Inc
Camrose, AB
Phone: 780-672-2990
Web Site: www.wagyucanada.com
Comments: producers of highly marbled beef from Japanese Wagyu and Angus cross cattle

Western Quality Meats
2825 Bonnybrook Road SE
Calgary, AB T2G 4N9
Phone: 403-255-3060
Web Site: www.wqmeats.com
Comments: wholesalers of premium meats
and wild game

Winter's Turkeys
Box 321
Dalemead, AB T0J 0V0
Phone: 403-936-5586
Web Site: www.wintersturkeys.ca
Comments: free-range, grain-fed turkeys,
fresh and frozen, and turkey products

CONDIMENTS AND SNACKS

Brassica Mustard
Web Site: www.brassicamustard.com
Comments: gourmet mustard in several
flavours including roasted garlic, horseradish, dill, and cranberry honey

Cattle Boyz Foods
1735, 33 Avenue SW
Calgary, AB T2T 1Y8
Phone: 403-262-9366
Web Site: www.cattleboyzsauce.com
Comments: barbecue sauces and seasonings

Del Comal Foods
Box 788
Claresholm, AB T0L 0T0
Phone: 403-625-3311
Web Site: www.delcomal.com
Comments: stoneground yellow and blue
tortilla chips, organic corn chips

El Molino Foods
3615, 9 Street SE
Calgary, AB T2G 3C7
Phone: 403-287-2000
Web Site: www.elmolinofoods.com
Comments: tortilla chips, flour and corn
tortillas, and Mexican and Italian foods

Longview Meats
Box 173
Longview, AB T0L 1H0
Phone: 403-558-3706
Web Site: www.longviewjerky.com
Comments: beef jerky in several flavours
and pepperoni-style sausages

Sage Kitchen
Box 550
Black Diamond, AB T0L 0H0
Phone: 403-933-4882
Web Site: www.sagekitchen.com
Comments: lavender, nasturtium, rose petal,
and jalapeno jellies, dried flower petals

Saucy Ladies
1254, 3 Avenue N
Lethbridge, AB
Phone: 403-329-8719
Web Site: www.saucyladies.com
Comments: home-style sauces, antipasto,
pickles, jellies, and chutney

Simmons Hot Gourmet Products
22 Greenview Close
Lethbridge, AB T1H 4K8
Phone: 403-327-9087
Web Site: www.firenbrimstone.com
Comments: award-winning hot pepper
sauces

Some Like It Hot
4432, 10 Street NW
Calgary, AB T2E 6K3
Phone: 403-735-6022
Comments: hot sauces, pickles, chutneys,
condiments

Zinter-Brown Taste Treats
25 Wedgewood Crescent
Edmonton, AB T6M 2N4
Phone: 780-487-9334
Web Site: www.zinterbrown.com
Comments: antipasto, salsa, roasted garlic
and onion jam, specialty mustards and
gourmet condiments

CHOCOLATE, CANDY, AND SWEETS

Alberta Bee Keepers Association
102, 11434 - 168 Street
Edmonton, AB T5M 3T9
Web Site: www.albertabeekeepers.org

Chinook Honey Company
Okotoks, AB T1S 1A1
Phone: 403-995-0830
Web Site: www.chinookhoney.com
Comments: on-farm tours and retail store
selling honey, bee products, candles, with
plans to make mead

Chocolaterie Bernard Callebaut
1313, 1 Street SE
Calgary, AB T2G 5L1
Phone: 403-265-5777
Web Site: www.bernardcallebaut.com
Comments: handcrafted Belgian choco-
lates, truffles, and high quality baking
chocolate

Golden Acres Honey
Box 42
Three Hills, AB T0M 2A0
Phone: 403-443-7705
Web Site: www.goldenacreshoney.com
Comments: honey, some organic

Heyn Old Fashioned Honey
Box 657
Eckville, AB T0M 0X0
Phone: 403-746-5726
Comments: honey

Olivier's Candies
2828, 54 Avenue SE
Calgary, AB T2C 0A7
Phone: 403-266-6028
Web Site: www.oliviers.ca
Comments: old-fashioned hard candy,
hand-pulled candy canes, ribbon candy

Riddles Sweet Impressions
6311 Wagner Road
Edmonton, AB T6E 4N4
Phone: 780-465-8085

Web Site: www.riddlessweet.com
Comments: old-fashioned hard candy,
chocolate, chicken bones, humbugs,
coconut marshmallows

GRAINS, PULSES, AND SEEDS

Artesian Acres
RR 3
Lacombe, AB T4L 2N3
Phone: 403-782-5075,
(toll free) 1-888-782-5075
Comments: organic kamut flour, flakes,
grain, cereals

Classic Grains of Canada
Box 621
Innisfail, AB T4G 1S8
Phone: 403-227-0098
Web Site: www.wheatcrunch.com
Comments: roasted grain snacks and salad
toppings, roasted corn

Grainworks: The Organic Grain Company
Box 30
Vulcan, AB T0L 2B0
Phone: 403-485-2808,
(toll free) 1-800-563-3756
Web Site: www.grainworks.com
Comments: growers and distributors of
organic grains, flours, cereals, heirloom beans

Hamilton's Barley Flour
RR 2
Olds, AB T0M 1P0
Phone: 403-556-8493
Web Site: www.hamiltonsbarley.com
Comments: barley flour

Highwood Crossing Farm
Box 25
Aldersyde, AB T0L 0A0
Phone: 403-652-1910
Comments: certified organic wheat flour,
rye flour, flax muffins and pancake mix,
organic cold-pressed canola and flax oils

Lakeland Wild Rice
Box 3042
Athabasca, AB T9F 2B9
Phone: 780-675-4148
Comments: wild rice

Prairie Harvest
12538, 126 Street
Edmonton, AB T5L 0X3
Phone: 780-454-4004
Comments: Canada's only full-scale manu-
facturer of organic pasta

Rockport Flour Mills
Box 460
Magrath, AB T0K 1J0
Phone: 403-758-3340
Web site: www.coyotepancakemix.com
Comments: Coyote brand pancake flour
and waffle mix

Sunny Boy Foods
250, 9411 63 Avenue
Edmonton, AB T6E 0G2
Phone: 780-672-3985
Web Site: www.sunnyboyfoods.com
Comments: hot cereal, organic flour, pan-
cake mix

BAKERIES

Brulee Bakery
722, 11 Avenue SW
Calgary, AB T2R 0E4
Phone: 403-261-3064
Comments: elegant handmade cakes and
desserts, open Saturday only

Byblos Bakery
2479, 23 Street NE
Calgary, AB T2E 8J8
Phone: 403-250-3711
Web Site: www.byblosbakery.com
Comments: pita and flat breads, naan, tor-
tillas, pizza shells

Decadent Desserts
831, 10 Avenue SW
Calgary, AB T2R 0B4
Phone: 403-245-5535
Web Site: www.decadentdesserts.ca
Comments: gourmet cakes, cheesecakes,
pies, cookies

Eiffel Tower Bakery
121, 1013 17 Avenue SW
Calgary, AB T2T 0P5
Phone: 403-244-0103
Comments: traditional French baguette,
peasant breads, French cheeses and deli

Kinnikinnick Foods
10940, 120 Street
Edmonton, AB T5H 3P7
Phone: 780-424-2900
Web Site: www.kinnikinnick.com
Comments: gluten-free, dairy-free, yeast-
free, sugar-free, egg-free baked goods

Lakeview Bakery
6449 Crowchild Trail SW
Calgary, AB T3E 5R7
Phone: 403-246-6127
Web Site: www.organicbaking.com
Comments: allergy-free and organic baking,
rice baking, organic spelt and kamut products

Manuel Latruwe Belgian Patisserie &
Bread Shop
1333, 1 Street SE
Calgary, AB T2G 5L1
Phone: 403-261-1092
Comments: intricate and elegant Belgian
pastries, quiche, croissant, bread

Prairie Mill Bread Co.
129, 4820 Northland Drive NW
Calgary, AB T2L 2L4
Phone: 403-282-6455
Comments: rustic, organic breads made
with stoneground flours, milled on site

Rustic Sourdough Bakery
1305, 17 Avenue SW
Calgary, AB T2T 0C4

Phone: 403-245-2113
Comments: hearty sourdough breads, rye
breads, pretzel buns, coffee cakes

Tree Stone Bakery
8612, 99 Street
Edmonton, AB T6E 3T8
Phone: 780-433-5924
Comments: artisan "pain au levain" breads,
milled organic whole grain flours

Urban Baker
802 Edmonton Trail
Calgary, AB T2E 3J6
Phone: 403-276-5499
Comments: natural sourdoughs, apple flax
rosemary, baguette, sweets

Wild Earth Bakery
8902 99 Street
Edmonton, AB
Phone: 780-425-8423

BEER, WINE, AND SPIRITS

Alberta Distillers Ltd.
1521, 34 Avenue SE
Calgary, AB T2G 1V9
Phone: 403-265-2541

Alley Kat Brewing Co.
9929, 60 Avenue
Edmonton, AB T6E 0C7
Phone: 780-436-8922
Web Site: www.alleykatbeer.com
Comments: small batch ales and lagers
including Aprikat fruit beer, Alley Kat
amber, and Old Deuteronomy Barley Wine

Big Rock Brewery Ltd.
5555, 76 Avenue SE
Calgary, AB T2C 4L8
Phone: 403-720-3239
Web Site: www.bigrockbeer.com
Comments: Traditional Ale, Grasshopper
Wheat Ale, McNally's Extra, Warthog Ale,
Black Amber Ale, and others

Fieldstone Fruit Wines
Strathmore, AB
Phone: 403-934-2749
Web Site: www.fieldstonefruitwines.com
Comments: Alberta's first cottage winery
making raspberry, Saskatoon, sour cherry,
Bumbleberry, and other prairie fruit wines

Highwood Distillers
Box 5693
High River, AB T1V 1M7
Phone: 403-652-3202
Web Site: www.highwood-distillers.com

Wild Rose Brewery
9, 5815 40 Street SE
Calgary, AB
Phone: 403-720-2733
Web Site: www.wildrosebrewery.com
Comments: from Velvet Fog to Raspberry
Ale and Industrial Park Ale, brewery on the
old Currie Barracks site

RESTAURANTS

The Belvedere Restaurant
107, 8 Avenue SW
Calgary, AB T2P 1B4
Phone: 403-265-9595
Web Site: www.thebelvedere.ca

The Bison Mountain Bistro and General
Store
211 Bear Street
Banff, AB T1L 1E4
Phone: 403-762-5550
Web Site: www.thebison.ca
Comments: fine cheese, specialty meats
and housemade spreads for picnics, bistro
menu

Bistro Provence
52 North Railway St.
Okotoks, AB T0L 1T3
Phone: 403-938-2224
Web Site: www.bistro-provence.ca

Forage (farm to fork foods to go)
Infuse Cuisine Group
3510, 19 Street SW
Calgary, AB T2T 4X6
Web Site: www.foragefoods.com
Comments: organic breads and baking,
prepared foods

Hardware Grill
9698 Jasper Avenue
Edmonton, AB
Phone: 780-423-0969
Web Site: www.hardwaregrill.com

Homefire Grill
18210, 100 Avenue
Edmonton, AB
Phone: 780-489-8086
Web Site: www.homefiregrill.ca

Jasper Park Lodge
PO Box 40
Jasper, AB T0E 1E0
Phone: 780-852-3301
Web Site: www.jasperparklodge.com

Muse
107, 10A Street NW
Calgary, AB
Web Site: www.muserestaurant.ca

Open Range
1114 Edmonton Trail NE
Calgary, AB
Phone: 403-277-3408
Web site: www.cuisineconcepts.ca

Pasu Farm
Box 656
Carstairs, AB T0M 0N0
Phone: 403-337-2800
Web Site: www.pasu.com

Quarry Bistro
718 Main Street
Canmore, AB
Phone: 403-678-6088
Web Site: www.quarrybistro.com

The Ranche Restaurant
Fish Creek Provincial Park
Bow Bottom Trail SE
Box 2780
Calgary, AB T2P 0Y8
Phone: 403-225-3939
Web Site: www.crmr.com/theranche/

River Cafe
Prince's Island Park
Calgary, AB
Phone: 403-261-7670
Web Site: www.river-cafe.com

Rouge
1240, 8 Avenue SE
Calgary, AB
Phone: 403-531-2767
Web Site: www.rougecalgary.com

Route 40 Soup Co.
146 Main Street
Turner Valley
Phone: 403-933-7676
Web Site: www.route40sc.ca

Saint Germain
115, 12 Avenue SW
Calgary, AB T2R 0G8
Phone: 403-290-1322
Web Site: www.saintgermain.ca

Sonoma Market Café
240, 520 5 Avenue SW
Calgary, AB T2P 3R7
Phone: 403-233-0111

Teatro
200, 8 Avenue SE
Calgary, AB T2G 0K7
Phone: 403-290-1082
Web Site: www.teatro-rest.com

Wildwood Grill & Brewing Co.
2417, 4 Street SW
Calgary, AB
Phone: 403-228-0100
Web Site: www.wildwoodgrill.ca

FISH

Billingsgate Fish Co.
630, 7 Avenue SE
Calgary, AB T2G 0J7
Phone: 403-571-7700
Web Site: www.billingsgate.com
Comments: wholesale and retail fish and
seafood sales

Cunningham's Scotch Cold Smoking
Pincher Creek, AB
Web Site:
www.cunninghamscoldsmoking.com
Comments: high quality smoked salmon
and trout

Delta Native Fishermen's Association
Box 480
Fort Chipewyan, AB T0P 1B0
Phone: 780-697-3678
Comments: walleye, lake trout, goldeye,
whitefish, pike

Freshwater Fish Marketing Corp.
8542, 126 Avenue
Edmonton, AB T5B 1G9
Phone: 780-495-5103
Web Site: www.freshwaterfish.com
Comments: freshwater fish

Valley Spring Trout Farm
Innisfail, AB
Phone: 403-227-2105
Comments: farm sales of frozen and hot-
smoked naturally raised Alberta trout

FRUITS AND VEGETABLES

Alexandra's Natural Garden
Box 1115
Black Diamond, AB T0L 0H0
Phone: 403-933-0004
Comments: salad greens

Beck Farms
RR 3, Site 3, Box 6
Innisfail, AB T4G 1T8
Phone: 403-227-1020

Web Site: www.innisfailgrowers.com/beck
Comments: fresh vegetables, carrots

Blush Lane Organic Produce
Web Site: www.blushlane.com
Comments: available at the Calgary
Farmer's Market

DNA Gardens
Box 544
Elnora, AB T0M 0Y0
Phone: 403-773-2489, (toll free) 1-866-687-
5268
Web Site: www.dnagardens.com
Comments: orchard and nursery specializ-
ing in unusual fruits like haskap, pie cher-
ries, saskatoons, and wild black cherries

Duncan's Market Garden
Box 2, Site 13, RR 5
Calgary, AB T2P 2G6
Phone: 403-936-5485
Comments: salsas, jams, pickles, jellies,
antipasto

Edgar Farms
RR3, Innisfail, AB T4G 1T8
Phone: 403-227-2443
Web Site: www.edgarfarms.com
Comments: largest asparagus farm in
Alberta with a seasonal general store on
the farm, selling asparagus, natural beef,
peas, and beans

The Garden
Glenmore Trail & 180 Street SE
Calgary (Langdon), AB T0J 1X0
Phone: 403-936-5569
Web Site: www.thegardencalgary.com
Comments: u-pick strawberries and veg-
etables, flowers, garden plots, fish pond

Gull Valley Greenhouses
Gull Lake, AB
Comments: hydroponically grown cucum-
bers, tomatoes, peppers, beans, lettuces,
with no pesticides or herbicides, at Calgary
Farmer's Market

Hotchkiss Herbs & Produce
Box 1, Site 22, RR5
Calgary, AB T2P 2G6
Phone: 403-236-2963
Web Site: www.hotchkissproduce.com
Comments; year-round, greenhouse production of organic, heirloom tomatoes, herbs, greens, and vegetables

Innisfail Growers
Central Alberta
Web Site: www.innisfailgrowers.com
Comments: five farm families that grow and market their vegetables in a co-op including Beck Farms, Edgar Farm, Uppergreen Farms, The Jungle Farm, and C&J Greenhouses

The Jungle
West of Innisfail
Phone: 403-227-4231
Web Site: www.thejunglefarm.com
Comments: on-farm general store and u-pick strawberries, cucumbers, pumpkins, etc.

Kayben Farms
Box 60, Site 2, RR2
Okotoks, AB T1S 1A2
Phone: 403-938-2857
Web Site: www.kayben.com
Comments: black currant orchard, garden centre and products, from punch base to jams and jellies

Kuhlmann's Market Gardens & Greenhouses
1320, 167 Avenue NW
Edmonton, AB T5Y 6L6
Phone: 780-475-7500
Comments: market produce, locally grown and sold at Edmonton area farmers' markets

The Little Potato Co.
Box 33166
Edmonton, AB T5P 4V8
Phone: 780-414-6075
Web Site: www.littlepotatoes.com
Comments: several varieties of gourmet miniature potatoes

Lund's Organic Farm
Innisfail, AB
Web Site: www.lundsorganic.com
Comments: certified organic seasonal vegetables, organic vegetable juices, at Calgary Farmer's Market

Macfarlane's Market Garden
General Delivery
Lyalta, AB T0J 1Y0
Phone: 403-934-3301
Comments: strawberries and vegetables, jams, jellies, pickles, condiments

Mo-Na Food
9320, 60 Avenue
Edmonton, AB T6E 0C1
Phone: 780-435-4370,
(toll free) 1-866-436-4370
Web Site: www.monafood.ca
Comments: wild mushrooms (fresh and dried), wild berries, Canadian wild rice

Pearson's Berry Farm
RR1
Bowden, AB T0M 0K0
Phone: 403-224-3011
Web Site: www.homestylebeverages.com
Comments: saskatoons (u-pick and picked), jams, syrups, pie filling, berry concentrates

Peas on Earth Certified Organic Market Garden
Sturgeon Road East
St. Albert, AB
Phone: 780-973-6680
Web Site: www.peasonearth.ca
Comments: organic vegetables including greens, peas, carrots, and exotic veggies, farm store

Poplar Bluff Farm
Strathmore, AB
Phone: 403-938-5400
Comments: gourmet potatoes

Prairie Mushrooms Inc.
Sherwood Park, AB
Phone: 780-467-3555

Web Site: www.prairiemushrooms.com
Comments: fresh portabellas, white, crimini, oyster, and shiitake mushrooms

Saskatoon Farm
RR1
DeWinton, AB T0L 0X0
Phone: 403-938-6245,
(toll free) 1-800-463-2113
Web Site: www.saskatoonfarm.com
Comments: saskatoons (u-pick and picked), jams, jellies, syrups, pie filling, restaurant/shop

GOURMET GROCERIES & SPECIALTY FOODS

Amaranth Whole Foods
John Laurie Blvd. and Arbour Lake Drive NW
Calgary, AB
Phone: 403-547-6333
Web Site: www.amaranthfoods.ca

Community Natural Foods
1304, 10 Avenue SW
Calgary, AB T3C 0J4
Phone: 403-229-2383
Web Site: www.communitynaturalfoods.com
Comments: large selection of local, organic and natural produce, packaged foods, meats, fish (two locations)

The Cookbook Company
722, 11 Avenue SW
Calgary, AB T2R 0E4
Phone: 403-265-6066
Web Site: www.cookbookcooks.com
Comments: cookbooks, house-made condiments and stocks, unusual herbs and spices, cheese and fresh local products, cheeses

Jan's Meat & Deli
2436, 2 Avenue NW
Calgary, AB
Phone: 403-270-8334
Comments: fresh meat, homemade bacon and Polish sausages, cold cuts, imports

Lina's Italian Market
2202 Centre Street NE
Calgary, AB
Phone: 403-277-9166
Comments: Italian groceries, produce, deli , cheese counter, restaurant

Mercato
2224, 4 Street SW
Calgary, AB
Phone: 403-263-553
Comments: upscale Italian specialty market and cafe

Planet Organic
Four locations in Calgary and Edmonton (plus across Canada)
Web Site: www.planetorganic.ca
Comments: organic supermarkets, started in High Level, AB

Second to None Meat Shop
3, 2100 - 4 Street SW
Calgary, AB T2S 1W7
Phone: 403-245-6662
Web Site: www.second-to-none-meats.ca
Comments: local Galloway beef, pastured pork, wild boar, poultry, rabbit, lamb, seafood, bison, elk, organic eggs, Cunningham's cold smoking, and other local products

Sunny Side Market
10, 338 - 10 Street NW
Calgary, AB
Phone: 403-270-7477

Sunterra Market
Several locations in Calgary and Edmonton
Web Site: www.sunterramarket.com
Comments: gourmet groceries, bakery, prepared foods, private label beef and pork

Worldwide Specialty Foods
7410, 5 Street SE
Calgary, AB T2H 2L9
Phone: 403-255-6262
Comments: wholesalers of imported cheeses, produce, and gourmet foods

INDEX

A

Air-Dried Buffalo Carpaccio Sticks, 5
Appetizers
  air-dried buffalo carpaccio sticks, **5**
  apple, walnut, and cheese strudel, 8
  bison carpaccio with cold-pressed canola oil, 69
  classic Swiss fondue, 12
  corn and chili pepper pancakes with smoked trout and horseradish cream, 7
  cowboy quesadillas with avocado cream dipping sauce, 3
  devilled eggs, 9
  not foie gras pâté, 8
  potato skins with double-smoked bacon and sheep feta, 12
  prairie pickerel ceviche, 11
  red lentil hummus, 6
  white bean slather with roasted onions and goat cheese, 4
  wild mushroom toasts, 9
Apple(s)
  , berry crisp, 140
  , compote, warm on ginger cake, 144
  , in mountain muesli with CPR strawberries, 129
  in golden prairie squash bisque, 31
  in Thierry's tarte tatin, 145
  in warm red cabbage and pecan salad, 17
  maple walnut, kuchen, 145
  walnut and cheese strudel with, 19
Apple Berry Crisp, 140
Apple, Walnut, and Cheese Strudel, 8
Apricot(s)
  in nutty fruit cake soaked in Scotch whisky, 148
Arugula
  in fettucini with creamy blue goat cheese and mascarpone sauce, 105
Avocado(es)
  , in barley salad with red onion, and orange vinaigrette, 25
  cream dipping sauce, with cowboy quesadillas, 3
  in tenderloin salad with spicy ranch dressing, 23

B

Baby Greens with Blue Potato and Goat Cheese Croutons, 17

Bacon
  double-smoked, with potato skins and sheep feta, 12
  in baked potato torte, 106
  smoky, in potato salad with warm mustard dressing, 26
Baked Potato Torte, 106
Baked Stuffed Potatoes with Roots and Ginger, 113
Banana Bread, 130
Barbecue
  pork, pulled with mustard sauce, 56
  rub, 56
Barbecue sauce
  cowboy coffee, with beef burgers, 44
Barley
  , and wild rice pilaf, 117
  , flour in multi-grain pancakes, 134
  , risotto with butternut squash and Alberta Grana 117
  , salad with red onion, avocado, and orange vinaigrette, 25
  in minestrone with ham and white beans, 39
  tomato chickpea soup with, 37
Barley Risotto with Butternut Squash and Alberta Grana, 117
Barley Salad with Red Onion, Avocado, and Orange Vinaigrette, 25
Basil
  , with roasted carrots, 106
Bean
  sausage and pinto, chili, 52
Bean(s)
  about, 29
  black, in cowboy calzones with grilled chicken and, 77
  black, in cowboy quesadillas with avocado cream dipping sauce, 3
  black, soup, 33
  black, Taber corn and smoked tomato cassoulet, 109
  black, turkey and rice salad, 24
  chickpea, and tomato soup with barley, 37
  chickpea, in prairie paella, 82
  dried, in fresh corn and roasted pepper succotash, 107
  garbanzo. See chickpea
  in bulgar and pinto, salad, 16
  mixed prairie, in chowder of wild Alberta mushrooms, 30
  pinto, in easy cookhouse beans, 109

slather with roasted onions and goat cheese, 4
  to soak and cook dried, 29
  white, and squash sauté with cold-pressed canola oil, 102
  white, braised with lamb shoulder, 55
  white, minestrone with ham and, 39
  white, with rosemary, 102
Beef
  , and Big Rock, 49
  , brisket, pot roasted, 48
  , shortribs in port and ale sauce, 47
  , tenderloin with wild mushroom sauce, 46
  burgers with cowboy coffee barbecue baste, 44
  cooking, about, 43
  flank steak, grilled with heirloom tomatoes three ways, 46
  ginger, 48
  grass-fed, about, 43
  grilled steak fajitas, 49
  ground, in spiced shepherd's pie, 50
  organic, about, 41
  prime rib roast, classic Alberta, 45
  stew, with beer, 49
Beef and Big Rock, 49
Beef Burgers with Cowboy Coffee Barbecue Baste, 44
Beef Shortribs in Port and Ale Sauce, 47
Beer
  beef shortribs in port and, sauce, 47
  black amber, soup, 35
  -braised onions and peppers with Spolumbo's sausage on crusty buns, 54
  in beef stew with Big Rock, 49
Beet and Cabbage Borscht, 38
Beet(s)
  , and cabbage borscht, 38
  , roasted and grapefruit salad, 24
  in lake trout fillets on roasted root vegetables, 89
  striped, and chèvre salad, 15
  to roast, 24
Berri(es)
  apple, crisp, 140
  raspberry and saskatoon crème fraîche tart, 150
  saskatoon, pie, 138
  saskatoon, and lime cheesecake 139
  strawberry napoleons with lemon mascarpone cream, 142
  white chocolate flan with, 140

Biscuit(s)
  cheddar cheese, 124
  lemon scones with crabapple and rose geranium jelly, 131
  savoury potato and cheese, 130
Bison
  , carpaccio with cold-pressed canola oil, 69
  braised, with mushroom sage gravy and wild rice fritters, 67
  grilled, on mixed greens with saskatoon berry dressing, 66
  ground, pie with potato crust, 68
  pemmican patties, 69
Bison Carpaccio with Cold-Pressed Canola Oil, 69
Black Amber Ale Soup, 35
Black Bean Soup, 33
Black Bean, Taber Corn, and Smoked Tomato Cassoulet, 109
Blackfoot Fry Bread, 129
Braided Easter Bread, 123
Braised Bison with Mushroom Sage Gravy and Wild Rice Fritters, 67
Braised Lamb Shoulder with White Beans, 55
Braised Turkey in Mole Sauce, 84
Braised Venison Shank with Caribou Mincemeat and Wild Mushroom Grits, 70
Bread
  , dough, frozen in cowboy calzones with grilled chicken and black beans, 77
  , pudding, Rudy's, 150
  banana, 130
  Blackfoot fry, 129
  braided Easter, 123
  buttermilk herb and seed, 125
  chili pita chips, 5
  harvest, 122
  Icelandic brown, 121
  Logan, 134
  multi-grain cereal, 124
  orange molasses spice, 128
  prairie flax, 121
  rustic white, 126
  walnut roll, 193
  whole wheat zucchini, 133
Breakfast dishes
  dried fruit and nut granola, 133
  mountain muesli with CPR strawberries, 129
  multi-grain pancakes, 134
  pemmican patties, 69